$53.00

Critical Essays on
JACQUES LACAN

CRITICAL ESSAYS
ON
WORLD LITERATURE

Robert Lecker, General Editor
McGill University, Montreal

Critical Essays on

JACQUES LACAN

edited by

ELLIE RAGLAND

G. K. Hall & Co.
New York

Twayne Publishers
1633 Broadway
New York, NY 10019

Library of Congress Cataloging-in-Publication Data
Critical essays on Jacques Lacan / edited by Ellie Ragland.
    p.   cm. — (Critical essays on world literature)
   Some essays have been translated from French and Spanish.
   Includes bibliographical references and index.
   ISBN 0-7838-0451-2 (alk. paper)
    1. Lacan, Jacques, 1901–1981—Contributions in criticism.
2. Psychoanalysis and literature—France—History—20th century.
3. Criticism—France—History—20th century.   I. Ragland-Sullivan.
Ellie, 1941–   II. Series.
PN98.P75C74   1999
801′.95′092—dc21   99-37143
                                            CIP

With gratitude, love, and respect, to my students and coworkers
from Missouri and from many other places as well whose questions and
support keep pushing me forward to the next answer and another question,
and even to the building of a space for a field of Lacanian Studies.

Contents

♦

Publisher's Note

◆

Producing a volume that contains both newly commissioned and reprinted material presents the publisher with the challenge of balancing the desire to achieve stylistic consistency with the need to preserve the integrity of works first published elsewhere. In the Critical Essays series, essays commissioned especially for a particular volume are edited to be consistent with G. K. Hall's house style; reprinted essays appear in the style in which they were first published, with only typographical errors corrected. Consequently, shifts in style from one essay to another are the result of our efforts to be faithful to each text as it was originally published.

Preface

◆

The essays collected here deal exclusively with the new theory of language and knowledge elaborated by Jacques Lacan (1901–1981) in the seminars that marked his official teaching from 1953–1954 to 1980. The topics range from why Lacan was first received by literary scholars, although his lifetime practice was that of an analyst, to the influences on his teaching by thinkers as diverse as Augustine to those of modern-day linguistics. Not only does a new theory of knowledge emerge that breaks with positivistic "pictures" of mind as made-up factual or biological material, his teaching also gives a formal logic for how fantasy, desire, drive, and symbol function within the field of language, always bringing something of the unconscious into conscious thought.

In this sense, Lacan uncovered the larger meaning of the *literary* as that which embraces more of the truths about how we as humans *actually* think than do the positivistic theories imposed on literary language, serving it reductively, not expansively or as true to experience. The logic that characterizes these essays is of a piece with memory as it really works—associationally in logical time, rather than linearly in straight narrative time; the *sinthome*/symptom that structures unconscious fantasy as a relation of desire to the Father's Name signifier for difference (whose logic is that of the normative masquerade, the neuroses, the psychoses, or perversion); fiction as the author's effort to create a new identity for him- or herself; the unconscious signifier that *can* be reconstructed by a new relationship to *jouissance* based on the transference encounters one lives by; sublimation as an overlapping of two voids that produces a double-effect of the object *a* such that the drives (oral, anal, invocatory, and scopic) materialize language by the real of sexual traits.

Miller, Wajcman, and Morel demonstrate in three diverse ways how Lacan's interest was not in the possibility for infinite metonymization, for example, but in the limits created between the gaps of objects and words; or the limits imposed by the real in the orders of identification, language, and ideology; or the necessity of at least one uncovered space (concomitant with the logic of the "not all" that marks feminine sexuation) in a topological square in order that images, words, and affects can be pulled into a certain bounded space. This theoretical material has the widest of implications for a new aesthetics, one that literature has awaited perhaps since Kant distinguished between the sublime as unbounded and horrifying and the beautiful as bounded and familiar.

Most of the translated material refers to the Norton editions in which Lacan's 26 seminars are appearing in English translation. One might note that the full translation of the *Ecrits* (925 pages in French) is slotted to appear in the year 2000.

Acknowledgments

♦

I should like to thank all those whose support and encouragement made this volume possible: Jacques-Alain Miller and Robert Lecker, as well as the editors, Michelle Kovacs and Mary Jo Heck, who became involved with the project at the final stages of its editing. I thank the various authors for their generous permissions to reprint well-known essays or for allowing me to include the precious material of an original text. Individually and collectively, the authors grasped the import of a volume whose goal is to render accessible Lacan's difficult thought in clear terms so that anyone who wants to study it can find a place of entry here. That all the fine Lacan scholars working in the Anglophone world could not be included is a source of regret for me. Thanks also go to Marga Dick of Columbia, Missouri, whose encouragement was crucial to me at a key moment. My mother has offered the generosity of her home, her cuisine, and her assistance with my teenage daughter to allow the time and space necessary to the endeavors of compiling a text of this kind. The chair of my department and the dean of Arts and Sciences were generous in granting a sabbatical year. In particular, I wish to thank Zak Watson for his assistance in helping me edit Jacques-Alain Miller's essay at the inception of this project, as well as Jack Stone for starting to build the select bibliography. Finally, I would like to thank David Metzger and Elaine Ross for reading and critiquing early versions of my introduction to this volume. I thank each one of you for your assistance and support.

Chronology

◆

1901	Jacques-Marie Lacan born April 13 in Paris, France to Alfred Lacan, a businessman for a house of oil and soap, and Emilie Baudry, a deeply religious Catholic woman.
1903	Lacan's sister, Madeleine, born.
1907–1919	Attends the Jesuit *Ecole Stanislaus* in Paris.
1908	Lacan's brother, Marc-François, born. Despite his brother's efforts to dissuade him, Marc-François later enters Benedictinc orders at Hautecombe and spends his lifetime collaborating on the *Vocabulaire de Théologie biblique.*
1926–1930	Studies psychiatry at the medical school at The University of Paris.
1930	Works in the *Clinique de Burg Hölzi*, animated in Zurich, Switzerland, by Eugen Bleuler and Carl Jung (August and September).
1932	Submits his doctoral thesis, *De la psychose paranoïaque dans ses rapports avec la personalité suivi de Premiers écrits sur la paranoïa,* on which his director makes only one comment: "Une hirondelle ne fait pas été" (One swallow does not a summer make).
1932–1936	Lacan's thesis wins him the prestigious appointment as clinical chief of Psychiatry at the Sainte-Anne Hospital, the central hospital serving Paris.
1932–1938	Undergoes a seven-year analysis with Rudolph Lowenstein, the leading analyst of the 1930s.
1932–1945	Publishes articles, including "Logical Time and the Assertion of Anticipated Certitude: A New Sophism" (a response to Jean-Paul Sartre's concern with time), in Surrealist journals such as *Le Minotaure* and *Cahiers de l'art.* Lacan's work with Surrealist artists and poets inspires his

reconceptualization of the creative spark that gives rise to metaphor. (See *Cahiers de l'art* [1945]: 32–42.)

1933–1948   Attends philosophy classes at the Sorbonne, studying Phenomenology and Existentialism along with Jean-Paul Sartre, Merleau Ponty.

1934   Marries Marie-Louise Blondin, whose charm, Catholic mysticism, and membership in the Parisian *Haute Bourgeoisie* appeal to him, on January 19.

mid-1930s   Lacan's originality gives him the basis for an initial understanding of a delineation to be made between an Imaginary axis of narcissistic identifications (the ego or *moi*) and a Symbolic axis of the cultural "realities" of language and social conventions.

1936   Sets up a private practice at Bonneval. Gives his first version of the "Mirror Stage" article at the Congress of International Psychoanalysis in Marienbad but refuses to contribute this essay to the conference proceedings.

1937   Daughter Caroline born.

1938   Is invited by Henri Wallon to publish his findings on the mirror stage in a long encyclopedia article on the family.

1939   Son Thibaut born.

1940   Daughter Sibylle born.

1941   Daughter Judith (Bataille) Lacan born. Divorce granted to Marie-Louise Lacan on December 15.

1949   "The mirror stage as formative of the function of the I as revealed in psychoanalytic experience" is accepted at the 16th International Psychoanalytic Conference at Zurich, Switzerland.

1951   Makes his first move from the use of the Freudian "topic" to topology in "Intervention on the Transference," in which he depicts the underlying logic in the Dora case as Hegelian. Begins a private teaching of Freud's famous cases.

1953   Puts forth his manifesto, "Function and field of the word and of language in psychoanalysis," in which he introduces himself as a practitioner of the symbolic function. (This manifesto becomes known as the "Rome Discourse.") Lacan, along with others, officially founds the *Société française de psychanalyse* (SEP) on June 16. Marries Sylvie Maklès (formerly Bataille), whom he had known since 1939.

1953–1963   Holds public Seminars at Ste.-Anne in the Amphitheater provided by Jean Delay.

1963–1981 Holds weekly Seminars at the *Ecole Pratique de Hautes Etudes.*
1965 Founds the *Ecole freudienne de Paris.*
1966 Collects various lectures, papers, and résumés of Seminars in a volume published by Seuil under the title *Ecrits.*
1979 Establishes the *Fondation du champ freudien,* whose president is Judith Miller.
1980–1981 Dissolves the *Ecole freudienne de Paris* and establishes in its place the *Ecole de la cause freudienne.*
1981 Lacan dies September 9.

Introduction

ELLIE RAGLAND

Jacques Lacan was not a literary critic or a world author in the traditional sense. He developed his psychoanalytic teaching by referring to literary works as paradigmatic examples, rather than citing case studies of actual people. Thereby, he not only gave new interpretations of classical works but, in a larger sense, elaborated a radically new way of responding to the enigma of what literature is. His 30-year seminar developed a logic of how mind and body are connected by structures that appear, disappear, and reappear continually in language, particularly in literary language. It is not surprising, then, that Lacan was received by literary people before clinicians, a paradox Jacques-Alain Miller points out in his contribution to this volume, "Lacan Clinician." This is probably because Lacan's theory of language and his rethinking of perception in terms of the scopic field and the gaze, for example, were more immediately germane to literary students and scholars than to medical doctors.

In the contemporary literary arena of poststructuralist, postmodernist ways of making sense of literature, Lacan has only begun to emerge in literary studies on the American scene, as texts by him become available in English. The measure of what he has to offer literary theory has not yet been taken, then. For his profoundly new picture of the "subject" requires one to assimilate a new theory of mind, memory, perception, and so on, such that older theories of knowledge that underlie the uses we generally make of language in defining the "literary" must, perforce, be reformulated as an effect of Lacan's teaching.

Lacan was born in 1901 and died in 1981. During his lifetime he reinterpreted Sigmund Freud's German oeuvre in a weekly seminar. In the history of recent innovative bodies of thought, Lacan's seminar stands as a monument to the power of an oral teaching to command an ever-growing international audience for nearly 30 years. From 1953 to 1981 Lacan's seminars were attended by thousands of world intellectuals who heard him give new answers to old questions regarding what knowledge is, what sexuality is, what the unconscious is, and so on.

In today's critical arena of assessing and reassessing not only the humanities but the literary canon as well, one may expect the select essays in this

1

volume to address once again "The Agency of the Letter" (1957), in which Lacan first rethought metaphor and metonymy not as mere figures of speech but as commensurate with the functioning of laws of desire, equatable with Freud's condensation and displacement, that move language and discourse along the path of fantasy, which is reconceptualized by Lacan as the bedrock of unconscious thought.[1]

Richard Glejzer's essay "Lacan with Scholasticism: Agencies of the Letter" takes issue with Samuel Weber's *Return to Freud: Jacques Lacan's Dislocation of Psychoanalysis,* which would leave fantasy out of Lacan's teaching altogether.[2] Weber takes a Derridean perspective, from which he portrays Lacan's theory of language as a rehash of Saussurian and Jakobsonian structuralist linguistics. Glejzer points, rather, to Lacan's return to Augustine in his development of a theory of language that ultimately leads to a radical reformulation both of Saussure and Jakobson, while allowing for powerful functions in language whose logic is not reducible to narrative, the alphabet, or grammatical conventions. Given Lacan's Catholic upbringing and his Jesuit education, Glejzer's point is not surprising. Lacan, Glejzer notes, stresses Augustine's concern to know what speaking (to God) might be as a theory of language that goes continually from the universal to the particular, thereby portraying God as a "negative" knowledge, an open space that poses a series of questions rather than giving a set of answers.

Working with texts of the early and late Lacan, Glejzer portrays a common preoccupation in medieval Scholasticism and Lacanian psychoanalysis: Teaching itself works from ignorance—resisting meaning—not from knowledge. Whereas Scholasticism evolves a negative theology, Lacan developed a topological structuralism, that is, a nonlinear theory of cause and effect. Aquinas, too, never ceased to be a reference for Lacan. Although Aquinas's object of study was of God as an unknown, he evolved the answer of metaphor in seeking a tangible referent for agency. Rather than dismiss the notion of agency, Glejzer looks to John of Salisbury, who defined cognition as a limit in relation to what is knowable, aligning him with Lacan's critique of Aristotle's and Kant's notions of the immortal soul and the Good. Not only is God the object (*a*) one believes will bring about one's good in one's fantasy of what that might be; Lacan points to the added problem of grounding the truth on which any knowledge is based on a master signifier—be it of a Christian God, a Pantheistic pantheon of nature gods, and so on. David Metzger treats this problem in his essay by considering the roles of fantasy and the *sinthome* in definition of agency.

Having mapped the propensity of human knowledge to duplicity, ignorance, and superego functioning, Lacan does not, however, end up in skepticism or nihilism. Refining older concepts of subjectivity, he makes the particularity of fantasy one with the particularity of associational memory. The question of agency concerns a relation of desire to language whereby a subject "speaks" as an obsessional, a hysteric, a psychotic, or a normative participant in the social masquerade hiding the perverse traits of fantasy. None of these is equated with being right or wrong. Lacan pointed out that humankind has always faced the problem that the Other of the world outside imposes itself on any subject as his or her knowledge, bifurcating knowledge into conscious and unconscious fantasy that is constructed in the first place such that the subject cannot directly attain its good, or its object *a,* nor can the object(s) that fill the gap-in-being for a time do so permanently. Both fantasy objects and the subject are paradoxically constituted and divided by the logical structures of alienation and separation that Lacan writes in his mathemes as $\mathcal{8} \diamond a$.[3]

In "Freud's Jewish Science and Lacan's *Sinthome,*" Metzger asks if psychoanalysis is not Freud's fantasy for the Jewish people, for what will make them whole for the Other. Metzger defines fantasy here in the sense that history, understood as fantasy, operates according to the logic of the *sinthome* and not the logic of the symbolic order of a given local universal concept of reality. Metzger defines Lacan's use of *sinthome,* a medieval spelling of the Greek word "symptom," as that which guarantees that there be at least one word or one thing with which one can identify as a subject who is "all"—a masculine position in sexuation—or "not all"—a feminine position in sexuation—in language. Each subject tries to answer the question "who am I?" by his or her relation to the Other sex, which Lacan calls the discourse of the unconscious: I am a mother, a symbolic father, an imaginary father, a real father, for example. Moreover, these "Oedipal" answers to identity must serve two systems—that of alienation into representational language and that of separation, where one is an "object" of/for enjoyment, which Lacan equates with truth. In this sense, truth is a position taken in discourse, as well as that which guarantees one's *sinthome.*

Metzger applies Lacan's mathemes to his argument, showing how they are a shorthand for depicting the multiform functioning of the unconscious. For example, the Φ is an equivalent of "I think," guaranteed by the authority in whom one vests one's concept of "reality," whereas "I am ___" is based on one's *jouissance,* depicted by Lacan's object *a,* that part of one's being that is "not all" co-opted by language. The discourse mathemes (S_1, S_2, $\mathcal{8}$, a) answer certain questions as to what one is for the Other, then. At the level at which one is alienated into the "reality" of a master signifier, one's division $\mathcal{8}$ is filled by the S_1, which describes a seemingly whole master representing him- or herself to the Other (S_2), taken as the one(s) who know. At the level of separation, one is rent by a hole where an object *a* has fallen out of the Other to decomplete it from being the imaginary whole it takes itself to be.

The essays in this collection demonstrate how Lacan's theories, in giving the different aspects of the subject, also map the various literary genres, simultaneously offering a new answer as to how art is connected to life, other than by mimesis. Giving a theory of the *why* of literature—a set of answers that are illuminative, not just for literary critics, interpreters, and theorists but for creative writers as well—Lacan does not reduce the *literary* to the correct interpretation, or the divine artifact, or the pathological artist—"Art itself is not pathological."[4] Bringing together Aristotle, Plato, Freud, Kant, and the other great thinkers and writers who have commented on poetics and aesthetics throughout the centuries, coupled with twentieth-century discoveries in linguistics, cultural anthropology, and contemporary topology, among other fields, Lacan's teaching developed as an explanation both of the manner of construction of what actually composes literature and of the logic of how each—the symbol, the dream, the fantasy, fiction, sublimation, desire, and a-ffect, to name but a few—functions. He thereby points the way to an understanding of what he meant by the following: "[A]esthetics, in other words, what you feel, is not in itself transcendental. Aesthetics is tied to what is only contingency, to wit, that it [aesthetics] is this topology that has value for a body."[5]

One wonders what, besides language, and the images it depicts, connects the body to the text? Early in "Lacan Clinician," Miller points out that Lacan says that one is only to adore art—one does not deduce the psyche from it, as Freud thought. The "catch-22" comes not from a cold aesthetics but from the fact that the adoration is a narcissistic one, an adoration made out of seeing ourselves refracted and reflected in the many shapes and pieces that make us up. Moreover, Lacan's style has its own literary value—often called "baroque." The effect of this style is to make one question one's own suppositions, to poke a hole in the well-made narratives of one's thought and beliefs. Lacan has attracted literary critics, furthermore, by showing not only that the unconscious has the structure of concrete language but that it has logical structure that includes time and space, as well; finally, then, one's language is what one can do with one's unconscious.

Although truth may have the structure of fiction, even as such truth emerges from mistakes and misrecognitions—the common coin of literary narratives and dramas—Lacan does not infer that truth is a fiction or that our truths are merely fictions. Stuart Schneiderman takes up Lacan's treatment of Poe's story of the purloined letter in his essay "Fictions," noting that Lacan's fiction focuses on the crucial moment of the story when Dupin sees and identifies the purloined letter, thereby describing a scene that is other than the actual scene. Rather than an unconscious emanation, Dupin intentionally substitutes another signifier—a crumpled ball of paper—for the missing one, the lost letter. Lacan seeks to show in his seminar on "The Purloined Letter" the primacy of the symbolic over the imaginary, which, among other things, is at the base of his theory that a third term referent—a (phallic) signifier with no signified—divides the sexes.

Lacan's empirical referent for this theory relies on his treatment of psychotics for whom any division between the sexes is repudiated such that both anatomical men and women are WOMAN. But most subjects accept that there is a division between the sexes, as Metzger argues in his essay, whatever may be their preponderance of identifications with the masculine (taken by

Lacan as the position of lover) or the feminine (taken as the position of the beloved). Schneiderman notes that, if one reads or listens to a story at the level of ego narrative, one will miss its message, that the cause of a story concerns unspoken desire, not Writing that is performative up to the point of its own obliteration into the chaos, or dissipating sounds. Schneiderman advances a thesis of his own: that a fictional character is always based on a real person who has been renamed by the story. In other words, the author writes out of a quest to rename him- or herself, to create or invent a new identity.

It was not, however, to ego psychology that Lacan turned in his rethinking of identity, nor to Kripke's concern with proper names as rigid designators in his philosophical study of the referent. Lacan turned to linguistics, not only to redefine its premises in what looks, at a first glance, like a misunderstanding or a subversion, but also to correct its errors, as he attempts in his redefinitions of philosophical commonplaces. If, for example, as Descartes argued, thought is extended by corporeal illusions, they are those of the body. Such illusions are sustained, Lacan demonstrates, by the consistency of imaginary fantasy, which works differently than the thought equated with conventional narrative and grammar. Lacan's concept of the body as imaginary is not, however, the Husserlelian or phenomenological concept of an immediate intuition of the world wherein an interior imagination is correlated with the body as a container of subjective thought. Rather, the "facts" of knowledge are meaningful events of the real, which functions not only by the laws of primary-process thought but also by the laws of logical time (the instant of seeing, the time for understanding, the moment of concluding), whose timing concerns desire and *jouissance,* not the linearity of narrative or spontaneity of imagination. This means, moreover, that subjective time has a formalizable logic that is not equatable to a description of feelings.

Finding his laws of meaning in Peirce, Saussure, Jakobson, and Lévi-Strauss, Lacan rejected the phenomenological illusion of a pregiven creative imagination marked by an immediacy of temporal thought, stressing instead that language is always already in a state of deferral, in the future anterior, representing something else. Its effects are those of an outside Otherness with its own alienating propensities that are inscribed on the flesh of an infant from the start of its life—and even before its birth insofar as the baby-to-be-born is talked about—to build it up as a subject of words given him or her by others, by the Other. Lacan shows, thus, that the idea of original innate structures, whether of a soul, of Being, creative imagination, language genes, or any other, is an illusion. It is, rather, interrelatedness that gives structure, not some a priori faculty of mind or self. Thus, he modified Saussure's concept of the sign, stressing instead that two fundamental combinations of signifiers—following Lacan's redefinitions of the laws of metaphor and metonymy—regulate conscious and unconscious thought. Metonymy is the ever displaceable cause of desire—a potential infinitization, Miller notes—for which metaphor substitutes something other than the primordially lost object a that causes desire precisely insofar as it is lost.

Against ego psychology, Lacan proposed that "reality" is an internal coherence fantasy that the *sinthome* gives to one's own speech. Early on, he stressed the sign insofar as the writer addresses something to someone. By 1972, his focus was, rather, on discourse, defined as that which makes a social link because someone wants to speak. The discourse mathemes for the field of language are one's own S_1s aiming at the Other's S_2. With such formulas, Lacan sought to show how one valorizes one's fantasy of one's identity at the point at which there is a lack-in-being ($\mathcal{S}$) by implicitly asking the other/Other to validate and reify the object a one already thinks one is. Lacan stressed the logic of alienation at work in thinking (characterized by the logic of alienation) and in being (which includes the logic of *jouissance*), demonstrating that it is not a question of whether one speaks to the other from reality or fantasy. It is that one addresses the other dissymetrically, from the point of a (mis)communication about one's own Ideal image of self. One's own *weltanschauung* is the measure of one's fantasy constructions, in other words.

In "Literature as Symptom," Colette Soler argues that literature is itself a symptom of the use of language as an anticipation of uncovering pieces of the unconscious. Whereas Freud used literature as a kind of applied psychoanalysis, equating the artist's work with his or her own unconscious, Lacan reversed Freud's position, arguing instead that literary works are not products of the unconscious but are enigmas that resist interpretation. Literature and psychoanalysis cojoin, rather, at the level of the symptom *because* the symptom is an invention, a substitute creation of *jouissance* meant to replace (in life) what has been lost of the primary object—which literary art seeks to recover, uncover, cover up—by making new, proximate meanings.

A number of the essays in this volume begin to elaborate a new aesthetics deducible from Lacan's teaching and germane to the field of literary studies. Insisting on the importance of the unconscious, Charles Shepherdson writes in "Vital Signs: The *Place* of Memory in Psychoanalysis" that the early Lacan spoke of "conjectural sciences" to juxtapose psychoanalysis to the experimental sciences based on clock time or to the sociological sciences based on notions of intersubjective time. Shepherdson notes that Lacan debunked the notion of biological memory as well as that of intuitionist mystification. Freud, as well, was concerned with the link between the unconscious and forgetting. He defined the unconscious as a "memory that has not been remembered," giving Lacan the basis for depicting memory as an active re-remembering that appears "strangely," as a symptom. Not only Freud and Lacan but also Nietzsche separated memory from nature, Shepherdson points out. Freud stressed that hysterics suffer from unconscious reminiscences, whereas Lacan discovered that the Other place of each person's memories is founded on the loss of a cause, the loss of the object a of fulfillment. Thus, the symbolic order reaches a dead end, pushed to search for its very existence via the world of a certain kind of object—the cause of desire in which mind and body overlap with sexuality as the connector. That desire can enter language, joining mind to body via sexuality, was demonstrated by Anna O.'s false pregnancy—her impregnation by Breuer's desire, Lacan argued.

In his study of Henry James's *The Sacred Fount,* John Holland argues that the narrator's unconscious fundamental fantasy is radically shifted when an equation of the mask with a grimace takes on the unconscious signification of death—thus replicating the lack in the signifier ($ \mathcal{S} $) with the meaning of this ultimate emptiness or horror. Holland claims, however, that the narrator's evolving relations with Grace and May have the effect of modifying his previous linking of this signifier for death and the one for a grimace to an unconscious apprehension of the feminine itself. This isolated signifier, invaded by the *jouissance* expelled by the masculine reconceptualization of the feminine, of necessity becomes—not just another signifier, or an object, for the narrator, but—a symptom that will alter his relation to enjoyment. Holland demonstrates Lacan's theory that fantasy is formulated from the outside in each subject's assumption of signifiers and *jouissance.*

Lacan showed the formal logic of how the fantasy is first constructed and then operates one's thought: the manner in which the symbol is constructed as the base unit of meaning, rather than as a second-level double reflection of some a priori. He viewed the joining of conscious (secondary-process) and unconscious (primary-process) thought as constitutive of the dialectical subject of desire (where want infers lack). This particular knowledge of what objects (*a*) will fulfill one's desire places a fantasy grid over seemingly objective meanings. That the Lacan effect has spread so rapidly is surprising only if one does not realize that he began his official work in the 1920s and 1930s, preparing himself for decades before being persuaded to launch the official teaching that held center stage until his death. He might be said to have invented a new epistemology—a twenty-first-century theory of knowledge, if I may be permitted to go so far—that resides at the interfaces of linguistics, cultural anthropology, continental philosophy, and literary and art criticisms, as well as topological structuralism, as they have coalesced into the new psychoanalysis that parallels nothing more than the new physics concerned with quarks, black holes, strings, and shards by which physicists of today define ever more precisely the material nature of the physical universe.

Although the goal of this volume is not to take stock of Lacan's past or present reception, one must state that the growth of his teaching in other countries is in advance of its influence in the United States. This is reflected somewhat by the translation history of the various essays in this volume, emanating from psychoanalytic and academic conferences. Some of the essays presented here have been translated from French or Spanish. In a broader sense, it is worth noting that Lacan's teaching currently gives rise to new journals and publications in languages as diverse as Polish, Russian, Hebrew, Greek, Dutch, African, Japanese, and others. The essays chosen here, written by well-known Lacanian scholars, offer certain answers as to why one might consider Lacan to have broken new ground in fields from which he has borrowed basic ideas and which he has, in turn, radically transformed.

In the final section of the volume, Geneviève Morel explains Lacan's concept of compacity, as introduced in *Seminar XX,* as the point at which an infinite ensemble finds its closure *in language.* Morel gives mathematical topological proof of how this works, explaining at the same time the distinction Lacan made between the unbounded feminine (as an epistemological position based on a logic of "not [being] all" enclosed within the symbolic field of conventions) and the bounded masculine (adhering strictly to the laws of the symbolic)—both separated from the *biological* man or woman. Demonstrating that one open set within an ensemble of meanings itself imposes a limit on what would otherwise be an infinity of metonymic meanings, Morel concretizes her argument in reference to Lacan's thesis that "Don Juan" is a feminine myth whose logic is that of the "not all," founded on the feminine epistemological position, rooted in the *jouissance* that comes from not identifying altogether with the superego.

Gérard Wajcman discusses the value of the visible for Lacanian theory as that which links the subject to the object—even invisibly—across the impasses and detours created by alienation and separation. The ◇, or *poinçon* (hallmark), of Lacan's algebra depicts between alienation and separation a formalizable join of enjoyment where thinking and being overlap. Continually functioning in a paradoxical logic—which gives the terms of representation at one remove from the experiential real, as well as the unary traits of the object *a* that dwell in the intersection between the thinking subject and the subject as an Ideal ego of narcissistic traits of being registered in fundamental fantasy—the *poinçon* means deferring and linking structures of language and perception that keep desire open, while enabling it to be momentarily filled or closed by the objects (*a*) that fill up its lack. Lacan's theory here yields a third category beyond symbolic logic that makes contradiction (or true/false tables) truth-functional. This gives a logic to the excluded middle of philosophy whose structure becomes that of a gap oscillating between desire and its fulfillment by the substitution of words, things, and images, for what has been lost. It also gives a logic to the ambiguous, fictional, and often paradoxical nature of literary language.

The visual structure of the topological world installs the subject, as Lacan argued in *Seminar XI: The Four Fundamental Concepts, 1964.* In his later teaching, he maintained that this is so only insofar as visual structure leads to topology. Wajcman argues that Lacan's schema represent what can be seen but not said; his graphs inscribe places by indivisible points and the picture itself presents sites as real places that correspond to the knotting of the trifunctional Borromean unit of orders Lacan called the real, symbolic, and imaginary. Finally, what can be shown—as a picture—without being said in conventional language are the four currencies of the object-*cause*-of-desire: the breast, the feces, the voice, and the gaze whose status is privileged, that of a singularity. Wajcman's article makes sense of Lacan's statement in *The Four Fundamental Concepts* that the "subject does not change the object; but the aim of the drive."[6]

By demonstrating how we identify with art by *real* components of identification from all three orders, not by learning to recognize separate—and arbitrary—categories of fiction, myth, allegory, or any other form of mimesis or rhetorical mapping of the human psyche, Lacan implies that what literary theory, criticism, and interpretation—not literature itself—have always lacked is a theory of *what* referent in the real links art to life, body to text, and reader to character. The answers usually given to such questions dead-end in analogical reductionisms. Rather, the dimensions of *jouissance* evoked by Wajcman, in reference to the four "currencies of the object-cause-of-*desire*," enter language as a density or compacity wherein the products and effects of images and words are allied with what Miller stresses: the *passion* of the signifier.

Anchored in the real of *a*-ffect, the object *a* cuts into language at the places and planes where imaginary consistencies give the appearance or *semblance* of being whole identifications. Whether one only momentarily encounters a gap ($\mathcal{S}$) that appears as a lack-in-being that fantasy generally fills with identifications, or the pure *angst* produced by a void place—an empty set in an ensemble—in the seemingly full meanings of the Other ($\emptyset$), one is touched by a grammar of *a*-ffect clustering around the eight partial objects-*cause*-of-desire that Lacan named as the breast, the feces, the voice, the gaze, the urinary flow, the phoneme, the (imaginary) phallus, and the nothing.[7] "For is it not obvious that this feature, this partial feature, rightly emphasized in objects, is applicable not because these objects are part of an imaginary total object, the body, but because they represent only partially the function that produces them" ("Subversion," 315).

In one way or another, all the essays in this volume seek to demonstrate that Lacan's theory of language is new precisely because it shows what gives rise to allegory, myth, or metaphor, thereby conveying that these metalanguages nonetheless contain unary traces of the object *a* that link the reader to the text by invisible bonds of the greatest particularity of response to image, word, and effects of the drives. Whether one points to tropes, figures, or other rhetorical names of the symbolic or identifies with imaginary traits of character or place or era, such identifications, even when giving the illusion of a whole, reveal that the symbol itself is not a unity of signifier to signified but a disunity wherein some piece of the real breaks off, tears away, splits, or makes a breach. Such movement creates the material surface of language out of gaps and holes between the partial objects and the matrices of *jouissance* meanings. One finds a tension or torsion within the tiniest piece of meaning, be it the rhythm of a sound or the semiturn of a gaze.

If one considers this topological gap or space as the base of language, which functions by a dynamic movement of reparations that continually reframe their own frame—be it as the counterclockwise doubling of a sphere, O, or at the point at which one of the intersecting sets of signifying associations from the imaginary, symbolic, or real crosses another, a word from the symbolic traversing an image from the imaginary, X—one refers to a point of overlap that contains a piece of meaning. Whether it is the unary trait of an object that first caused desire at the time its loss was experienced, the trait has become the nexus of an origin around which a weaving of "material" dimension is created by the linking of image to word and sound. This material is made out of the oral, anal, invocatory, and scopic *real* links of *jouissance.* These unary traits bind positive knowledge to concrete loss by attaching the unary trait to the concrete real of a hole. Fixations in memory chains join loss to knowledge—be it erudition (*savoir*) or the *jouissance* knowledge one might also call *connaissance*—thereby giving rise to repetitions as the foundational base sought and resought in all the orders where repetitions function as the base of being. In such a context, one might call that which propels language toward some goal the drive to (re)find the lost objects of early experience, placing the movement of language magnetized by desire in the future anterior tense.

That such an early laying down of primary process thought—whether it is called *la lalangue* or *jouissance* knowledge—occurs in the first two years of life becomes the referent of the real on which subsequent memory associations are founded.[8] The Lacanian Ur-lining of mind/memory, initially built up around the first objects that *cause* desire, exists prior to grammar and well-made narrative, which appears at around three to five years of age, once the mirror-stage image of two beings has merged into one singular, consolidated identity of self-believed fictions. One can grasp what Charles Pyle means in stating that the "Freudian revolution turns on the gap created by censorship," which makes it clear that, from the beginning, the field of psychoanalysis has been the field of language, not of biology.[9] To Freud's censorship, Lacan appends the cut of losing the desired object, thus adding libido to language.

In *Le séminaire, livre XXIII: Le sinthome, 1975–1976,*[10] Lacan states that words of the symbolic and images from the imaginary copulate, giving the gap its hole-shaped formal consistency (*Le sinthome,* March 16, 1976). In the same seminar, he describes "the real [as] put in place by being knotted to the symptom, to the imaginary and symbolic. . . . Paradoxically, this real ties itself to nothing" (*Le sinthome,* April 13, 1976). Subsequently, the real will exist outside the knotting. It is for this reason that it is encountered as rupture and malady (*Le sinthome,* March 16, 1976). In other words, the real corresponds to the hole made by the signifier, the letter, or the object, which are coequivalents of the primary repressed layers of knowledge one might describe as identical to themselves in having the structure of doubleness that Wajcman designates in speaking of the topology of the picture, a doubleness that occurs when images, words, and effects are organized around an emptiness the early Lacan called the No-Thing. The object (*a*) becomes that which tries to replicate itself in such a way as to close the hole. Lacan calls such an encircling of a central emptiness *sublimation*.[11] Theology has studied this place of central emptiness for centuries.[12]

In her essay on *Antigone* and sublimation, Ellie Ragland elaborates Lacan's theory that sublimation satisfies the drives—without repression—at the sites of the empty sets of the body (mouth, ears, eyes, etc.) where two voids overlap: ◊ . The primary space formed by a lost object intersects with the lack created by the desire to replace it. The erogenous zones respond, then, to the residual unary traits of a subject's particular real and to the void place of a hole. Antigone mimes the void place not only in her discourse—which Lacan describes as *sublime*—but also in the cavelike tomb in which she is imprisoned. Her discourse mimes a sublimation that marks a limit Lacan calls "between-two-deaths," not unlike the open or uncovered hole(s) in the square encircled by a certain number of Borromean signifying units, evoked by Geneviève Morel.

Lacan states that, in the beginning, there is a line that is cut or twisted in such a way as to give it the dimensions of being (the imaginary), thinking (the symbolic), and feeling (the real): ◎ . That is, Lacan's topological logic, in working with aspects of the real, places four formalizable dimensions within language: "When you scribble . . . , it is always on a page with lines, and we are thus immediately enmeshed in this business of dimensions. What cuts a line is a point. Since a point has zero dimensions [that is, it cannot be divided], a line is defined as having one dimension. Since what a line cuts is a surface, a surface is defined as having two dimensions. Since what a surface cuts is space, space has three dimensions."[13] Depicting this in the schemas that stratify the planes of the image [$-\sqrt{-1}$], Lacan posits that a surface cuts space, which corresponds to the real sites that show the picture of the fantasy, inscribed by the imaginary and symbolic. Space separates the inside from the outside, in other words. The surface and edge constitute a real hole, nonetheless placing inside and outside on the same surface, even though a point of obscurity will always remain where the twist or overlap covers something else—be it signifier, letter, or object *a*: ℗. In writing, however, something different occurs. One line crosses another before it passes underneath, showing the flattened dimension of a knot, rather than the three-dimensional space created by a cut: ⊗ (*Encore*, 122).

The essays in this volume that treat the literary from a Lacanian perspective, such as those by Soler, Metzger, and Ragland, for example, demonstrate in various ways that art does not imitate nature, or the reverse. Rather, art is portrayed as the most expansive use of image and word possible to show that the unconscious "speaks," placing in the ordinary use of language a language of cuts, reversals of time, disassociation of memories, fadings of meaning, and so on. These are, nonetheless, attached to language by the meanderings of *associative memory*, which characterizes everyday thought—thought as it actually functions—when it is not on guard, not putting on the superego armor of secondary process well-ordered grammar and syntax.

Whether discussing older classical pieces or new cutting edge theories, each essay, in its own way, demonstrates Lacan's teaching at work. The picture I hope will emerge is of the Lacan who both reinterpreted famous literary works and used them as paradigmatic examples of stories or narratives that explain of *what* material literary language is made; and it is not of separate formal orders and historical or rhetorical conventions that dwell apart from mind and body. Rather, an intrication of materials constitutes separate and separable categories—each with its own laws—that Lacan called the real, symbolic, imaginary, and symptom.

Antigone, for example, serves Lacan as a drama that is exemplary of his new theory of *sublimation,* which "passes beyond repression to the beautiful, posed at a limit beyond the field of any culturally determined 'good' " (*Ethics,* 278). Antigone's condemnation, or death sentence, places in life the concept of between-two-deaths—the natural animal one and that of a place outside life where one goes after death: Antigone's watery "Beyond," or de Sade's fiery furnace of a hell "Below."[14] Lacan's innovative interpretation of this classical tragedy takes account of "the second death" as a place between life and death, be it heaven and hell, or any other cultural picture or myth of the same.

Lacan's demonstrations of how the *real* speaks in language—literary language being its home—suggest that the drives speak there from the foundational place of a fundamental fantasy whose "universal" grammar might be that of win or lose, love and loss, as implied in Freud's "A child is being beaten" fantasy. The terms of the fantasy are particular for each subject, made up as they are of the memory associations that replicate experience and require one to negotiate the real of trauma by trying to cover it over, while unveiling this "truth": The *real* continually returns into the symbolic and imaginary to enunciate itself as the excess (*plus-de-jouir*) Miller describes as an exchange made between language and *jouissance.*

There is a gap, not a unity, between the symbolic and imaginary. This means that the imaginary is a world of masks and semblances. Words lie, rather than pinning down final truths or realities. They can, themselves, be semblances. Lacan's matheme for the subject's being barred from its own supposed or imagined totality—its believed identity to self—is $\mathcal{S}$. Not only is there no whole subject unity, the aporia in language move its meanings by a rhythm of anticipation/retroaction as it goes through the constant motion of trying to place good enough "objects" (identifications, things, events) in the gap of a structural lack-in-being. One could even describe art as a formal map of the Lacanian subject, ego (Ideal and ideals), the Other: formations that dramatize the various Lacanian structures—myth aiming at the real, fantasy at the imaginary, and so on.

Taking the subject as a negativity ($\mathcal{S}$)—which Freud named castration—Miller asserts that this structure of a gap produces meaning, suffering, fantasy, *jouissance,* symptoms, and so on, making sense of the fact that one reads by correlating words, images, and the real effects produced by the passion of the signifier with his or her beliefs, identifications, symptoms, and enjoyments. Whereas Freud pinpointed the slips of connections between words and things in pauses, enigmas, fadings, uncertainties, and jokes, Lacan—adding the aggressivities and jealousies that valorize a place of Otherness between "I" and "you"—mapped the space of this negative castration $(-\varphi)$ as a kind of *slippage* of material between the imaginary and symbolic orders. Placing the superego tyranny of a local universal language that equates itself with power and reality ($\overline{\Phi}$) between the symbolic and real, Lacan discovered a more disturbing gap between the imaginary and real—that of a pure identification with the cut itself. In such an identification, one feels the void in the Other whose products are the real of trauma and anxiety ($\varnothing$).

Jeanne Granon-Lafont opines that, although Lacan invented only two signs of his algebra—the bar (/) and the *poinçon* (<>), or hallmark—these were enough to show how language is its own material referent. That is, language has no innate or pregiven metalanguage that serves as the source of its material. Concepts of surface and deep structures in language—such as literary imagination hiding behind conventional language or the Chomskian biological conditions for language—are for Lacan, imaginary models based on the concept of an inner and outer whole body. To the contrary, he taught that there is no thickness, no anchor, no depth, no point fixed in a pregiven space to which language ties itself.[15] Rather, language ties the unary traits of imaginary, real, symbolic, and symptomatic material to real holes. This material both constitutes and surrounds the holes that are first introduced or created by the loss of objects that appear and then disappear around the "one dimension" of the hole and its edge—a single dimensionality that evokes the absolutism of the real (Granon-Lafont, 14).

Thus, it is through the radical particularity of the associative material of his or her own memory that a reader will relate to the material of a text through the multileveled centerings and decenterings of the real, symbolic, and imaginary orders. What Miller calls the poststructuralist intoxication consists of the idea that texts speak to texts. He explains in "Lacan Clinician": "I would say that it is academic intoxication par excellence, the frenzy of erudition, because, in fact, it consists of stressing the signifier as a *semblant*, which means that the signifier taken as a *semblant* has no consequence on anything but the other signifiers. If you like, it is the frenzy [of believing] that a signifier is equivalent to another. And thus, through a game of substitution, of displacement, we are embarked on an infinite metonymy where the ultimate truth is that there is no ultimate truth, where the last word is that there is no end. It is sometimes called . . . deconstruction." As recently as May 30, 1998, Jacques Derrida, the father of deconstruction, described deconstruction thus: " 'Everything is a text; this is a text,' he said, waving his arm at the diners around him in the bland suburbanlike restaurant."[16]

As Wajcman notes, Lacan demonstrated with his graphs how *place* is inscribed such that it corresponds to symbolic space and is dominated by the dimension of the point, that of zero. *Place* is what is given to be read. With his schemas, Lacan figured the stratifying dimensions of the planes of the image; the dyadic dimension of surface predominates here. This dimension is the given to be seen that literary critics and philosophers so often relegate to the supposed creative faculty of imagination. Lacan evolved the notion of real space in presenting the picture as the real place of a *site*.

In the schema of two dimensions, Lacan gave the imaginary reality of self and mirror other. Whereas the pure real has the absolute effect of the cut, "reality" proper has three dimensions as far as the knotting of the imaginary and the symbolic realm of language to a hole creates the real as an excess, insofar as one dimension is always subtracted from language. This occurs at the level at which the referent of language is the real of the cut and the residual imaginary traits that fill the void created by the loss of the objects that cause desire. Thus, signifiers are spoken in real time, giving a temporal—as well as a spatial—dimension to the word, marked by the varying kinds of cuts that intervene between its sounds (Granon-Lafont, 32–33).

As Lacan's new theory joins language and knowledge to the drives and *jouissance,* it makes ever greater sense to think of the real as that which links the reader to the text via the material components of the unary trait, proximate to the object *a* that first causes desire and then returns in an attempt to provide the *jouissance* that has been lost. Thus, this volume represents a passage from Freud's metapsychological way of presenting psychoanalysis based on the idea of an inherently dynamic unconscious whose ubiquity of intrapsychic conflict comes from childhood sex and aggressivity to a Lacan who gives us a concrete map of the extralinguistic dimensions in language that explain the mysterious, opaque language of literary art.

His is a new geometry, Lacan stated, one that has never been tried before. It depends on the possibility of formalizing certain structures at the base of what looks like chance, randomness, or even chaos. And this "new geometry" depends on the truth-functionality of contradiction that makes the Borromean knot of mind/meaning/memory the base unit of meaning, made of a quatrocentroperspective; that is, this triad of real, imaginary, and symbolic categories, each with its own laws and properties, is knotted by the *sinthome* of each person's relation to desire and sublimation of the *jouissance* of the drives.

The essays here demonstrate this basic Lacanian grammar, some in terms of "high" theory, others, in application of it. Overall, they do not reflect a heterogeneous plurality of interpretations, conforming to some set of "general laws" of eclectic interpretation. Rather, these essays have been chosen because they are central to the shaping of a volume that sets forth and exemplifies what is at stake in a new theory of knowledge. They portray some of the best thinking going on in the use of this theory. This includes the category of paradox as truth-functional and shows that a theory of knowledge can be as precisely presented in axioms that function logically and rationally, as can the sciences of physics or mathematics.

Thus, these essays demonstrate a commonality of logic, rather than a plurality of interpretational possibilities. Breaking with theories of origins based on varying kinds of positivisms, be they Comtian, Darwinian, animistic, monotheistic, philosophical, or scientific, Lacan takes us to a beginning that starts from a central experience of lack and loss. This ultimately leads us away from any theory based on biological first causes or a typological first cause, to the topology of which he said the following: "I remind you that it is from logic that this discourse touches on the real. To encounter it is impossible, which means it is this discourse which carries it [logic] to its final power: science, as I have said, of the real."[17] Lacanian thought operates on the basis of structure, but it is not the structuralism of linguistics or anthropology. Rather, it is the various structures that evolve out of imaginary, symbolic, real, and symptomal orders due to the flaw in the Universe—the structural lack-in-being, alongside the void at the center of the symbolic—that determines that humans be parasited by language, submitted to the logic of the signifier: that the living body be taken up in and by the symbolic and articulate the subject as Other and as object *a,* the object of a subject's condensed *jouissance*(s). In other words, the subject is neither a self nor a metaphor for Lacan, but a structural effect of the object *a* that divides its imaginary consistencies and symbolic identifications by the voice, the gaze, the breast, and the feces—four objects that correspond to the four partial drives and that evoke traits particular to subject identification and desire— which orient thought and action and which organize the hole at its border where *jouissance* resides in the particular.[18] As Skrirabine points out, in *Seminar XX,* Lacan writes that "for each speaking being, the cause of his desire is strictly as to structure, equivalent . . . to his fold . . . his division of subject" (Skrirabine, 64).

Yet, how could Lacan's topology give a greater clarity to the mysterious nature of *what* constitutes the literary? On the one hand, Lacan uses topology as a domain of science by which science takes account of its own failure to suture the lack of the subject. But the subject, as subject of unconscious desire and fantasy, is only a correlative of science—the subject that science forecloses; even though this subject "remains the correlative of science, it is an antinomic correlate since science announces itself as defined from the nonissue of the effort to suture it . . . [because] the subject is . . . in internal exclusion to its object" (Skrirabine, 65). Divided by the signifier (in alienation— [/]) and the object (in separation or intersection—[◇]), the subject must seek a complement of being in both spheres: in filling the $S(\varnothing)$, the real emptiness in the Other, by the identifications that enable fantasy and its partial realizations that give one enough positive material to live by.

When Lacan writes the Other as $S(\varnothing)$, his matheme for the void, or the lack of a whole universe, he works from certain mathematical premises that also apply to how meaning functions: a ≠ (does not equal) b, a ≠ c, a ≠ d. Starting with "a," then, we have an ensemble (b, c, d), each of which defines itself in terms of its difference from "a." This is another way of demonstrating what Morel depicts topologically: Each square covered by the associative signifying chain of thoughts it can pull in can only function an inverted reflection of mind/memory precisely because at least one square is not covered over. This principle alone puts an empty set in the place of the catalyst that moves language along an interwoven chain of thought and desire.

In other words, we have ensembles of meaning only as long as "one element is lacking in it each time; one exception. Language, like mathematics, aims at the 'sense' of its meaning, following the logic of a signifier which sustains itself based on a logic of difference" (Skrirabine, 66). The difference in question for Lacan is not the Derridean *différance* of minimal shadings between the mark and the trace of whatever is represented, however. Rather, it is the difference of one element from another creating a concrete gap, a space of emptiness, into which, and out of which, primordial effects—unconscious narratives and sublimated drives— appear, disappear, and reappear. Insofar as the signifier itself marks a difference—is, indeed, a differential—a signifier will always be lacking between the gap and another one. Lacan denotes the gap that eventually becomes the $\mathcal{S}$ as the negative phi, $(-\varphi)$ or $\underline{-\varphi}$. Denoting this incompleteness in the universe as $\varnothing$, Lacan points out that, even if one equates nonidentical elements—a ≠ A—a heterogeneous element has been introduced that differs from itself. The relation of this element to the $\varnothing$ will be that of a notable, even if minimally so, inconsistency: the Other only exists as barred (Skrirabine, 66). This bar serves as a limit point, thus determining the difference between Lacan's incompleteness theorem and that of Gödel, who deduces an infinite infinitization.

When one tries to equate signifiers (a = a), the signifier can only define itself by its differences from itself—that is, by exclusions. Thus, the subject ($\mathcal{S}$) is spoken by its fundamental signifiers. For example, S_1, the master signifier, is inaccessible as a point of unconscious identification of the Ideal ego. It nonetheless sustains thinking and being. Insofar as S_1 is primordially repressed, it can only grasp itself at the level of its differences from itself. It is of such microdifferences that Derrida constitutes his vast text(s) of slippages, maximal and minimal. Lacan learned that no difference can occur at all unless its referent is a negative space, what he called the one-minus (*un-en-moins*). He learned this in his decades of practice in a clinic of psychosis where the deficit is of the lack of a negative space.

To depict the logical time in which a signifier tries to grasp itself, Lacan drew the unit of an interior 8: ◉.[19] In the intersection of two circles here— ◐ —Lacan placed logic and topology; reunion and intersection. Although the hole itself—a torus [◉]—excludes the intersection, it places the real in language and being: "The impossible which shows up there is the same on the basis of which the subject founds itself" (Skrirabine, 67). Lacan's topology is this structure that he calls in "L'étourdit" "the real brought to light in language" (33).[20] Skrirabine describes it as the necessity of founding the subject in the signifier, making each subject a respondent of the hole, to the point of lack in the Other from which the subject—as a lack—remains suspended and excluded. The subject, therefore, can only be re-presented in the signifying chain (Skrirabine, 67).

Lacan developed this topology from *Seminar IX* on identification, mentioning it as a tridimensional effect in the word (*parole*) as early as the "Rome Discourse" (1953) in reference to symbolic mortality. This void center that remains exterior to language is what Lacan called "extimacy": The outside is actually the inside of a distant interior that the literary text—in all its forms—tries to recapture at the levels of meaning and essence. Thus, the object *a* aimed at in language can only be a missing object whose leftover properties—whose unary traits—include passage, perspective (image), geometrical, and optical dimensions of space, all of which come from the early experience of a mirror structuring of "self" (or Ideal ego) by others and the Other.[21]

Notes

1.   Jacques Lacan, "The Agency of the Letter in the Unconscious or Reason since Freud," in *Ecrits: A Selection,* trans. Alan Sheridan (New York: W. W. Norton, 1980), 146–78.

2.   Samuel Weber, *Return to Freud: Jacques Lacan's Dislocation of Psychoanalysis,* trans. Michael Levine (Cambridge: Cambridge University Press, 1991).

3.   Bruce Fink, *The Lacanian Subject: Between Language and Jouissance* (Princeton: Princeton University Press, 1995).

4.   Jacques Lacan, "Hommage fait à Marguerite Duras, du ravissement de Lol V. Stein," *Ornicar?* 34 (July–Sept. 1985): 7–13. All translations are the author's except where indicated.

5.   Jacques Lacan, *Le séminaire, livre XXII: R.S.I., 1974–1975,* seminar of March 18, 1975, unedited.

6.   Jacques Lacan, *The Seminar of Jacques Lacan, Book XI: The Four Fundamental Concepts of Psycho-Analysis, 1964,* ed. Jacques-Alain Miller, trans. Alan Sheridan (New York: W. W. Norton, 1981), 186.

7.   Jacques Lacan, "The Subversion of the Subject and the Dialectic of Desire in the Freudian Unconscious," in *Ecrits: A Selection*, trans. Alan Sheridan (New York: W. W. Norton, 1980), 315; hereafter cited in text as "Subversion."

8.   My stress here is on the temporal nonlinearity of regular thought associations, which is not to be confused with Mesmerian concepts of memory attributed to hypnotized cataleptics to whom miraculous memories were imputed. The "photographic" memories reproduced were thought to demonstrate clairvoyance and genius. See, for example, Moriz Benedikt, "Catalepsy and Mesmerism," appendix 3 in Mikkel Borch-Jacobsen, *Remembering Anna O.: A Century of Mystification*, trans. Kirby Olson (New York: Routledge, 1996), 111–18.

9.   Charles Pyle, "The GAP in Lacanian Psychoanalysis and in Linguistics," photocopy.

10.   Jacques Lacan, *Le séminaire, livre XXIII: Le sinthome, 1975–1976,* unedited seminar; hereafter cited in the text as *Le sinthome.* Some of the lessons can be found in *Joyce avec Lacan,* ed. Jacques Aubert (Paris: Navarin, 1987).

11. Jacques Lacan, *The Seminar of Jacques Lacan, Book VII: The Ethics of Psychoanalysis, 1959–1960,* ed. Jacques-Alain Miller, trans. Dennis Porter (New York: W. W. Norton, 1986), 134–35; hereafter referred to in text as *Ethics.*

12. Ellie Ragland, "Medieval Rhetoric and Psychoanalysis," in *The Year's Work in Medievalism, 1994,* ed. David Metzger, with Gwendolyn Morgan (Holland, Mich.: Studies in Medievalism, 1997), 9:29–40.

13. Jacques Lacan, *The Seminar of Jacques Lacan, Book XX: Encore, On Feminine Sexuality, The Limits of Love and Knowledge, 1972–1973,* ed. Jacques-Alain Miller, trans. Bruce Fink (New York: W. W. Norton, 1998), 122; hereafter cited in text as *Encore.*

14. Jacques Lacan, "Kant with Sade," trans. James B. Swenson, *October* 51 (Winter 1989): 55–104, especially 63–64.

15. Jeanne Granon-Lafont, *Topologie Lacanienne et Clinique Analytique* (Cahors: Point Hors Ligne, 1990), 32–33; hereafter cited in text.

16. Dinitia Smith, "Philosopher Gamely in Defense of His Ideas," *New York Times,* May 30, 1998, A13, A15.

17. Jacques Lacan, "L'étourdit," *Scilicet* 4 (1973): 5–6; hereafter cited in text as "L'étourdit."

18. Pierre Skrirabine, "La clinique de Lacan et la topologie," *trAvaux: Le transfert* 5 (1990): 64–65; hereafter cited in text.

19. Jacques Lacan, *Le séminaire, livre IX: L'identification, 1961–1962,* unedited.

20. English translation by Jack Stone, "L'étourdit," 24.

21. Cf. Jacques Lacan, "The Mirror Stage as Formative of the Function of the I as Revealed in Psycho-Analytique Experience," in *Ecrits: A Selection,* trans. Alan Sheridan (New York: W. W. Norton, 1980).

Lacan Clinician

JACQUES-ALAIN MILLER

Before I begin, I should set straight a few minor details regarding Lacan's reception in North America. Lacan was not a surrealist poet; he was trained as an M.D. and a psychiatrist. It is true that, during the 1920s and 1930s, he had contacts with a few surrealists. In particular, he communicated to Salvador Dali his concept of paranoid knowledge, which, in the hands of Dali, was to become what you may know as "critical paranoid knowledge." But I really cannot allow you to say that Lacan was a surrealist poet; on the contrary he has a straight trajectory.

Let us recall first that Freud's works were initially received in France—and it is Freud himself who noticed it—by people in literature, when the groups that should have been most receptive to it, the medical profession, psychiatrists, whose interest Freud expected to attract, were closed to psychoanalysis.

It is noticeable, if only through this audience and the place where we are gathered, that Lacan's teaching has been first welcomed in North America by literature professors. It does appear to me that most of the participants in this conference belong to this profession, although there are a few analysts among you. This fact, in its magnitude, seems to me indicative of what one must call an intellectual abdication, the abdication of North American psychoanalysis, whose main current derives from the egopsychology that gave its main polemical impetus to the beginning of Lacan's teaching and precisely to the return to Freud, which Lacan made the slogan of his teaching. (We shall perhaps have the opportunity later to see what specific meaning he gave to this "return to Freud.") I am simply noticing that a few analysts are present and, in particular, a few from the International Psychoanalytical Association who bothered to come to hear about someone who spent his whole life dealing with psychoanalysis. I call this for what it is: an intellectual abdication.

Because of this fact, I have all the more appreciated the invitation I have received from this university and specifically from Mr. Henry Sullivan, this

Revision of keynote address given by Jacques-Alain Miller, Conference on The Reception of Post-structuralism in Francophone and Anglophone Canada, held at The University of Ottawa, May 10, 1984, sponsored by The University of Ottawa and The Canadian Council. Translated by Françoise Massardier-Kenney.

invitation that gives me the opportunity to speak to you—and I must also say to listen to you, which is what is most important to me—and to participate with you in this conference.

This is the very first time that I speak thus in the Anglo-Saxon and North American area, not era: language can sometimes be ambiguous. I must say that, previously, I declined Lacan's invitation to accompany him to the Baltimore conference, in 1966, where Mr. Donato, if I remember correctly, had attempted to gather the best representatives of what you now call *poststructuralism*. I remember perfectly Mr. Donato coming to Paris and gathering what is today called poststructuralism to bring it to Baltimore. Thus, it is that I speak here for the first time in North America; I did not speak in Baltimore in 1966.

To begin, I cannot avoid making a few remarks about poststructuralism. When I accepted his invitation, I did not hide from Mr. Sullivan, who is with us today, that I could absolutely not condone the expression of *poststructuralism*. And he did not object, very courteously, to my holding my assent on this point until you explain to me the way in which you are using this term, and I am open to discussion on this.

First let me remark that the term *poststructuralism* is not in use in France. We have known structuralism, which took shape and impetus from a fad in the educated public around 1966. I remind you that, at that time, the Parisian obsession with structuralism was great, that there was a general taste for the austere knowledge of specialists, and that, at that time, people believed in a new age of enlightenment. It was not really understood that Lacan, in this very year 1966 when everyone in Paris had their heads turned by structuralism, announced that structuralism "would last the length of time roses, symbolism, and Parnasses last." This citation must be understood by the French literature specialists who are in this room. Lacan announced that structuralism would only last the length of a literary season.

As for me, I have a weakness for this period—meaning a certain inclination—and I never speak of it without some fondness because, during 1966, a year that I am giving you as a historical marker, I was a philosophy student, and every week with my fellow students of the Ecole Normale Supérieure, I would go hear Lacan at his seminar. Beginning in 1963, I had attended Roland Barthes's seminar at the Hautes Etudes School; at the start, we were 20—and I think that I was the first one to mention Jacques Derrida's name to Barthes. I was taking Derrida's classes at the Sorbonne and then at the Ecole Normale, where I must say that I did not leave him while he was doing his tutoring of what's called a caiman. The tutor of the students at the Ecole Normale is called thus because he prepares the students for the extremely competitive *agrégation* exam, and when they fail the exam, he cries crocodile tears.

So at that time I saw Derrida. The other caiman of the Ecole Normale was Louis Althusser, whose name, by the way, is not on your list of poststructuralists. It is to him I owe having read Lacan for the first time. He told me to read Lacan, saying that I would find it interesting. To tell you how insightful he was, it is also thanks to Althusser that I met Michel Foucault, who came to the Ecole Normale to present his *History and Madness,* which was his first great important book. And if I may, to end these remarks that bring a personal touch to what you group as poststructuralism, I want to add that, on Thursday evenings between 1964 and 1966, Barthes and Foucault had dinner together, and I was often invited as the student, as the third party, to participate in their festivities. It also happened that, at that time, Lacan would sometimes come in the evening to our quarters, what's called a *turne* at the Ecole Normale—that is to say, a dorm room—to answer, almost in secret, the questions that four or five of us had about his seminar of that week. I even remember that it was after Barthes's lecture on "The Structuralist Activity," a lecture that set the trend of structuralism, that we all came back to rue d'Ulm with Althusser, where he did the cooking, something he did very well. I am telling you all this to show you that structuralism existed as a movement, and even as a feeling of congeniality at that time. Lévi-Strauss was present during the first lesson of Lacan's seminar, *The Four Fundamental Concepts.* Every time he came to Paris, Roman Jakobson stayed with Lacan. Foucault was at Lacan's seminar a few days after his book *Words and Things* came out. I must say that Foucault (who had known Lacan since he was 15 years old) always claimed he did not understand a thing of Lacan—which means that, if this is the case for you, you are in good company. This first structuralism of the 1960s, as I lived it, was a time rich in friendship and discoveries, a time vibrant with the feeling of novelty that accompanies all emerging truths. And I brought my own contribution by creating, with my friends, a journal, in January 1966, called *Cahiers pour l'Analyse,* which published, as its first text, the essay by Lacan entitled "Science and Truth," which is the last text of his volume of the *Ecrits.*

Here is how it ended. At that time, it was possible to imagine that all these intellectual endeavors were consonant, harmonious—that they converged. And after that period, I must tell you, it was not poststructuralism, it was animosity—and I don't want to go into details here—animosity that Roland Barthes was probably the only one not to share and who remained friends with everyone. One can say that these authors were at one time united in the spirit of the time, but each went on the way that was his own before, which stayed his afterward, and which was never that of the others. As for me, I base myself on my student experience—I described myself as a kind of Figaro at that time, going hither and thither, from one to the other—to tell you that there isn't any poststructuralism. There was structuralism, a structuralist movement, a motion among researchers in the social sciences, among students, writers, those who write, and the public. Poststructuralism is only the fallout of this movement. So what is its validity? In my opinion, only that of a heading that must be called by its name—the validity of a garbage can.

And this heading is misleading; it does not help any of the concerns of each of its authors.

As I am making the opening speech of this conference, it seemed appropriate to me to mention each of these names and to do it rather through the memory of friendship. But if I read the program correctly, these names are ordered in separate series for each of them, and this is fine because poststructuralism does not form an ensemble, unless it is an ensemble of dispersion. Thus, I consider, at least for me, that the question of poststructuralism must be cleared away in order to find one's way and especially, because I am among you in Lacan's name, in order to find one's way in Lacan. I am now going to speak about him.

I was told that it was expected of me that I would tell some truth about Lacan. To do so here, many ways are opened to me. Because my acquaintance with Lacan has a long history, to present him in 50 minutes is obviously difficult. But first, I take this into account; you are almost all professors of literature, and you know Lacan as the author of the *Ecrits*. Well, here, preconceived ideas must also be cleared away. What concerns you is to know, I suppose, whether it is possible to use what Lacan brings in your literary discipline. It is not so much a question of the importance of Lacan. What concerns you, for the most part, is exporting Lacan for literary criticism.

I will put you immediately at ease about this—it is up to you to decide what you can import into your literary discipline from Lacan. I must nonetheless advise you that Lacan did not devote his work to giving you something with which to reread literary texts. Lacan devoted his work to the practice of psychoanalysis. It must be made clear because it seems precisely in the obsession, the enthusiasm, to read him, that one imagines he wrote for oneself. This is not so. He wrote and devoted his work to the practice of psychoanalysis, to its elucidation and its transformation. And I am not saying that he devoted his work to the reading and the restitution of the meaning of Freud's works—although obviously it was a concern of his—because even his reading of Freud was for him only a means and not an end, the end being his practice of psychoanalysis.

Let us say that right away; unlike Freud, Lacan does not conceive of an applied psychoanalysis. *Au sens propre,* he thought that psychoanalysis can be applied only as a critical treatment. This is applied psychoanalysis—that is to say, psychoanalysis applied to a subject who speaks and hears. This seriously limits the activity that can be engaged in the name of Lacan. Of course, this does not prevent us from being inspired by the method of psychoanalysis: to decipher the signifier without presupposing the signified, if this is the way we can characterize most simply the method of psychoanalysis inasmuch as one can use it as an inspiration for literary criticism. But before the work of art, what can the analyst do? The thesis of Lacan is that the analyst shouldn't do a critique of literature; he can only take examples from it: that is to say that with the work of art, it is a question of emulation—not of criticism—for the analyst. This emphasizes Lacan's point. It implies the opposite of a scorn for literature. It implies, rather, its most extreme valorization. You probably know that Lacan studied James Joyce a great deal; he would certainly have wished to produce a magnum opus on Joyce that he did not write; and I saw him throughout the years in the 1970s fill his library with everything that was being published or ever had been published on Joyce—that constituted a huge library, some 300 volumes on Joyce—titles that Professor Jacques Aubert (who is Joyce's translator into French) would pass on to him. Lacan was thus quite interested in Joyce, but he said precisely that Joyce would not have gained anything by a psychoanalysis, which his patroness offered him, not because Jung would have done the analysis but because it was Lacan's opinion that Joyce was already going directly to the best that can be expected of a psychoanalysis at its end. I will come back to this essential point later in my speech.

This is not to say that psychoanalysis has no effect on literature. I think that the very existence of psychoanalysis, on the contrary, has affected literature as it has affected hysteria. One psychoanalyst in the world was enough for the treatment of hysteria to change—because clinical treatment is not unchangeable; it is itself caught in history, and the presence of the analyst has already caused hysteria to pale. I also think that there is a postanalytic literature and that, in some way, since analysis, literature is split between a literature of pure fantasy and a literature of the symptom, as Lacan called Joyce's writing. I am only mentioning this briefly; perhaps we will have the opportunity to come back to it.

Thus, when you find references to theater, short stories, novels, and poems in Lacan's *Ecrits* and in his *Séminaire,* you must know that, for him, they are only there in a discourse concerned with the analytic experience: a *mise en fonction* for illustrative purposes, as examples aiming at clarifying or explaining the analytic experience. And I would say that he is a *bricoleur.* That's what is justified by the fact that, for everyone, whether they know it or not, the signifier functions first as separate from its meaning; it is for this reason precisely that it lends itself to new meanings. People are misled if they think that they criticize Lacan because he does not hide that he is taking from literature what can act as an apologia for psychoanalysis; it is founded precisely on the autonomy of the signifier in regard to signification. We need this reminder to start with, considering your discipline; there isn't any literary criticism in Lacan, just as there isn't any anthropology in Freud. Through the spoken myth in Freud's work, through the literary text in Lacan's, there is an approach, a clamping of limit points of the psychoanalytic discourse by these other disciplines. But there isn't, strictly speaking, any literary criticism. Psychoanalytic interpretation belongs only to the analytic experience as a saying (*le dit*) of the analyst, a saying from which he expects, on the side of the subject in analysis, a mutation. Interpretation—in Lacan's sense—is not a construction.

PART 2

Interpretation is the seizing of the opportunity during the analytic session. Obviously, here, I am afraid I am taking aim at a few among you; I tell you this on my part only to stress that I consider things Lacan's way. All the same, I recognize that it is up to literary critics to say what is useful from the elaboration of Freud and Lacan because I acknowledge that you, too, have the right to be *bricoleurs* and even to be poachers. I ask you only to keep in mind how Lacan understood it. He said it once, and I will repeat it to you: "If literary criticism could actually renew itself, it would be from the fact that psychoanalysis is here for texts to measure themselves against, the enigma being on its side"—on the side of psychoanalysis. But obviously, the problem is that this sentence itself presents an enigma. I am giving you a word of caution and also of incitation to mark that Lacan is not primarily addressing you. It is thus necessary to make some effort in order to manage to become the recipient of his message. In this way, it has happened that a few became psychoanalysts.

To move toward Lacan, as that is my goal today, one must take—and I apologize again—a third precaution; I must undo for you a third presupposition that is a trap. This trap is the one contained in this volume of the *Ecrits,* exegeses of which are beginning to be published in English, this book that, as Professor Sullivan reminded us, came out in 1966, a date that is a turning point. What is the trap? It will be my way of telling you not how you must read Lacan but how I read him. There is a fact: Lacan writes. If he never claimed he was a writer, he still has his own style, as those who have tackled it have found out, and this style supports a knowledge that, apparently, is a whole. This is enough for Lacan, once imported into academia—where, I emphasize, he does not belong—to have been converted into an author and his teaching converted into an oeuvre. It is thought that the *Ecrits* is a book, and this lure has many effects on the very way people read him; that it is to say that Lacan is read and is quoted, Lacan's sentences are brought together, the first page of this book is thought to be contemporary with the last one. People imagine that Lacan has a doctrine and, occasionally, they propose to produce its synthesis. They think he has a doctrine that he applies, in the course of time, to different objects. Thus, Lacan is explored as if in a time of suspension: that is, he is supposed to already have the knowledge he is constructing. One must, by the way, call it for what it is—it is exactly an effect of transference. And one must notice, I notice it all the time, that Lacan's style generates this transfer: by that, I mean a supposition of knowledge that goes beyond the knowledge that is explicit, a style that precisely creates the supposition of a knowledge that would not be known. That is what Lacan accounts for with the name of unconscious. In this regard, Lacan's style—which one could nevertheless call so formal, so abstract—effectively mobilizes the subject supposed-to-know, and as a consequence, people think that, in this volume, everything is contemporary.

One must say that Lacan himself stands for something in this illusion because, every 10 pages, here goes his mirror stage again: the master and the slave, the "you are my wife"—I am speaking for those who have leafed through the *Ecrits* before—we see these same references come up again and again. We can thus think that all this is said in the same time frame. Doesn't Lacan admit that he stumbles, trips, changes, corrects himself, transforms? He admits it all the time, but he is not heard—because we are under the spell of a style that, however tortuous it may be, however gnarled, obviously unfolds normally, habitually, in the mode of assertion. And people don't realize that Lacan not only never rewrote the same text but also never rewrote the same thesis, that he never gave the equivalent of a text. He never found his principle of theoretical activity in the single treatment of new objects, with a doctrine already established and invariable. There are obviously some authors (I won't give any names) who already have—even if their style is continually in the conditional and interrogative—in their pocket, every time, the answer that they are only waiting to give all along during a difficult move forward. I would say of Lacan, rather, that there isn't one single writing of his that does not modify the one that it follows. I would almost go so far as to say that the end of a writing by Lacan is not often contemporary with its beginning. I mean that the definition posed at the beginning, having evolved in the course of the text, is distinct from its end. If that is the only thing that you remember of what I am telling you, that would already be enough. There is no oeuvre by Lacan; there is a teaching by Lacan. And I must let you understand what Lacan meant by this and the resistance that he opposes precisely to those readings that people want to make. Lacan never said anything different about himself. In what terms does he speak about what he does? In terms of itinerary, of moving forward, of clearing a way. One gets lost in the definitions that Lacan provides. In fact, a definition in Lacan is an operation that does not compare at all to what academic disciplines think a definition is, even scientific disciplines.

Lacan's definitions construct and modify what they introduce; they do not describe it. They are, in this regard, like many signifiers that create their signified; but also, Lacan's definitions are not superposable. I mean that. When you look for a passage in which he speaks of the phallus and then another, and when you believe that you will be able to superpose these two definitions one on the other, you are mistaken, because you act as if what it is about exists independently of the way it is introduced. And that is why there are battles of quotations that I attend in Paris; still, I have put things in good order. One must understand that the statement "This is not a book" means that it is a route, an itinerary. You must reintroduce the factor of time in Lacan's *Ecrits*. The very formulas that he repeats—the unconscious structured like a language, or the subject represented by a signifier for another signifier—do not have the same exact value twice. It is easy to understand there that his seminar, which took place every week for a long time, was his particular elective mode of elaboration. Lacan was not one to relax on a beach of knowledge and rework it by increasing repetitions as other authors do; his teaching was first an oral, achromatic teaching, and most of his writings fall from it as so many conundrums, as so many pieces of waste. These are his own terms that are memorials of more than one resistance of the Other, embodied in a public who became more and more numerous, even though they did not understand. Lacan's success has been that, at the beginning, there were 50 people who did not understand him and that, at the end, there were thousands.

Was this public held by the prestige of the assertions? Or more secretly, wasn't it solicited by a problematic whose spring is doubtlessly fundamentally aporetic? It is a fact, I say it, that, up until now, nobody has noticed a thing except the fire. Lifted as they were by Lacan's *dits,* in the form of oracles, they believed, or by his mathemes which seemed definitive, the reader of the *Ecrits,* no less than the former listener of the seminars, did not know how to understand Lacan's questions. In reading Lacan, he only notices Lacan's answers, and usually he doesn't know where they come from.

This is the way I invite you to read Lacan; this is the way, in the weekly class I hold on Lacan, I reconstitute the underlying problematic of his teaching, yet, which is right at the surface. What I show is quite different from what has been perceived of Lacan up to now; I show a Lacan thinking against Lacan. I show not a prophet claiming his certitudes to every wind that blows but a Lacan who answers to himself more than to anybody else and who is never more assertive than when he is arguing against himself.

So how does one read Lacan? I will answer from his questions and as much from what he says as from what he doesn't say. Otherwise, how does one understand that he gave so much importance, at the beginning of his teaching, for example, to the formula "supposed-to-show" by which the dialectic of recognition—"You are my wife/woman"—demonstrates the necessity, in order to say "I am a man," to speak to the other first, in order to found himself in his being. This meant, very simply, that he thought it possible to found a sexual rapport with the symbol. And to the contrary, for many years at the end of his life, his slogan became the proposition that precisely in the symbolic there is no possibility of founding the sexual relation as a rapport.

One does not understand the insistence of what Lacan repeats during the 1970s if one doesn't realize that he says the opposite, on this point, of what he was saying in the 1950s. This will obviously mean something only for those who are already somewhat familiar with Lacan.

It is thus my position that Lacan's teaching is not a summa, it is not a dogma; it is not a knowledge supported by a master signifier that plugs up its truth, but a teaching that arises from a permanent effort made against repression. And this is how Lacan could affirm that he spoke in his seminar as an analysand—which must be understood exactly: as a subject as he conceived of it, and you know how he writes this subject, S —as barred subject, that is, a subject not defined by what he or she knows but, on the contrary, defined by his or her "I don't want to know."

Lacan's teaching, in a way, shows a great deal of continuity because every step implies the previous step; but it does not develop like a linear deduction because the consequence, on occasion, erases the premises and always reframes and moves them. Here is the perspective that I find right in regard to how to read Lacan, and I think you will benefit, at least, from thinking positively about this way of perceiving Lacan; this will mislead you less than what is occasionally proposed as a synthesis of Lacan.

How is it possible, after what I have just said, to make Lacan appear to you in broad daylight? First, I must mention two dates: 1901 and 1981. You have here the milestones of his life in its vastness, poststructuralism being only a small wave that occurred at a specific moment. The middle of his life is 1941; that is when he settled at 3, rue de Lille in Paris in his office, which Stuart Schneiderman has briefly described in his book [*Jacques Lacan: The Death of an Intellectual Hero*[1]], and one must say that Lacan progressively had an enormous practice. I am not saying important, but enormous,—and that took most of his time. This is already what sets him apart from academics; he had an enormous practice, and I would even say—and it is perhaps the way in which Lacan should be presented in the United States—that he was the psychoanalyst who has had the largest clinical experience of all time. I am saying this fully aware of the superlative. But this is indisputable. Lacan has been reproached for holding sessions that were too short; one can consider this reproach as one wants. The consequence in any case is that he saw more patients during that time than any other psychoanalyst. And I don't think that you can do this for 50 years while being what is called a show-off; this kind of clinical practice could not go on for 50 years for a mere show-off.

My idea was to talk to you primarily as literature specialists, but Mrs. Ellie Sullivan pointed out to me that first I still had to give you an idea of what is at stake in Lacan's teaching in relation to this practice. At bottom, what is at stake from this practice is what one can learn and transmit about what man is from the experience, limited by its definition, that psychoanalysis constitutes. What one can learn about man goes far. One can learn about his or her desire, especially about one's difficulties with one's desire. For instance, one can learn why man defends himself against his desire—that is to say, why it can be that, in the very movement of one's desire, one can be stopped by a limit, an invisible limit, about which he or she knows nothing, and desire falls. This happens especially if the subject is an obsessional neurotic. Or one can learn why this man or woman can support his or her desire only on the mode of dissatisfaction—if she is a hysteric; or if he is a pervert, why that subject's desire is linked to the presence of a specific object, of a radical particularity, lacking which he or she does not desire. This object is there as the condition of the possibility of his or her desire. Sometimes it occurs that the subject in question is crazy, that he or she is convinced that another persecutes him or her and experiences pleasure in persecuting him or her—that is paranoia; and that this Other is interested in him in a way that is so exclusive that he will even talk to him in his head. That is called mental automation; or the idea that, in her body, her organs play on their own—that is often called schizophrenia. Or this subject may make him- or herself into the refuse of discourse and will not even engage in it—and that is called, too lightly, autism.

Of course, this is clinical practice, which is what Lacan saw all his life and what he did. But this term *clinical practice* is too convenient to use for putting aside what I just said. It allows one to imagine that these difficulties and avatars of desire would be a kind of zoology. On the contrary, from Freud on, human difficulties with desire are anthropology itself, except that the concept of "man" does not come back out as certain as it was when it went in. And why is it, starting from Freud, that clinical practice acquires this status? It is because Freud extended the field of established facts, or facts that seemed that way. Freud showed that what seemed to be the conundrums of mental life—dreams, slips of the tongue or pen, stumbling behavior, witticisms (and this is accepted by everyone, beyond those who maintain a certain affected skepticism)—are ordered facts, conveyed in what deserves to be called a logic. By this hypothesis, he showed that these facts and difficulties with desire are valid for all speaking beings. I understand this, in terms of the definition of "speaking being," because this is valid as well for all those who listen. What has the same value for all is the fact of the symptom. What distinguishes the analytic symptom from the psychiatric symptom and the medical symptom is that the former is established by the person who speaks of it himself, not by the clinician who observes him. In the analytic experience, it must be said in this way: the subject is his own clinician. There is a symptom in the analytic sense when the subject experiences himself as overwhelmed by what is happening in his own thought, in the sphere of what he thinks makes his being. Let us add that his thought can just as well go down into his body. This symptom takes a clinical form when it becomes impossible to bear—without this impasse, one manages to live with it, which does not mean that one does not have these symptoms. That is how Lacan defined the clinic—the real as that which is impossible to bear. But from there, obviously, there are artifices that enable one to bear this condition; there are a certain number of cataplasms and plugs, such as culture, for instance. Culture, in its most general definition, is what arranges, tames, and attenuates the impossible to bear; it is the ensemble of artifices that can make the real bearable, that can enable one to bear it with patience. And I will even say that styles and fashions respond increasingly to what turns out to be, at every moment, unbearable for the contemporaries—which means that one cannot imagine that, by saying "It is a matter of clinical practice," one separates what is involved in psychoanalysis by the closed space of the analyst's office. For instance, Freud could write his work *Mass Psychology* because psychoanalysis is itself a social experience—that is to say, an experience in which the minimal constituents of the social bond are present. That is what he says in his introduction: There are two individuals, and we have there *a minima* of the constituents of the social bond—two individuals to whom you must add language, the concrete universal discourse. It is from this that Lacan, in the 1970s, defined four fundamental modes of the social bond that he called the four discourses.

From this point, one can have a notion of what produces the social disruptions that take the form of epidemics; it is perhaps in this direction, by the same thread, that one can have an idea of why people are so sensitive to the irruption of a new signifier. To experience it, it is sufficient, for instance, to study the birth of Islam in the seventh century. There you see that a man, through his discourse, can bring together crowds and catapult them into a movement that makes wars and conquests. It is from Mahomet's signifier that this happens, not from anything else. It is generally thought that those effects of disruption show man's irrationality; we have such an example in World War II. One gives up reason when one speaks of the action of evil in history. Here, to be a rationalist is, to the contrary, to try to understand why people are so sensitive to the action of the signifier, because that is what it is. Why are people so sensitive to the action of the signifier? If this word *signifier* bothers you, then, let us say, so sensitive to the action of *discourse*? That is what must also be established and approached in the analytic experience. That is what is at stake in psychoanalysis as Lacan understands it—psychoanalysis that is apparently such a limited experience.

PART 3

One must say that discourse also has a consequence for the way in which we can understand what science is about, because science is also a matter of the introduction of a new signifier—which alters the world and nature well beyond what we can master of the changes. Clinically, science is a psychosis. When Galileo formulated the statement "Nature is written in mathematical terms," what was he saying if not that, in the real, there is already a knowledge that functions in and of itself? It is from the point when this was asserted in the seventeenth century that we can speak of science, from the moment when it was postulated that, in the real, there is a knowledge, which functions on its own. Today, we have the incidence of this science through those objects that are called gadgets, about which a computer manager from the Silicon Valley recently said something that I found so deep, so exemplary, that I made a commentary about it in one of my classes. This also gives us the extent of what is at stake from the point of view of the signifier: "Home computers are a solution without a problem." I saw there precisely the particular mode of incidence of the signifier unleashed by science. It is from there that I have restituted the mode of the particularity of the subject in analysis, which is, on the contrary, that of a question; the subject brings the emptiness of his or her question.

Why does psychoanalytic practice not belong to a kind of zoology? There is also the clinical question: Why don't things between men and women go so well? It had to be said. Things don't go well and never do; in the end, everyone knows it. Everyone knows that there is no preestablished harmony between the sexes, that it is not possible to play at an ethology of human behavior from a sexual standpoint. It has been tried sometimes; we are shown animal couplings, and they try, as in Desmond Morris's book *The Naked Ape*,[2] to put a few pages at the end to attempt to include men and women. And the only thing found as a female signal would be the variations of the pupil; it is not much compared to what is displayed in the animal world.

The essential problem, and that is what Lacan meant by his statement "There is no sexual relation [or rapport]," is that, of course, there are sexual relations, but there is not in the human species a relation that is fixed and invariable, as if it were written beforehand, thanks to which a woman or a man recognizes the other as the one necessary to him or her. This is why there is room for invention, and throughout history many different ways, many social ways, have been invented that allow men and women to relate to each other, precisely in the absence of this fixed and invariable relation.

What we must observe as well is that humans invent little in this matter, and, unlike those who expect much from the liberation of desire, the analytic experience shows that the reparatory of fantasies men and women are capable of is extremely limited.

Of course, there is the case of perversions that are really inventions put in the place of this sexual relation that is not written or pregiven. But there, too, the catalog of perversions is extremely limited. Lacan said once—I don't know if his audience understood him, but with what I am telling you here, you can grasp the thread—"The best thing that could be expected from psychoanalysis would be the invention of a new perversion," which meant a new way to catch the relation between man and woman that is not a fixed and invariable relation. This means that, from the clinical point of view of the relations of man and woman, there is no "know how." That is to say that, in our scientific age, one attempts to treat this relation technically. But we must say, rather, that it is a renewed form of wisdom. What we catch through sexology in the technical appearances of handling it is a renewed form of what was hoped for from antique wisdoms and oriental wisdoms, which were also fashionable at one point. One hopes for a "know how" with sexual pleasure.

The existence of psychoanalysis proves, to the contrary, the bewilderment of the subject in regard to his or her *jouissance,* especially in the age of science.

I made a quick survey. One can always say that Lacan's innovation consisted of showing us a decentered subject. Lacan has never presented what he said as a decentering of the subject; to speak of decentering, Freud on occasion compared his discovery to that of Copernicus. The problem with the Copernican decentering is that it promotes a center more central than any, because it is the sun. With Lacan, it is a completely different matter. First, it is a matter of noting in man this ex-centering from the signifier; but beyond, psychoanalysis discovered a being of man strictly new in history. It is not simply that, in his being, the subject is sensitive to the signifier—and that is essential. It is not simply that man gives himself mere words that he or she says or listens to. It is not simply that, for the speaking being, language preexists him or her. That language preexists the human being who enters it is a fundamental notion because if you don't place this proposition first, you are led to Chomsky's elucubrations on language biology, questions for which, as a linguist, he has no chance of ever finding the answer. The question that really concerns the linguist is that language is already there, before anyone begins to speak; language is already there on the outside, in the world, in what Lacan calls the Other, which precedes the subject.

Freud discovered in this regard that there are, for every speaking being, words that are decisive. And on occasion, these are words that were uttered before he was born because sometimes, and even as a rule, they are the words of the parents' discourse that determine as well what he will have to pay later during his life. In this regard, the relay of the debt formed by his or her parents is passed on to him or her. So we must recognize the decisive function for everyone of what he or she was in the desire of his or her parents; and psychoanalysis is here to teach us the ravages that are the effects of the nondesire of the parents on those children. Children who are not desired, if nothing comes to oppose it, have a tendency to suicide, and even through psychoanalysis, we must admit that it is not easy to change that.

This is part of things; man appears in psychoanalysis as a shred of discourse, a piece of discourse. And that is what Freud himself formulated—although people did not understand him—with the concept of the superego. It was thought that the superego meant morality. Not at all! The concept of the superego was psychologized. Superego means that there are formulas that force themselves upon humans and guide them, whether they want it or not, on the paths of *jouissance* that on occasion they reject, a *jouissance* that on occasion they do not want. And that's how the paradox is explained: the way Lacan formulated the imperative of the Freudian superego as *Jouis!* (Enjoy!)

How does one conceive this? It is even nice to say that, on top of it that, this paradox of *Jouis!* relies on experience. Lacan's teaching consists in trying to give a form that I call rational to those facts that, as I deliver them to you in a heap, obviously give a somewhat catastrophic image of the human species. But it is an image that is not so far from our daily reality.

How does one conceive this, not only say it or describe it? That's what Lacan did by posing the concept of subject, a concept that is more extreme and extraordinary than people think and that surprised our structuralists at the time when it was thought that structure involved the evacuation of the subject. The concept of subject is the way in which Lacan tries to account for man as a shred of discourse, of this being so sensitive to discourse, who tries through discourse to forge a bond with a partner whose formula he does not have. This subject, first, must be a subject who would go beyond the individual, who has always been defined, from Aristotle on, from the living, the living body. Precisely because this subject depends on occasion on words said before he or she was born, he must, of course, be defined as transindividual. Moreover, it is necessary to define him or her as well as a subject to identify with. This is where the Freudian concept of identification comes in. But what does it include? What does the fact that man is inclined to identify involve? Precisely that there is in him a lack of identity. It is through this that he is caught in a movement of identification. And this is what Lacan writes as $. He writes it $ because you can't write S = S. This is the way you write the subject who identifies.

The subject is also indispensable because man, in the dimension that psychoanalysis approaches, is not a master; man is a serf—that is, subject. This is also what subject means in Lacan's sense. And his is also the subject of the superego. Why must we write $ for this subject of the superego? Because he presents the paradox of being a subject who is led to act against his own good, and in this, he is divided. That is essentially what remained inconceivable for philosophy, in its ancient tradition—that, precisely, for man, his most acute *jouissance* could be exactly the opposite of his well-being.

Moreover, that is where what Lacan calls an ethics of psychoanalysis imposes itself; it is true that there is a choice to make and that looking for the truth of *jouissance* most certainly disturbs well-being. Besides, this is why the people who come into analysis do so, because this *jouissance* has disturbed their well-being, having created the impossible to bear.

What necessitates positing the subject is also that he or she is the subject of the symptom, that is to say, the subject overwhelmed by what wells up in him or her—she does not know what is happening to her.

Attempting to elaborate logically, and not rhetorically as I am doing here, a subject that could be this serf subject of discourse—this transindividual subject, this subject who is subjected to identification, this subject of the superego, this subject of the symptom—is what constitutes the thread, the nerve of Lacan's teaching. That is what he called the "subversion of the subject." It is the concept of a subject as it never existed before.

Structuralists—even poststructuralists, if the term has any meaning—imagined that structures excluded the subject, that they excluded man. For them, the subject, that is to say, its structures, in the end functioned on their own and were in a relation of exteriority with man. Lévi-Strauss never said anything else. When you think from structures, the concept of man is useless, which is simply to pose things in a relation of exteriority; for example, one proposes that the cycles of language are running and there is no need to posit man in order to account for this functioning.

Afterward, there was what I shall call the poststructuralist intoxication—and there the term applies itself, I admit it—that consisted, after having read the structuralists, in their thinking that signifiers combine with each other, that they are impossible to master, that they don't form sets, and that texts speak to texts; that's what, I think, was vaguely called intertext. I would say that it is academic intoxication par excellence, the frenzy of erudition, because, in fact, it consists in stressing the signifier as a *semblant*, (as if it were *das Ding* in itself), which means that it has no consequence on anything but the other signifiers. If you like, it is the frenzy of thinking that one signifier is equivalent to another. And thus, through a game of substitution, of gaps, we are embarked on an infinite metonymy in which the ultimate truth is that there is no ultimate truth, in which the last word is that there is no end. It is sometimes called, I think, deconstruction. Myself, I would call this metonymism, the metonymism where, in fact, one always knows ahead of time the response one brings to the process. The answer is precisely nothing; that is to say, the construction is only one of contingency and in short reflects the weight of the tradition. It is always the same.

What I am describing here roughly, and which, I think, will shock a few, is that, in fact, we are speaking here of knowledge as pure seeming or appearance (*semblant*). "As pure seeming" means unlike analysis. Analysis is a knowledge whereby one must make an effort. It is an experience in which one engages. Metonymism, as I call it, only accentuates the derealizing effect of the signifier, with the result that what you finally find is the same plate in all the cupboards. There are only names that differ. Under different names, one always finds nothing.

Well, there is no infinite metonymy. On the contrary, there are stops, concretions, accumulations. The signifier has effects, and it also has products. The signifier creates meaning. But not only that. The signifier creates suffering, and it creates *jouissance*, symptom, and fantasy. What makes the difference in this regard, if you follow me, between Lacan and any poststructuralist, is what he calls, by an expression that has not been noticed very much, the "passion of the signifier." The passion of the signifier is not the equivalent of the love of the signifier. The passion of the signifier means that psychoanalysis, in all cases, is concerned with what suffers from the signifier. That is to say, this signifier creates effects and products.

That is what Freud has also called castration, which is the name he gave to this passion of the signifier. In what way, especially, does the living being that has to support the signifier, that the signifier inhabits, that the signifier parasitizes, that the signifier encumbers, in what way does this being suffer? In what way does this produce the effect of suffering? One must say that, as a rule, it diminishes it. You can see it with animals. Tame ones no longer have the beauty of the wild; you can feel that coming closer to language devalorizes them and that language, in this regard, is in itself a mortification. This passion of the signifier produces the effect of a deficit of *jouissance* in the living and even an annulation of *jouissance*.

One must say that it is true, except that it is precisely through this loss that we can have the idea of this *jouissance* because when this loss is not there, we don't know. Lacan sometimes asked the question, and this is not extravagant: "What is the *jouissance* of the tree?" or "What is the *jouissance* of the oyster?" That is to say, what is the *jouissance* of these living things where there is not this weakening caused by the signifier?

That is where Lacan took up Freudian castration; he took it up in the form that the signifier has an effect of canceling out *jouissance,* of almost complete annulation. That is where *jouissance* comes to the subject in the form Lacan calls the *plus-de-jouir: a.* His concept is constructed on the Marxist concept of surplus value. In surplus value, there is an exchange. One gives something and one receives the equivalent, except that there is a residue, a leftover.

What Lacan called the *plus-de-jouir* is this: For the living being, an exchange is made between language and *jouissance;* he loses his *jouissance,* and this loss is a correlative of language, but there remains a *jouissance* sheltered in certain zones of the body; and this residual *jouissance* that Lacan calls *plus-de-jouir* is the *jouissance* Freud isolated under the name of erogenous zones, these limit zones of the body where *jouissance* coils up, and as well through what he called the stages of oral or anal development. These are the points at which the body of the living being who speaks, and who is disinhabited by *jouissance,* nonetheless keeps his or her links to *jouissance.* And in this regard, you can easily see that the body has always been used by the speaking being as a signifying surface of inscription. That is where writing can be found first, as tattoos or scarification. It is in this that Lacan poses the antinomy of the Other of language and *jouissance* he isolates under the name of object *a*—these objects that are different forms of the *plus-de-jouir* for the speaking being.

Now, what about the phallus? Because Lacan spoke of it around 1956–1957, people thought it was the key of keys of his teaching. The phallus, certainly, is where Freud poses that castration proceeds electively. When Lacan calls it the signifier of *jouissance,* what does it mean? Only that it embodies the signifying part of the loss of *jouissance* and that, in this regard, it coordinates the *jouissance* that is not part of the object *a* to the signifier. It is also a consequence of what Freud discovered in the *Three Essays on the Theory of Sexuality* (1905),[3] the development of sexuality. What Freud discovered under the name of sexuality is quite different from what people think; he discovered that *jouissance* is not sexual first, in the sense that sexual *jouissance* is the *jouissance* of the Other sex. His discovery is exactly the contrary; it is that sexual *jouissance* is the *jouissance* of the body proper. The word *jouissance* is very difficult to translate into another language, and in general I advise translators to leave it in French. But to situate it in relation to Freud, *jouissance* is the satisfaction of a drive that occurs around erogenous zones. *Jouissance* is not in itself opened onto sex as the Other sex. That's what led Freud to postulate a genital drive: that is to say, the idea of a sexual drive that would be turned toward the other sex as such. What he discovered, instead, was castration, which signifies definitively that there is no sexual drive as such and that what is constitutive for both sexes is their relation to this lack of sexual relation. In this regard, if the phallus is the symbol, it is the symbol of what sets the two sexes apart through a lack—less through a lack than an impasse or set of obstacles.

Apart from this, there is the *jouissance* of the phallus, which is very different. We must consider that it appears in psychoanalysis first in the way that the subject takes this *jouissance* by him- or herself; and it is through masturbation that this phallic *jouissance* was first situated. That is even what it essentially designates—*jouissance* as closed unto itself. And this is why, to see it through to the end, phallic *jouissance* is not reserved for men; women [as Freud stressed] also know phallic *jouissance*.

Simply put, there is, however, another thesis of Lacan on feminine sexuality: not all of their *jouissance* is phallic or objectal. He tried to give a formula also for what has always been known and occasionally formulated through myths: that is, that there is for women access to an Other supplemental *jouissance* that nobody could think is for others.

I realize that I must stop here. I must say that I consider this speech as the introduction, and after this somewhat rhetorical excursus, I wanted to show how one must put Lacan's teaching into perspective, how the dominant position generally given to a few texts in his *Ecrits,* and in particular to the "Instance of the Letter . . . ," is in fact a complete misdirection of the "moving forward" dimension of Lacan's teaching. I wanted to show that you should not lay Lacan's teaching in the Procustean bed of the "Instance of the Letter . . . ."

I was also ready to give a new reading of "The Purloined Letter" to show you what Lacan really said and which has obviously been misunderstood by the best minds.

But I am limited by time constraints, and because, in any case, I would need to speak to you for 8 or 10 hours to get somewhere, I am going to stop now.

Notes

1. Stuart Schneiderman, *Jacques Lacan: The Death of an Intellectual Hero* (Cambridge, Mass.: Harvard University Press, 1983).

2. Desmond Morris, *The Naked Ape* (New York: McGraw Hill, 1967).

3. Sigmund Freud, *Three Essays on the Theory of Sexuality* (1905), in *The Standard Edition of the Complete Works of Sigmund Freud,* ed. James Strachey (London: Hogarth Press and the Institute of Psychoanalysis, 1953–74), 7:125–245.

Lacan with Scholasticism:
Agencies of the Letter

Richard R. Glejzer

To consider Lacan as scholastic may seem to some as a statement of dismissal, a way of marginalizing psychoanalysis or Lacanian theory in light of the current pragmatic concerns of the post-high-theory climate. To others such a statement could be taken as a distortion of scholasticism itself, where contemporary theory once again reads the past without regard to its particularity. However, my reading of Lacan in terms of scholasticism/of scholasticism in terms of Lacan points at something quite precise in the structure of the human subject within language, a structure that is explicit within Lacanian psychoanalysis as well as in the medieval epistemology that grounds the scholastic project. For both Lacanian psychoanalysis and medieval scholasticism, language functions as the limit of the human subject, the limit within the epistemological and ontological considerations of subjectivity itself. In this essay, I will explore Lacan's debt to medieval cosmology through an exploration of the structural similarities in both Lacanian and scholastic considerations of causality, focusing explicitly on their reliance on Augustine's theory of language and knowledge.

Contemporary considerations of Lacanian psychoanalysis have consistently entered into Lacan's theory of language through structural linguistics, tracing Lacan's use of Saussure and Jakobson as a way of grounding his project in linguistic terms. Samuel Weber's *Return to Freud: Jacques Lacan's Dislocation of Psychoanalysis,* for example, has two chapters dedicated to Lacan's dependence on structural linguistics for his consideration of language. Lacan, however, did not begin with Saussure or Jakobson. From his first seminar of 1953–4, Lacan placed his investigation of language within Augustine's examinations of signs and teaching. By focusing on how language works particularly for each subject, Lacan developed a way of placing language at the center of knowledge and being, a conclusion that the Twelfth Century scholastics similarly drew from Augustine. In considering the problem of speaking as intrinsically a problem of moving from universals to particulars back to universals, Lacan has more in common with the cosmology of the scholastics

From *American Imago,* Vol. 54, No. 2, 105–22. © 1997 by The Johns Hopkins University Press.

than he does with the linguistics of Saussure or Jakobson, since the very grounding of his notion of absence and language is found in Augustine's questioning of how to teach of God.

Unlike structural linguistic models, both scholasticism and psychoanalysis are founded on an imperative to consider a knowledge that resists signification, to bare the signifiers that ground ontology within an epistemology. For scholasticism, God is the ultimate referent and agent to all signifying systems: scriptural or worldly. For Lacanian psychoanalysis, the primary agency is the unconscious—not a totalizable or coherent system that acts separate from conscious thought, but, like medieval Christian notions of God, an agent that can only be witnessed by effect, an agent that is always coming into being. In this way, both the scholastic Christian God and the Lacanian unconscious are agencies that cannot be reduced to the series of effects that are traced, and thus cannot be precisely defined as a content-based causality.

But to view the unconscious as God or God as the unconscious would not be a correct formulation for either medieval scholasticism or Lacanian theory. They are, however, structurally connected in the way in which both agencies impinge on language, where language itself offers the means of investigating subjectivity while also functioning as the grounding of that subjectivity. Such a tautological problem is acknowledged both in scholasticism as well as in Lacanian theory; both modes of investigation resist linear causality as a way towards proof, favoring instead the limit or loss within totalizing systems. For both Lacanian theory and medieval scholasticism, the limit of knowledge within language qua symbolic system is the precise problem of language, of the subject itself. Lacan and scholastic thinkers thus problematize language as the end of knowledge, ultimately placing language on an overtly Augustinian foundation.

Scholasticism and psychoanalysis place the problem of language as the significant cosmological issue, ultimately grounding all considerations of epistemology and ontology as a limit that is first articulated by Augustine. Scholasticism constantly has one foot squarely planted in Augustine's consideration of language, where language is necessary for moving towards God, but also is that which limits the possibility of knowledge; scholastic theories of causality and representation carefully traced Augustine's consideration of sign and meaning in such texts as *On Christian Doctrine* and *On the Trinity,* both of which formulate the limitations of rationality in terms of language. Similarly, Lacan's definition of the retroactive function of signifiers as evidence for the unconscious, emphasizing that the content of the utterance is not the unconscious, is initially grounded on Augustine's notion of the impossible effect of signification. Citing Augustine's discussions of language in "The Teacher," Lacan places language in the realm of the particular, structurally situating real knowledge in the realm of particularities in language. In this way, both scholasticism and Lacanian theory find language to be the means and the limitation of knowledge about representation.

In order to accommodate language in terms of a nonlinear causality at the foundations of epistemology, scholasticism ultimately rests on negative theology as a means of leaving God as knowledge open, of not knowing some-thing but still being able to speak about it. Lacan, however, situates his teaching within a topological theory of the subject, allowing him to do more than just speak about gaps in knowledge to which metaphor points, but rather actually trace such gaps as meaning, as the structural interplay in the metonymic effects of metaphor. Throughout each phase of his teaching, Lacan works to show how the entry into language (the entry into the symbolic) and the constitution of wholeness (the entry into the imaginary) are not a linear sequence of stages. Lacan appeals to topology as a way of tracing the movement of the unconscious, the insistence of the real into language, tracing the knotting of the subject as a series of topological impasses. Thus, both scholasticism and Lacanian theory construct a nonlinear causality at the foundation of their epistemology and ontology, defining an agency of the letter, an agency that is marked—but not contained—by signification.

Augustine and the Agent of Scholastic Epistemology

In scholastic theory, notions of God are foundationally tied to the neoplatonism inherent in Christian mythology. In fact, R. W. Southern sees the scholastics as working with contradictory theoretical foundations: newly discovered Aristotelian texts, scripture, and the neoplatonic tradition that grounds such thinkers as Augustine and Boethius. Perhaps most important epistemologically is the reliance on the anti-representational theology of Pseudo-Dionysus the Areopagite who posits that God can only be represented negatively, where any positivistic accounting of God as agent—as a king, as a man, etc.—is inherently misleading simply by its rationality. Such thinking is also implicit in authorities like Augustine, whose attack on the Manicheans and reconsideration of signification is similarly based on the inability to rationalize God as agency (most explicitly addressed in his "The Usefulness of Belief"). This notion of negative theology grounds even the most rationalist of scholastics, like Thomas Aquinas and John of Salisbury. John, though less influential than Thomas, perhaps best illustrates the fundamental paradoxes that scholastic thinkers were forced to negotiate. It is in the negotiation of contradictory authorities that scholasticism privileges the nonrational, nonlinear examinations of the divine. Marsha Colish emphasizes that it is this ontological dilemma that served as the foundations of all medieval epistemology:

> And, not withstanding the scholastic demand for a theory of cognition explaining man's knowledge of the world of nature, the object to which medieval thinkers normally addressed themselves was the world of spiritual reality, with preeminent attention to God. The medieval theory of knowledge was a direct

consequence of this radically ontological emphasis. Epistemology was conceived as a function of metaphysics. The existence of an objective order of being was the primary condition which was held to make human thought possible at all. (1968, 1)

What makes the scholastics important for psychoanalysis is this ontological radicalism, where epistemology is itself an effect of an ontological impossibility, an impossibility that the scholastics recognized as real in knowledge and language. It is this ontological radicalism at the basis of medieval epistemology that Descartes will eventually bracket and dismiss, a radicalism that will then similarly serve as the basis of Lacan's return to Freud.

Another effect of such a radical ontology is reflected in the important Augustinian problem inherited by the scholastics: the particularity of divine contemplation and speaking of God or teaching. Speaking of God is necessary yet "impossible" for Augustine since the impossibility of representing divine agency grounds the very object of rapport, where one cannot teach of God universally, since the divine can only be contemplated individually, since knowledge is dependent on the particularity of a given subject. It is important to note that Augustine arrives at this inherent problem in language through his consideration of how one teaches about God, how one can transmit—communicate—a knowledge of Christian faith within language. Augustine shows that it is in this act of communication that agency breaks down, placing the ultimate problem of language in the movement of signifiers rather than in their origin. In his dialogue "The Teacher," Augustine shows that what makes teaching both a necessary and yet impossible act is that it must take place in the field of language, that the subject who teaches and the subject who learns are both constrained by their particular positions within language; both subjects in a teaching-learning relationship are limited by a fundamental difference in language itself. In fact, Augustine's dialogue as a whole revolves around the first question put to Adeodatus: "What would you say we are trying to do whenever we speak?" By beginning his consideration of teaching with the act of speaking, Augustine grounds his pedagogy in a radical way, questioning the very possibility of transmitting *real*—ontological—knowledge through language.

Augustine's initial epistemological question leads him to an ontological conclusion: speaking does not take place within the transmission of words per se, for if it did learning would be equated with recollection, a definition he rejects. Instead, Augustine divorces speaking from the content of words:

> The most I can say for words is that they merely intimate that we should look for realities; they do not present them to us for our knowledge. . . . So by means of words we learn only words, or better, the sound and noise of words. For if something cannot be a word unless it is a sign, I still cannot recognize it as a word until I know what it signifies, even though I have heard it as a word. (1967, 49)

Words, as signifiers, can only signify particularly to a subject. They—unlike their sounds—do not transmit an awareness or a knowledge in and of themselves. In other words, words themselves do not teach. At best, words cause a subject to recollect significations; they cause subjects to remember:

> So it is that we bear these images in the deep recesses of the memory as witnesses, so to speak, of things previously experienced by the senses. . . . But these images are only witnesses for ourselves. If the one who hears what I am recounting has seen these things for himself and was there on the spot, he does not learn them from my words, but recognizes them himself by the images he took away with him from these things. But if he has not experienced them with his senses, then it is clearly a matter of his believing my words rather than of learning. (1967, 53)

Augustine's juxtaposition between learning, or recognition, and belief is important epistemologically since it marks knowledge as separate from either the simple transmission of facts or from faith in the speaker. Thus, the content of what is transmitted does not define the agent who speaks/is spoken. Recognition, then, is not the same as either knowing or believing:

> (H)e knows the things whereof I speak by contemplating them himself, and not by my words. Therefore, even when I say what is true, and he sees what is true, it is not I who teach him. For he is being taught, not by my words, but by the realities themselves made manifest to him by the enlightening action of God from within. (1967, 54)

The important question for Augustine, then, is how the teacher functions to bring the student towards a position where she can learn, all the while recognizing that the student does not learn what the teacher teaches, which would be simple recollection.

For Augustine recognition and knowing are separate issues that both point towards the impossibility inherent in language. Augustine's evidence for the impossible relation between recognition and language is familiar: he cites the way in which a subject's language is riddled with slips and errors, where the "intention" of the speaker is unfathomable. He concludes the dialogue by considering moments when "we cannot know the speaker's thoughts, even though we share the same language and the words spoken in Latin are heard very distinctly" (1967, 58). For this reason, Augustine concludes—at least on the surface—that teaching is impossible:

> But men make the mistake of calling people "teachers" when they are not that at all, because there is generally no interval of time between the moment of speaking and that of knowing, and because their coming to learn from within follows quickly upon the suggestive force of the speaker's words, they think that they have learned externally from him who spoke those words. (1967, 59)

Augustine leaves an impasse between teaching and learning, between speaking and recognition, ultimately placing recognition itself in the realm of the divine (that which is impossible to know) rather than in the classroom (where knowledge is actual). In this sense, learning involves a recognition of ignorance since the divine, for Augustine, is unknowable. What speaking allows for Augustine is the contemplation of the limits of knowledge. For Augustine, then, an ethical teacher works from an understanding of ignorance, knowing that she does not know what she is supposed to know.

In its reliance on Augustinian notions of language and divinity, the scholastic project—although not uniform in method or theoretical grounding—attempts to offer a means of considering knowledge when the foundation of such a knowledge is ultimately un-signifiable, where God is unknowable. Although thinkers like Aquinas allowed for knowledge of the world to get at notions of God, his theory of signification still rested on the impossibility of knowing or representing God. Working from Pseudo-Dionysus and Augustine, Aquinas ultimately based his epistemology in negative terms, even while working with positivistic, Aristotelian notions of the universe.

From the very outset of his *Summa Theologica,* Thomas Aquinas establishes theology as a science that has God as its object and grounding, an essence that can only be pointed at rather than known:

> Although we cannot know in what consists the essence of God, nevertheless in this doctrine we make use of His effects, either of nature or of grace, in the place of a definition, in regard to whatever is treated in this doctrine concerning God; even as in some philosophical sciences we demonstrate something about a cause from its effect, by taking the effect in the place of a definition of the cause. (I, 1, 7) (1944, 13)

Theology for Thomas is the supreme science, working through the structure of metaphor as a way of marking God as agent without defining the divine as content. Such a position problematizes the manner in which the human is seen as an instrument to God, an instrument to an ultimately unknowable agency that insists but whose insistence cannot be discerned except in the moments of non-understanding. In this sense, God as primary agency (cause) is only traceable in terms of a limit within the secondary human agency (effect).

As a way of acknowledging the effect of such an unknowable agency, Thomas grapples with how theology works through metaphor. Following both Augustine and Pseudo-Dionysus, Thomas establishes that scripture uses metaphor as a way of representing divine truths:

> As Dionysius says, it is more fitting that divine truths should be expounded under the figure of less noble than nobler bodies . . . because thereby men's minds are better freed from error. For then it is clear that these things are not

literal descriptions of divine truths, which might have been open to doubt had they been expressed under the figure of nobler bodies, especially in the case of those who could think of nothing nobler than bodies. . . . For what He is not is clearer than to us than what He is. (I, 1, 9) (1944, 16)

By defining the very inquiry of theology in negative terms, Thomas bases his epistemology, the grounding of theology as a science, around the absence inherent in metaphorical representation, where the metaphor works to bring one closer to God only through the denial of the tangible referent. In other words, by grounding all theological discourse in metaphor itself, Thomas allows for the consideration of some excess in language as the ultimate situating of God in language, where language is not full but vacant and where such vacancies mark the real knowledge of God qua agency.

And, for Thomas, real ruptures in knowledge present a real ontological problem. Since the primary agency, the very grounding of causality, is only traceable as absence qua excess, the very root of human subjectivity rests on something missing in language, the mark to which the metaphor points but does not represent. Such a problematic foundation of human epistemology offers an ontological dilemma to knowing that extends throughout medieval Christian theology, also finding its roots in Augustine's sign theory. Medieval scholastics posit the human, not as creator of knowledge, but as an instrument to the unknowable nature of God, a subject of/by an infinite and thus unknowable knowledge, an agency of the letter.

Considerations of agency in medieval scholasticism are attempts to systematize knowledge as effect in order to trace cause. And this tracing of knowledge as effect offers a structural examination of the divine, reflecting an ontology that is fundamentally connected to knowledge defined as *auctoritas*. We can even see such an ontological methodology in medieval invocations of *auctoritas*, where medieval thinkers interpret earlier material from church figures like Augustine and Pseudo-Dionysus to Arabic redactions of Aristotle as a means not only to create their own authority rhetorically, but also to constitute the unknowable within knowledge, placing cause retroactively in their precursors. Such an epistemology implicitly acknowledges scholasticism's explicit theorizations of the human self as an instrumental agency, best elaborated in the use of Aristotle's four causes and in rhetorical investigations of invention. Medieval theorists and poets place God in the position of primary cause. Such a relegation places the human in a precarious position, especially from a contemporary critical perspective.

Thus, a scholastic understanding of the human subject requires a reference to something outside nature as a symbolic network, as seen in John of Salisbury's *Metalogicon*, which situates the human in terms of the assimilation of this some-thing outside into language. John of Salisbury defines this ability to assimilate in terms of reason, as the power of the soul which examines and investigates things that make an impression on the senses or intellect. A dependable judge of better things, reason has, after estimating similarities and differences, finally established art, to be, as it were, a circumscribed science of unlimited things. (1971, 35)

For John of Salisbury, that which defines the human, the soul, is not the same as nature, but, rather, is that which allows nature to be perceived, to be divided into genus and species. This scientific enterprise, the circumscription of that which is unlimited, is characteristic of much medieval investigation, since human knowledge is consistently placed as a limit on the limitless. In Book II of *The Metalogicon,* John of Salisbury offers a further elaboration of human knowledge in relation to the limits of real knowledge:

> In fact [our] cognition, in apprehending something, circumscribes and defines the latter for itself by a certain [comprehensive] capacity of the mind, so that if a thing presents itself to the mind as absolutely unlimited in every respect, neither primary nor secondary cognition can proceed. All knowledge or cognition possessed by creatures is limited. Infinite knowledge belongs solely to God, because of His infinite nature. . . . But we are imprisoned within the petty dimensions of our human capacity, wherefore we attain neither primary, nor secondary, nor tertiary, nor any distinction of knowledge of what is infinite, save the realization that it is unknown because it is infinite. Accordingly, all demonstrative and relative expressions must refer to a specific, definite subject if they are correctly posited. Otherwise they will miss their mark. For cognition naturally seeks or possesses certitude as its object. (1971, 127)

And cognition is by definition a limit in relation to the unknowable, infinite dimensions of real knowledge. And John of Salisbury's attack on the "Cornificians" ultimately resides in what he sees as a scientific method turned in on itself, where one ceases to circumscribe unlimited things in favor of the limit itself. Such a Cornifician understanding of knowledge places certitude in line with truth, collapsing agency into the letter, a move that John of Salisbury implicitly attacks. As John of Salisbury emphasizes, certitude is the limit of knowledge, not knowledge itself; the only true knowledge resides in the infinite that is precisely foreclosed by such certitude. Such a move places the human at a point of necessary misperception, since we cannot see or know by any means the infinite that grounds all knowledge, thus positing a subject that is based on a fundamental misprision, what Lacan will later define as *méconnaisance.*

Unlike contemporary science or contemporary theory, both of which foreclose questions of causality, scholastic hermeneutics replaced the effect with the cause, incessantly focusing on fundamental questions of the relationship between the material that is invented and the cause of the invention, since there is an obvious relation between creation and the production of knowledge, where all knowledge functions as an effect of a cosmology that places God as its metaphysical guarantee. In this way, the circularity between effect qua cause and effect qua effect is ruptured, leaving knowledge of God, of the unknowable, as a precipice at which all medieval theorists eventually found themselves. It is this precipice that Descartes eventually imagines away with his *Cogito* and which Lacan rediscovers in his reading of Freud.

LACAN ON THE UNCONSCIOUS

Like scholasticism, Lacan explicitly grounds his notion of language in Augustinian sign theory, constructing a theory of language that maps out the structuration of loss, desire, drive and their structure within signification (the order of the symptom). To map out such impossibilities, Lacan offers a topological structuralism, a non-linear theory of causality that allows for a rethinking of the relationship between cause and effect. Following Augustine, Lacan re-examines the particularity of knowledge and its relation to being, allowing us to trace where the ontological and the epistemological meet in metaphor, are knotted—where knowledge is both an effect and a cause of being. Like John of Salisbury and Thomas Aquinas, Lacan's investigation of the subject articulates a relation between knowledge and the ineffable, ultimately going beyond scholastic understandings of agency by further theorizing the particular structurings of desire and loss. Lacan's re-vision of Freudian and post-Freudian notions of the unconscious acknowledges a scholastic understanding of subjectivity, an understanding that stems in part from his reading of medieval Christian tradition rather than from contemporary linguistics or the differing branches of Freudian psychology.

As early as *Seminar I* (1953–54), Lacan reads Augustine as a way of reformulating the relation between signifier and signified and the construction of the symbolic and its relation to the real, showing how the subject is not simply static, immortal, or essential but rather contingent upon something, a function within the movement of signifiers. Dedicating a whole seminar during this year to "The Teacher," Lacan grounds his theory of language not in the linguistic structuralism of Saussure or Jakobson, but on the semiotics of Augustine, a semiotics that acknowledges the point of absence that epistemology must admit. What Augustine offers Lacan that contemporary linguists do not is a notion of the particular in language, where language only seems to work universally. Lacan reads Augustine's problems of teaching— "What is it that we do when we speak"—as ultimately *the* problem of language. For Lacan, language becomes particular to the subject that speaks and it is in this particularity that he will place the unconscious.

In his well known essay "Function and Field of Speech and Language," Lacan posits that the unconscious is structured like a language, offering an axiom that takes Freud's discovery of the unconscious one step further. Lacan's axiom marks the way in which signifiers are structured relative to their movement, defining the subject as that which represents a signifier for another signifier, as an agency of the letter only traceable in the intricacies of language itself. Lacan places the agent of speaking not in a definable, containable consciousness or even unconsciousness—both of which would be signifiers or totalities—but in the movement between signifiers, in the space where knowledge can't be traced by linguistic means or by rationalist epistemologies. In this way, the subject is also instrumental, contingent upon an entry into language, existing only in the dialectical move between signifiers. This movement between signifiers has the same structure as Augustine's observation about the impossibility of language to contain agency. Further, in "The Agency of the Letter," Lacan defines this instrumental subject in terms of metaphor and metonymy, offering a structure to what Augustine describes in "The Teacher" as the impossibility of a universal language. Ultimately, Lacan's theory of the unconscious grounds the Augustinian problem of language within a traceable topology, first through the cut of metaphor and circulation of metonymy and later in the knotting of the real, symbolic and imaginary.

Although both psychoanalysis and scholasticism offer similar epistemological frames, Lacan's structuralism offers a much more precise way of mapping out the effects of the real's entrance into signifying systems, offering us a way to move beyond the theological into problematic points of ethics and sexuality. In *Seminar VII,* Lacan's critique of Aristotle and Kant's reliance on an immortal soul aligned with various goods shows how both miss the paradoxes surrounding desire and its cause, the some-thing that is both the cause and effect of desire, the object *a.* Implicit in *Seminar VII* as a whole is the relation between language as particular and morality as universal, placing the ethical on the side of particularity, rather than on the side of faith in totalities. Lacan's reading of Augustine's theory of signification, then, constructs a typically scholastic understanding of agency, where the human functions instrumentally to a primary efficient cause that is unknowable or ineffable, while at the same time questioning the imperative of identifying the primary efficient cause with God, at least as a knowable content. Thus, Lacan's critique of the Cartesian subject aligns himself with the scholastics, even as it formulates what medieval thinkers were unable to, the excess that is evident in language that necessarily functions particularly—the Christian God of Scholasticism becoming Lacan's object *a,* that which is necessarily lost within any notions of universality.

Lacan's definition of the object *a* addresses Augustine's impasse between universality and particularity differently than scholastic theology, offering a theoretical and practical definition to Augustine's problem about language and its (in)ability to be taught. Like Augustine, Lacan also considers language to be particular, but he then traces the interplay between the two subjects within the transference relation, a relation that is a structure at work within teaching. His seminar on transference, *Seminar VIII,* focuses in part on Socrates, specifically on how the particularities of language and desire are structured in a relationship to a one-who-knows, one who occupies the position of the object *a,* the lost object, where such a position is grounded less on institutional endowments and more on a subject entering into a transference relationship. For Lacan, the transference relationship requires the analysand to endow the analyst with a knowledge, and the analyst occupies this position. This does not mean that the knowledge the analyst has is a cure. Rather, it is in the supposing of the knowledge on the part of the analysand that makes the transference relation work, that forecloses a universal cure in favor of the particular structuring of the subject. For Lacan, the analyst occupies this particular knowledge of the analysand rather than actually containing it or speaking it. In fact, it is the language of the analysand that re-structures the relation to the object *a,* not any universal knowledge on the part of the analyst.

In *Seminar XVII,* Lacan sets out a discourse that acknowledges this position of the one-who-knows, the discourse of analysis, against the discourse of the university, where the one who speaks believes that he is the one-who-knows. Lacan's formulation maps out the transference relation by showing that the analyst knows that she occupies the position of the one-who-knows, but is ignorant of the knowledge which she is supposed to contain by the analysand. In this sense, the one-who-knows knows nothing. In the university discourse, however, the teacher also occupies the position of the one-who-knows, but he really does not know that he does not know; the university discourse itself is foundational in that it places teachers in the position of knowing some-thing and then believing that that some-thing moves between teacher and student. In *The Lost Cause of Rhetoric,* David Metzger explains that the attraction of academic discourse rests in the fact that "one needn't then prove that the Other doesn't exist" (1995, 101). Academic discourse avoids recognizing the structure by which it establishes knowledge by investing a signifier as a guarantee of knowledge. Thus, Metzger concludes, "the academic subject (S) proceeds through a logic of 'neither this nor that will satisfy the desire of the Other' (a)—neither this nor that will bring back the Other in light of the object. For this reason, the academic goes on to create a master signifier, S1" (1995, 101). What Metzger shows is how any pedagogy working within an academic discourse grounds epistemology by endowing some signifier as offering truth, a signifier that is enough to ground the movement between signifiers, to cross over any gaps in knowing. Academic discourse, then, avoids all gaps and precipices in knowledge by skipping over them with the help of the master signifier; academic discourse disavows a precipice between signifiers within any symbolic chain. It is at this precipice that scholasticism finds itself: Thomas Aquinas can know that God is unknowable, can know that any signifier for God is only partial, but is then unable to articulate any way of speaking with such a knowledge, while still requiring that such speaking take place. Alternatively, psychoanalysis teaches us that speaking rests not in methodology or an imperative for a universal foundation, but in some missing signifier in epistemology. Lacan then traces how the master signifier within all discourse structures functions to instrumentalize the subject, to split her off from the impossibility that is the real.

At the beginning of his last phase of his teaching, Lacan goes even further with the instrumental subject, or the subject of the letter, examining its effect on sexual identification within the knotting of the real, symbolic and imaginary. Lacan begins *Television*—a broad and later consideration of his psychoanalytic teaching—with a statement reminiscent of Augustine's opening to "The Teacher":

> I always speak the truth. Not the whole truth, because there's no way to say it all. Saying it all is literally impossible: words fail. Yet it's through this very impossibility that the truth holds onto the real. (1990, 3)

For Lacan, it is in the failing of words, in the particular limitations of a subject's language, that the unconscious speaks as impossibility. From this typically scholastic position, however, Lacan works towards addressing very different concerns than those of the scholastics, focusing on issues of sexual identification and ethics within this realm of the particular. Rather than ending with the position that knowledge is impossible, Lacan shows how impossible knowledge can be traced in a subject's language, in a subject's symptom, since there is no universal imperative to speaking. It is in this last point that Lacan is ultimately not theological, since all notions of a universal are fundamentally misrecognitions of the particular.

From this non-theological position, Lacan formulates sexuality in structural terms, placing the effects of difference as a particular effect within subjectivity. In *Seminar XX*, Lacan posits Woman as an epistemological category reminiscent of Augustine's consideration of the divine, where content based notions of sexuality take the limit to be the thing, similar to John of Salisbury's notion of certitude as the foreclosure of the impossible. In "God and the Jouissance of The Woman," Lacan examines his axiom "woman does not exist" (which is another way of saying that there is no Other to the Other or that there is no metalanguage) offering a theory of gender that problematizes essentialist and rationalist notions of sexual identity. It is especially in this regard that psychoanalysis departs from the ultimate goals of scholastic theory. For psychoanalysis, it is ultimately this question of sexual difference, of the movement or counting from two to one, that grounds epistemology. While scholasticism works from sameness as its practice, toward ultimate unification with the ineffable as a way to solving difference, psychoanalysis places the ineffable in being itself, in two bodies existing in language that only seem to be one. This is the ultimate problem with language that Augustine discovered but could not articulate since for him the One did exist.

As two distinct agencies of the letter, scholasticism and psychoanalysis are tied together by the ways in which both offer similar notions of the human subject, making both difficult for contemporary theorists working with questions of identification through linear or developmental models. To see agency not as content based—not as a personified unconscious or totalizable God—places the human precariously close to deconstruction. But, Lacan is not post-structural, no more than Augustine or the scholastics were. Instead, Lacan defines for us a new scholasticism that once again acknowledges the *real* in agency, the particularity of language. Thus, Lacan allows us to explore the problematic nature—the problem of the limit—of being and knowing and identifying in language.

References

Augustine. 1950. *On Christian Doctrine (De doctrina Christiana)*. Translated by D.W. Robertson. New York: Macmillan.
———. 1963. *On the Trinity (De Trinitate)*. Translated by Stephen Mckenna. *The Fathers of the Church*, Vol. 45. Washington, DC: Catholic University Press.
———. 1967. "The Teacher" (*De Magistro*). In *The Writings of Saint Augustine*. Translated by Robert P. Russell. *The Fathers of the Church*, Vol. 57. Washington, DC: Catholic University Press.
———. 1947. "The Usefulness of Belief" (*De utilitate credendi*). In *The Writings of Saint Augustine*. Translated by Luanne Meagher. *The Fathers of the Church*, Vol. 4. New York: CIMA.
Colish, Marcia. 1968. *The Mirror of Language: A Study of the Medieval Theory of Knowledge*. New Haven: Yale University Press.
John of Salisbury. 1971. *The Metalogicon*. Translated by Daniel D. McGary. Gloucester: Peter Smith.
Lacan, Jacques. 1992 *The Seminar of Jacques Lacan, Book VII: The Ethics of Psychoanalysis 1959–1960*. Translated by Dennis Porter. Edited by Jacques-Alain Miller. New York: Norton.
———. 1991. *Le Séminaire de Jacques Lacan, Livre VIII (1960–1961): Le transfert*. Text established by Jacques-Alain Miller. Paris: Editions du Seuil.
———. 1991. *Le Séminaire de Jacques Lacan, Livre XVII (1969–1970): L'envers de la psychoanalyse*. Text established by Jacques-Alain Miller. Paris: Editions du Seuil.
———. 1990. *Television/A Challenge to the Psychoanalytic Establishment*. Translated by Denis Hollier et al. New York: Norton.
———. 1988. *The Seminar of Jacques Lacan, Book I: Freud's Papers on Technique 1953–1954*. Translated by John Forrester. Edited by Jacques-Alain Miller. New York: Norton.
———. 1977. "The Function and Field of Speech and Language in Psychoanalysis." *Ecrits: A Selection*. Translated by Alan Sheridan. New York: Norton. 31–113.
———. 1977. "The Agency of the Letter in the Unconscious or Reason since Freud." *Ecrits: A Selection*. Translated by Alan Sheridan. New York: Norton. 146–178.
———. 1975. *Le Séminaire de Jacques Lacan, Livre XX (1972–73): Encore*. Text established by Jacques-Alain Miller. Paris: Editions du Seuil.
Metzger, David. 1995. *The Lost Cause of Rhetoric: The Relation of Rhetoric and Geometry in Aristotle and Lacan*. Carbondale: Southern Illinois University Press.
Southern, R. W. 1970. *Medieval Humanism and Other Studies*. Oxford: Basil Blackwell.
Thomas Aquinas. 1944. *Summa Theologica*. Edited by Anton Pegis. *The Basic Writings of Thomas Aquinas*. New York: Random House.
Weber, Samuel. 1991. *Return to Freud: Jacques Lacan's Dislocation of Psychoanalysis*. Translated by Michael Levine. Cambridge: Cambridge University Press.

[From "Vital Signs:
The *Place* of Memory in Psychoanalysis"]

CHARLES SHEPHERDSON

Let us not forget psychoanalysis. The forgetting of psychoanalysis could not be one forgetting among others and cannot fail to produce symptoms.

> Derrida, "Let Us Not Forget"[1]

First, then, we must comprehend what sort of things are objects of memory; for mistakes are frequent on this point.

> Aristotle, "Of Memory and Recollection"[2]

I have carefully avoided any contact with philosophy.

> Freud, "An Autobiographical Study" (20:59)

The thread of memory can guide us through the labyrinth of Lacan's categories, the imaginary, symbolic and real—but not without difficulties, which we may as well confront in order to clarify a few technical details along the way: above all the twist that leads from the "Rome Discourse" to *Seminar XI,* from the Other to the object, along the path of the transference.[3]

THE SILENCE OF THE *GESTALT*

A first approach to memory might be sought in the imaginary: setting out from the image or sensory impression, one might be led to conceive of memory as the faculty that recollects an image or perception after it has passed away. Following this line of thought, both perception and memory (phenomena of "consciousness"?) would belong to the imaginary, the former taking in an image or impression in the immediacy of the present, the latter recalling it after the fact, the difference between the two residing in a

This section is taken from *Research in Phenomenology,* vol. 23 (1993), pp. 22–72; 22–32, 35–40, 60–67.

temporal factor. A link is thereby established, not only between the image and time, but also between the body and the mind, the sensory apparatus and the mental faculties.

There are good historical precedents for such an analysis. As Aristotle says in his treatise on memory, "only those living beings who are conscious of time can be said to remember" (449b28–30). Which living beings, one might ask, are "conscious of time"? Are we to place memory somewhere along a hierarchy of living beings, a natural order in which time might also be located? "Time" here refers particularly to *past* time, for Aristotle points out that one does not, properly speaking, "remember" the present or the future. In this way, a series of distinctions is quickly established between the three ecstasies of time, each with its respective faculty (of body or mind?): "*sensation* refers to what is present, *expectation* to what is future, and *memory* to what is past" (449b27–8, emphasis added). Through memory, then, the past and present would be connected, in that a sensation, once it has passed away, can be recalled in the mind. As for the future: "It is impossible," Aristotle remarks, "to remember the future, which is *an object of conjecture or expectation*" (449b10–11). The science of memory would thus be confined to the past and the present (like our discipline of history, that reconstruction in the present of what once was). And yet Aristotle adds parenthetically: "(there might even be a *science of expectation* as some say there is of divination)" (449b12, emphasis added). A curious remark for the philosopher dedicated to "science" (especially biology), Aristotle's observation recalls Lacan's statement in the "Rome Discourse" that psychoanalysis is part of a "movement that is now establishing a new order of the sciences" (E 72), the principal feature of which is the distinction it makes between "exact sciences," natural sciences modeled on the experiment and bound to clock-time, and what Lacan calls "conjectural sciences," which confront "the intersubjective time that structures human action" (E 73–5; see also SXI 43).[4] As an action or praxis which bears on human time, then, psychoanalytic memory cannot ignore the dimension of the future:

> The point is that for Freud it is not a question of biological memory, nor of its intuitionist mystification . . . but a question of recollection, that is, of history, balancing the scales, in which conjectures about the past are balanced against promises of the future (E 48).

Thus, although memory, strictly speaking, joins the present and the past, the question of the future cannot be left aside, since memory entails a reflection on the structure of time, and even poses problems for the term "science," by linking it to "divination" (Aristotle) and "conjecture" (Lacan).

Ten years later, Lacan opens *Seminar XI* by returning to this question: rather than simply claiming that psychoanalysis, buttressed by the new techniques of formalization provided by Lévi-Strauss and Saussure, has now become a science, rather than beginning with the measure already given as to what constitutes a science, and then asking whether psychoanalysis has attained this status, Lacan begins with a question as to the status of psychoanalysis, positioning it in relation to the two poles of science and religion: "psychoanalysis . . . may actually enlighten us as to what we should understand by science, and even by religion" (SXI 7). We have here a first indication of our direction: for whereas, in the "Rome Discourse," the "return to Freud" tended to unfold as an effort of formalization guided by the regularities of the symbolic order—the autonomous, objective field of the "Law"—now it is a matter of introducing something beyond the limits of formalization, an "element" that falls outside the systemic operation of the law and marks an impossibility of closure, an "object" that is missing, which Lacan addresses in terms of radical particularity, something that concerns the transference, and may be formulated in terms of *desire*. Unlike the structuralist projects of linguistics and anthropology, which still provide the major point of orientation for our reading of Lacan, and which succeed in establishing themselves as sciences only by bracketing the problem of the subject and focusing on the *a priori* laws governing language or exchange, psychoanalysis returns to the question of the relation between the subject and the law. For the "science" of psychoanalysis, if it is a science, this means that it cannot be a question of attaining a truth that would be universalizable, repeatable by "anyone"; it does not seek a proper degree of objectification by eliminating desire: "What must there be in the analyst's desire for it to operate in a correct way? Can this question be left outside the limits of our field, as it is in effect in the sciences?" (SXI 9). We have quickly passed from the image, through the symbolic, toward the element of lack that comes to be designated as the *object a,* the fragment of the real. With this trajectory in mind, let us take up the thread of our argument again.

For Aristotle, memory links perception to time, but it also entails a connection between the body and the mind: in fact memory has two aspects, bearing on mental content (*hypolepsis*) as well as perception (*aisthesis*)—"in the former case remembering that one *learned or thought* a thing, and in the latter that one *heard or saw or perceived* it in some way" (449b19–23, emphasis added).[5] Memory poses a question of time, then, but also a question of *place*. For in what part of the organism-soul does memory reside? If "sensation" is of the *body* and "expectation" is of the *mind,* does "memory" somehow provide a link between the two, binding the raw experience of the organism to the distant and peculiar legislations of the will? Does memory shuttle back and forth, uniting the three aspects of time, weaving a fabric of the past and present, and perhaps even of the future, the "conjecture" of the soul, its hope and yearning? Does memory, in fabricating time, also weave a unity for the organism-soul, joining the passing experience of the body to the retentive knowledge of the mind, as well as to what Aristotle calls "appetite," "passion," and "desire"? Where shall we *locate* this faculty which is said to "belong to both soul and body"? What is its *place*? We know this question was central to Freud, who refused to locate the unconscious anatomically. In spite of these difficulties, our point of departure locating memory in the image would seem to be confirmed when Aristotle remarks that, since memory is not exactly the perception itself, since it concerns *something that is absent* (*apontos*) and must be revived in the mind, "it is obvious, then, that memory belongs to that part of the soul to which imagination belongs" (450a23–24).

Wordsworth, recalling Aristotle, notes that the poet, who is by definition endowed with a lively imagination, does not simply "imagine" in the sense of "making things up." It would be more accurate, Wordsworth observes, to say that those possessed with imagination are "affected more than other men by *absent things as if they were present*."[6] It is as if the imagination, far from being the free and spontaneous faculty of creation for which it is often mistaken, were essentially bound to recollection. Hence Aristotle's remarkable claim: "All things which are imaginable are essentially objects of memory" (450a23).[7] Everything happens as if language were exterior to memory, a means of articulating or representing what is recalled, perhaps, but in no way intrinsic to recollection itself.

SUFFERING FROM REMINISCENCE

And yet the memory that concerns Freud is not a conscious act that recalls the image or thought after it has passed away, but is unconscious, that is to say, *a memory that has not been remembered*. This is the meaning of Freud's early formulation according to which "hysterics suffer mainly from reminiscences" (2:7). The memory that concerns Freud here is not so much a cognitive faculty—what we might call the "ability" to remember—as the fact of a memory *outside the cognitive apparatus* of our usual psychology (which is always a psychology of "consciousness"). Freud's path starts out from this *Other* memory, this Other *place* (*ein anderer Schauplatz*, or, as Lacan puts it in *Seminar IX*, "What Freud calls . . . *die Idee einer anderer Localität*," 56), a non-organic memory that appears, not in the image or thought that is recollected in the mind, but in the exteriority of *discourse*. "The unconscious of the subject," Lacan says, "is the *discourse of the Other*" (E 55, 193, SXI 131, emphasis added).

Accordingly, the classical point of departure for locating unconscious memories is found, not in what the subject recalls, but in the symbolic "material" of the lapsus and free association. Even the body has a symbolic status here: for to Freud's own astonishment, the symptom was not a phenomenon of "nature" and could not be reduced to the kind of organic illness treated by medical science, since it was a phenomenon of meaning, a "reminiscence" that, having been lost to consciousness, found itself inscribed in the flesh.

Outside consciousness, the lapsus, the symptom and free association provide symbolic material that has no apparent meaning, a spontaneous creation that appears in speech or in the body, but that is "non-sense" from the point of view of the speaker (not what I meant to say, not what I desired). Hence Lacan's definition: "The unconscious," he writes in the "Rome Discourse," "is that part of the concrete discourse . . . that is not at the disposal of the subject in re-establishing the continuity of his conscious discourse" (E 49).

Since Lacan's work is so often "explained" by reference to Saussure, let us take another step (holding on to the thread of the symptom). It is often said that the "body"—and the symptom is of the body—is an *imaginary body* for Lacan, but this cannot be sufficient. Setting out from this theme of the imaginary body, many readers have been led to separate the imaginary and the symbolic, concluding that Lacan's work "evolves" by passing from a "mirror stage" in which the body is central, to a later preoccupation with linguistics in which everything is reduced to a play of the signifier, and "reality" is lost. Such a "staging" of Lacan's work is a convenient way of avoiding his thought, replacing it with a narrative divided into two contradictory periods—Kojèvian intersubjectivity eventually replaced by the formalism of Saussure—though neither of these has any bearing on the unconscious. Translated into the already digested references of the academy, Lacan's work is magically made to disappear before our very eyes, like the real itself, replaced by an imaginary narrative.[8] But it is clearly not only a matter of linguistics, of *langue* and *parole,* when Lacan distinguishes between speech and language, for in separating the ego's narrative from the linguistic material produced by the unconscious, he is concerned with the relation between the signifier and the organism, noting that "speech is driven out of the concrete discourse that orders the subject's consciousness," only to find "support . . . in the natural functions of the subject. . . . The symptom is here a signifier" Lacan adds, "a symbol written in the sand of the flesh" (E 69; cf. 50–2).

This proposition from the "Rome Discourse" is elaborated in "The Agency of the Letter": "metaphor is the very mechanism by which the symptom, in an analytic sense, is determined . . . a symptom being a metaphor in which flesh or function is taken as a signifying element" that remains "inaccessible to the conscious subject" (E 166). The symptom is therefore not a purely organic phenomenon, but a bodily effect unique to the speaking being. This is the "reminiscence" from which the hysteric suffers, without knowing why, as if history had come to an end, and could only repeat itself, refusing to pass away: "there is no other way of conceiving the *indestructibility* of unconscious desire," Lacan writes, the fact that even when the ego forgets and time passes by, the unconscious remembers—as if, to recall Freud's formula, the unconscious did not know time (14:186; 5:661; 18:28). "It is in this sort of memory," Lacan writes, "that is found the chain that *insists* on reproducing itself . . . which is the chain of dead desire" (E 167). Such is the "enigma that desire seems to pose for a 'natural philosophy' " (E 166). Thus, in order to avoid the reduction which makes the "body" imaginary while relegating the symbolic to a purely "linguistic" phenomenon, we must consider more closely the relation between the signifier and the flesh, the status of these vital signs.

One can see here why Lacan claims that well "before Darwin . . . Hegel had provided the ultimate theory of the proper function of aggressivity in human ontology," by detaching the intersubjective structure of the desire for recognition from its biological counterpart, a model governed by survival and adaptation: "if, in the conflict of Master and Slave, it is the recognition of man by man that is involved, it is also promulgated on a radical negation of natural values" (E 26). Given this disjunction between Darwin and Hegel (which makes "cultural evolution" an oxymoron), one would have to draw a sharp distinction between the time of *history* (a temporality of the symbol) and the time of evolution or natural *development,* a distinction that psychology, by virtue of its adherence to naturalistic models of perception and adaptation, fails to appreciate, thereby remaining pre-Hegelian. The human animal is destined to *history* precisely because it has no natural development: in Freudian terms, if the instinct had something like a "natural development," regulated by the stages of adolescence, reproductive maturation, and object-choice (with all the consequences of "normalization" this entails), then sexuality would remain within the order of nature and its law; but the most elementary point of Freud's discovery, which leads to his distinction between the instinct and the drive, is precisely that whereas the instinct amounts to a sort of natural program, governed by the principles of life (self-preservation and reproduction), the sexual drive has no natural mooring, *no predestined aim and no proper object;* moreover, the drive is ultimately linked by Freud to a thoroughly non-biological relation to death, a "death drive" that, in spite of Freud's biological terminology, is unmistakably due to the play of representation to which sexuality, in the human animal, is subject. In "The Rome Discourse," Lacan accordingly notes "the difference . . . between reference to the supposedly organic stages of individual development and research into the *particular* events of a subject's history" (E 51); and again, "the anal stage is no less purely *historical* [that is to say, bound to the particularity of the subject, in his or her detachment from natural development] when it is actually experienced than when it is reconstituted in thought," and "seeing it as a mere stage in some instinctual maturation leads even the best minds straight off the track" (E 53).

Now the symbolic debris of the lapsus and the symptom, this realm of apparent nonsense and error, is not a matter of chance according to Freud: emerging as a mistake or accident that interrupts speech, the discourse of the Other is nevertheless *governed by law.* "Speak of chance," Lacan writes, "if you like," citing Freud's remark in *The Interpretation of Dreams,* but "in my experience I have observed nothing arbitrary in this field" (SXI 45), a field that is governed by law.[9] We find here the famous "linguistic" orientation of Lacan's early text, organizing Freud's meditation on the lapsus, the truth that emerges in the error of the signifier, the laws of displacement and substitution that govern the apparent spontaneity and chaos of the dream. The law here is neither that of consciousness and its intentions, nor that of the organism and its natural life, neither a law governing the constitution of "subjective" sense (a phenomenology of intentionality), nor a law given by medical science, but the law of the Other. Thus, if psychoanalysis breaks with the causality of organic medicine, it is also not a science of "subjectivity." As Lacan says in "The Freudian Thing," when it is a question of the memory carried in the lapsus, or in the reminiscence of the symptom: "The laws of recollection and symbolic recognition are, in effect, different in essence and manifestation from the laws of imaginary reminiscence" (E 141)—in "essence," because they are foreign to the mental sphere of psychology, and in "manifestation," because they appear in the alterity of the signifying chain.

Such a conception of memory will have immediate consequences for the theory of the "subject." In the "Rome Discourse," it is already evident that the "subject," for Lacan, is not the active "subjectivity" that doubts and recollects, establishing a certain mental content ("emotion recollected in tranquility" is the phrase we remember from Wordsworth): "The subject goes well beyond what is experienced 'subjectively' by the individual, exactly as far as the truth he is able to attain" (E 55). As he puts it in "The Freudian Thing," in his prosopopoeia of truth:

> Whether you flee me in fraud or seek to entrap me in error, I will reach you in the mistake against which you have no refuge. . . . The trade route of truth no longer passes through thought: strange to say, it now seems to pass through things: (E 122).

This is the function of the signifier in its materiality. The "memory" in question is not a psychological faculty which recollects an image, perception or thought, but must be located *outside* the psychological subject, at the level of the signifier.

Lacan explicitly marked the difference between the "subject" of psychoanalysis and the "psychological" category of subjectivity in schema L, in which the narrative of the ego was distinguished from the "place" of the subject as marked by symbolic debris.

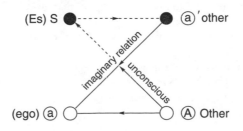

FIGURE ONE: Schema L

Here one sees clearly the distinction between the symbolic axis, in which the "non-sense" of the unconscious appears as the "discourse of the Other," and the imaginary axis, in which the narrative of the ego unfolds in the intersubjective relation of "I and Thou," not a relation of "dialogue" and "mutual understanding," as our theorists of "communication" would wish, but a relation of deception and love, idealization and narcissism.

To ignore the symbolic, moreover, is to be forced, with Jules Masserman and his raccoon, to advocate a conception of "reality" in which the psychoanalytic understanding of the subject disappears altogether:

> In analytic practice, mapping the subject in relation to reality, such as it is supposed to constitute us, and not in relation to the signifier, amounts to falling already into the degradation of the psychological (SXI 142).

Thus, if we wish to follow the course of Freud's thought, and assign a "true function to what, in analysis, is called recollection or remembering," we must not confuse it with the return of an image from the world of "reality": "Recollection is not Platonic reminiscence—it is not the return of a form, an imprint, an *eidos* . . . from the beyond. It is something humble . . . at the level of the signifier" (SXI 47). We have dropped the thread that would lead from perception to recollection, along the path of the image.

LOOKING BACKWARD

At first glance perverse and exceptional, an affront or disruption that contradicts the entire tradition of "natural philosophy," by separating memory from organic life, Lacan's claim may turn out to be the norm.[10] Nietzsche at least was equally perverse in his text on history, itself a radical contestation of the "philosophy of life," the "vitalism" with which it has so often been confused. For Nietzsche too separates memory from nature at the beginning of his "untimely" text, starting with the human's inability to forget, and stressing the derangement of pleasure that results:

> Consider the herd that is feeding yonder. They know not the meaning of yesterday or today; they leap and feed, rest, digest, and leap again; and thus from morning to night, and from day to day, they are fettered to the moment and their pleasure or displeasure, and therefore neither melancholy nor bored.[11]

"Thus the animal lives *unhistorically*," Nietzsche adds, not only because it is contained in the present, but also because it *does not speak*. Nietzsche's remarks are thus organized not simply around the image, but around *the articulation of a question*:

This is a difficult sight for man to see, for though he thinks himself better than the animals because he is human, he cannot help envying them their happiness. . . . A human being may well ask, "Why do you not speak to me of your happiness but only stand and gaze at me?" The beast wants to answer, "Because I always forget what I wanted to say." But he forgets this answer too and is silent, and the man is left to wonder.

Humanity is thus left hanging on the *question* of happiness, for "he cannot learn to forget but clings relentlessly to the past," as if bound eternally to the return of the signifying chain. Nietzsche adds:

however far and fast he runs, this chain runs with him. And it is a matter for wonder: a moment, now here and then gone, nonetheless returns as a ghost [*als gespenst weider*] and disturbs the peace of a later moment.

To say that memory (this "return" of the ghost from the past) does not belong to nature would seem to contradict a long tradition, for Aristotle, the good biologist (at least this is how we have come to remember him), situated memory within a hierarchy of living beings, differentiated according to their lack or possession of certain faculties—the need for nourishment and reproduction (shared by plants and animals), the capacity for locomotion (given only to animals), the potential for memory distinguishing the higher animals (those capable of learning), and finally the "rational soul" of the human, who is able to "decide," to exercise "judgment" and "will." Didn't Aristotle *locate* memory this way, assigning it a *place* on the great chain of being? We read in *On the Soul* for example: "not everything that has sensation has movement also," for "plants seem to live without sharing in locomotion or in perception, and many living animals have not power of thought (*dianoia*)" (410b20f). This is the tradition we remember, and yet one may begin to doubt, as one looks back.

At first glance perverse and exceptional, a disruption of "natural philosophy" and "the tradition," the link between memory and the signifier may already belong to Aristotle. We said that Aristotle associates memory with the image or perception, as the faculty that recalls these things after the fact, belonging to "that part of the soul to which imagination belongs." We said that "the tradition" (a singular noun) confirms, through Wordsworth, that the "remembrance of things past," "emotion recollected in tranquility," is the principal gift and debt of imagination. A ghost returns, beckoning: perhaps we have gone too quickly. Let us retrace our steps. For if memory is of the image, if memory is said to recall the "image" or "perception" or "thought," bringing back an "impression" after the fact, *what* exactly is being remembered if this "impression," as David Krell has shown, concerns "perception" (*aisthesis*) but also "thought" (*hypolepsis*), and perhaps some other things as well, such as "affects" (*pathei*). Addressing this plurality, Aristotle's formulation is striking: "for when a man is exercising his memory he always *says in his mind* (*en tei psychei legei*) that he has *heard, or felt, or thought* this before" (449b23, italics added).

We have remarked on the question of place: *where* is memory if it is of the body, rooted in the sensory apparatus, but also of the mind, recalling ideas or thoughts? And *where* is the affect if, like "guilt" or "anxiety," it is difficult to call such a bodily phenomenon "sensory," and absurd to call it an "idea"? Now, the question also arises as to *what*, exactly, is remembered in memory—*the thing itself* (idea or affect or perception) or rather some *re-presentation* of the thing ("mistakes are frequent on this point" 449b10). For it must be observed, Aristotle says, that in remembering, we do not return to the things themselves, but only have a "memory" of them: "it is only the affection that is present, and the fact [*pragmatos*] is not" (450a26). A new difficulty for the relation between the present and past, perhaps, since Aristotle asks whether the memory is actually *the thing that was*, or whether it is *a thing of its own*: "Is what one remembers the present affection [*to pathos*] or the original from which it arose [*he ekeino aph' hou egeneto*]?" (450b13–14). At this point in his discussion, Aristotle returns to an image—or metaphor—he has already used, in which the memory is compared to a picture. In one sense, he suggests, the memory is like a picture, which represents what was; and in this sense it can be said that one is able to "remember the absent fact" (15), to "remember what is not present" (18). But in another sense, the memory is a separate thing of its own, "just as the picture painted on the panel is at once a picture and a portrait, and though one and the same, is both" (21–22). Consequently, "we must regard the mental picture within us both as an object of contemplation in itself and as a mental picture of something else" (24–26). A host of problems, even at the level of our traditional, "imaginary" memory, even before we wind our way to the unconscious.

A plague of questions, to which we add one more: when we speak of memory as recalling a perception—idea or affect or sensation—that has passed away, when we speak of memory as "re-presenting" something that was once present, the terminology which revolves around the image is easily displaced by another terminology, one that is closer to "inscription" than to images. Here too, the term "representation" seems to lead in more than one direction. For when Aristotle writes of the memory as "being like a portrait" (*hoion zographema*, 450a29–30), his vocabulary is no longer that of the image that served as his starting point, but rather links together two references: the living being (*zoon*) and the verb for inscription or writing (*to graphema*).[12] (When Lacan speaks in *Seminar XI* of the "gaze," that peculiar object of the scopic drive that is beyond the visible field, he says "I am photo-graphed," SXI 106.) In spite of our initial direction, then, we wind our way to the symbolic, that field about which Aristotle seems already to have been speaking. We know Aristotle as the good biologist, but these ghostly remarks return to us now: what is it that "the tradition" wants us to recall; what has our memory of "the tradition" concealed? What indeed *is* "the tradition" (a singular identity)? One is easily disoriented by these recollections: what route would lead us back to the Greek origin, the natural philosopher, as we try to recall him, the father, who has been such a decisive part of our destiny?

Doesn't Wordsworth also say that the imagination, while certainly a faculty bound to the image, is nevertheless constitutively structured by words? In his famous note to "The Thorn," he suggests that the signifier, far from simply re-presenting or "remembering" an image or experience that took place somewhere in "reality," on the contrary plays a constitutive role for imagination itself. "It was my wish in this poem," Wordsworth writes, "to show the manner in which men cleave to the same ideas," to present characters who have been afflicted by some trauma, and are compelled perpetually to return to this trauma:

> I had two objects to attain; first, to represent a picture which would not be unimpressive . . . secondly, while I adhered to the style in which such persons describe, to take care that words, which in their minds are impregnated with passion, should likewise convey passion to Readers.[13]

Moreover, Wordsworth remarks, in treating the sort of character who speaks in this poem, in showing that tendency by which "men cleave to the same ideas," he also wished to illustrate how "an attempt is rarely made to communicate impassioned feelings without something of an accompanying consciousness of the inadequacies of our own powers, or the deficiencies of language." As a result, in the midst of the imagination's effort to speak, Wordsworth says, "there will be a craving in the mind, and as long as it is not satisfied the speaker will cling to the same words." All of which indicates "the interest [the investment or cathexis perhaps] which the mind attaches to words, not only as symbols of the passion, but as *things,* active and efficient, which are themselves part of the passion." Here again, the imagination veers off from the start, diverging from its natural origin.

A similar trajectory is evident in Freud. When he comes to the analysis of the sexual drive in the *Three Essays* (7:135–243), Freud does not speak of a "masculine" and "feminine" drive ordered as if by nature. One might wish to find two forms of sexuality, one for each of the sexes, but as Lacan says, giving Freud's observation its most extreme and counterintuitive force: "there is only one libido." Thus Freud, unlike Ernest Jones and Karen Horney, does not speak of a "masculine" and "feminine" form of the drive, but rather of an "active" and "passive" drive that, far from being divided between the two sexes according to nature (thus confirming the conventional "passive" female and "active" male), rather characterizes human sexuality as such *along the lines of grammar*: "active and passive," "subject and object" are grammatical functions (SXI 177, 192, 200). It is this "sentence structure" which organizes Freud's reflections on the relations between sadism and masochism, voyeurism and exhibitionism (SXI 170). Freud's text "A Child Is Being Beaten" (17:177–204), which deals with primary masochism, is equally clear on this point, the fantasy it explores being ordered by a series of variations ["My father is beating the child (whom I hate)"; "I am being beaten by my father"; "A child is being beaten (I am probably looking on)," etc.]. Perhaps even more intriguing is Freud's remark in "Some Points for a Comparative Study of Organic and Hysterical Motor Paralyses" (1:155–72), where the displacement from the image to the symbol is central. Pointing out that the hysterical symptom does not follow the lines of anatomy as the neurologist might expect, Freud remarks that "in its paralyses and other manifestations hysteria behaves as though anatomy did not exist or as though it had no knowledge of it" (169). The part of the body which is affected in hysterical paralysis corresponds, not to the biological unit, but to the *idea* of the body, the *popular conception* of the body. We come to a crossroad here: does the part of the body correspond (in this representation, this correspondence theory) to the *image* of the body, in defiance of medical knowledge, or does it correspond to the *concept*, the *common name*? The problem is explicit in Freud's text: hysterical paralysis, he writes, "takes the organs in the ordinary, popular sense of *the names they bear:* the leg is the leg as far up as its insertion into the hip, the arm is the upper limb *as it is visible under the clothing*" (169, emphasis added). When the symptom is a "reminiscence" in some way, does it follow the image or the word? Let us consider more closely some elements of this symbolic memory.

LAW AND CAUSE

We have stressed the lapsus, the dream, and the forgotten word—symbolic debris that has no apparent meaning, "material" that is "nonsense" from the point of view of the speaker. Appearing as a mistake or accident that interrupts discourse, the lapsus is nevertheless not error but the truth of the unconscious.

If the first hysterics "suffer mainly from reminiscences" instead of purely organic conditions, it is also the case that their symptoms could be relieved—against all biomedical causality—by purely symbolic means (voodoo or magic, rather than "science"): "nothing can be grasped, destroyed, or burnt, except in a symbolic way, as one says, *in effigy, in absentia*" (SXI 50; Lacan is citing Freud 12:108). What is more, this symbolic intervention upon the bodily symptom is not accomplished through *conscious memory* but through *verbalization* (the "talking cure"), a speech which the early patients would articulate under hypnosis, but often *would not remember* upon being awakened—which suggests that the work of symbolization is not a psychological process of recollection, but a labor that operates *outside* the psychological subject, at the level of the signifier. "The psychological prejudices of Freud's day were opposed to acknowledging any such *reality* in verbalization," but the fact remains that one does not "have to *know* whether the subject has remembered anything whatever from the past," Lacan says. "He has simply recounted the event . . . verbalized it . . . made it pass into the *verbe*" (E 46, emphasis added). Thus, the labor of symbolization is not accomplished *at the level of knowing,* or by "making the unconscious conscious." This fact should carry more weight than it does with those analysts who believe that their task is to go back through the past and discover "what really happened," as if an appeal to prediscursive "reality" would be sufficient for addressing what, at the same time, they admit to be "psychological" difficulties. Freud himself, in the *Studies on Hysteria,* tells of his early discovery of this point, when, having been given a diary by the mother of his patient, in which all the facts of the past were written down, he tried to accelerate the patient's memory, to hand her the "truth" when she stumbled, only to find that it impeded the patient's progress.

This is why, in *Seminar XI,* Lacan insists that even if the law of the symbolic order is essential, our path must turn elsewhere, toward the "cause":

> Cause is to be distinguished from that which is determinate in a chain, in other words *law.* By way of example, think of what is pictured in the law of action and reaction. . . . There is no gap here (SXI 22).

"Whenever we speak of cause, on the other hand, there is always something anti-conceptual, something indefinite" (SXI 22). The problem of the "subject" thus leads beyond the "law" of the signifier to the object *a,* the "cause" of desire. We must therefore confront this element which, in "The Freudian Thing" he calls an element

> of death, the quasi-mystical limit of the most rational discourse in the world, so that we might recognize the place in which the symbol is substituted for death in order to take possession of the first swelling of life (E 124).

The path of the symbolic order thus reaches a dead end, for if the formations of the unconscious (lapsus, dream, symptom) belong to the network of the signifier, it is quite another thing to speak of the "formations of fantasy," which are not reducible to the symbolic order. In Freud, the isolation of the fantasy meant the encounter with something beyond the suffering of the symptom, a more primordial formation that did not yield to the work of interpretation, that was not resolved by symbolization—something that led Freud to conclude with dismay that the subject did not want to get better, but clung to suffering as if to life itself. Thus, the symbolic resolution of the symptom, accomplished through speech, was not sufficient. Beyond the symptom, there lay a level of fantasy, a *jouissance* that was not susceptible to resolution, to which the subject remained attached. In Freud's account, the fantasy is linked to primordial masochism, a concept that "was only accepted by Freud once he had put forward the hypothesis of the death instinct."[14] This is why, in *Seminar XI,* Lacan's formula for fantasy is written $\mathcal{S} \lozenge a$, a formulation which indicates the heterogeneous relation binding the subject of the symbolic chain ($\mathcal{S}$) to the object of fantasy (a) that is not contained within the symbolic order. We see here that the famous "division of the subject" is not simply the "alienation" that occurs when the subject identifies with an image, nor merely the familiar "division by language" that marks the subject upon entry into the chain of representation ($\mathcal{S}$); it also includes the relation between these two heterogeneous elements of the fantasy. It is this last relation in which the enigmas of "sexuality" are most at issue for Freud, in that the fantasy "binds together two very different things, the satisfaction of an erotogenic zone and the representation of a desire."[15]

Thus, beyond the "formations of the unconscious" (lapsus, dream, symptom) that are grasped dialectically through the labor of symbolization, one finds the fantasy, and Lacan's formula accordingly marks the relation between the "subject" divided by language ($\mathcal{S}$) and the "object" (a) which is neither specular nor symbolizable but real. The paradox is not only that, whereas the symptoms in Freud's early cases could be resolved by the labor of speech, a more fundamental, "symptomatic" domain (that of the fantasy) emerged beyond resolution; what is more, the symptom in its classical form brings suffering, while the fantasy appears to do the opposite, to bring a peculiar sort of pleasure; and even masochism is thus paradoxically said to involve a kind of "pleasure," something Lacan therefore formulates as distinct from the pleasure of the ego, namely *jouissance*—not, as is so often said, the "orgasm" it appears to name, but the obscure satisfaction that looks out from the Rat Man's eyes as he tells the part of his story that is most tortuous to him. This is why Freud says the patient clings to suffering, or seems to enjoy the symptom, or more precisely, to enjoy something "in" the symptom that is beyond the suffering it entails. When Lacan develops what Freud understands as the death drive, he uses the term *jouissance* to designate that primordial suffering, that punishing enjoyment to which the subject clings, beyond the symbolic and resolvable construction of the symptom.[16]

THE DESIRE OF THE ANALYST

In order to take our final steps, let us retrace the path that led Freud to diverge from the first miraculous accomplishments of speech to the impasses which led to "sexuality." Let us return to the "chimney-sweeping" technique, the early revelations in which the "talking cure" took shape. "This was fine in the beginning," Lacan says: "How convincing the process of remembering was with the first hysterics . . . one remembered things right down to the dregs" (SXI 49–50). But Freud found something beyond the pleasure of symbolic labor, something real, a limit to the signifier and the work of memory, something that manifested itself as repetition: "in the recalling of his biography," Lacan writes in *Seminar XI,* the subject "goes only to a certain limit, which is known as the real" (SXI 49). "Freud's discovery of repetition" thus points out "the relation between thought and the real" (49). But this limit, Lacan adds, could not have been expected by Freud, for in the very process of symbolization, in this dramatic point of departure, something was at issue that Freud himself could not have divined, something that, according to Lacan, may even bear on the question of the father: "what is at issue in this remembering could not have been known at the outset—one did not know that the desire of the hysteric was the desire of the father" (50). Is the "return to Freud" in some way an attempt to re-trace some steps that Freud himself passed over too quickly? Or a return to passageways that Freud explored, but that his followers mistook for a detour?

Here we run headlong into the enigma of the transference: Freud, the good doctor, used every means at his disposal—hypnosis, suggestion, even the "manipulation" of the televangelist ("Now, when I remove my hands from your forehead, you will then remember . . .")—to enable symbolization. And the patient, eager to please, and quite unwilling to have the sympathetic physician's efforts come to nought, suddenly began to speak: "for the benefit of him who takes the place of the father," Lacan says (50). Thus, the most surprising successes, in which a simple recounting of the concealed event brought about an alleviation of suffering, suddenly came to a halt in the relation to the other, which, although it should have been a *means,* abruptly turned into an *obstacle.* The patient, Freud concluded with dismay, evidently did not want to get better, but clung to suffering as if to life itself. Clinicians began to speak of "resistance," and "defense," a series of technicalities bound up with the transference. In spite of the claims that link the unconscious to the laws of language, then, in spite of the fact that "the unconscious of the subject is the discourse of the Other," we must not be tempted by the closure of the Law, the completeness of signifying system so often attributed to Lacan whenever his work is reduced to the "structuralist" position of Saussure or Lévi-Strauss. We must proceed slowly at this juncture, in order to see clearly where we are going.

These remarks are made in the chapter of *Seminar XI* entitled "Of the Network of Signifiers." Later, Lacan returns to this issue, and the chapter is now entitled: "Sexuality." Here Lacan writes that there is a remainder, something missing from the circuit of the signifier, an "object" that must be distinguished from the Other. And in this sense, the unconscious is not simply a symbolic order phenomenon, but is *real:* "the nodal point by which the pulsation of the unconscious is linked to *sexual reality* must be revealed. This nodal point is called desire" (SXI 154, emphasis added). Here it is a question of the relation between what shows up in the field of speech, "the field of demand, in which the syncopes of the unconscious are made present," and the field of "sexual reality" (SXI 156), a dimension which, though it cannot be understood by recourse to the biological functions of mating and reproduction, nevertheless does not reduce to the level of the signifier. "Look again," Lacan says:

> It was in the case of Anna O. that the transference was discovered. Breuer was quite delighted with the smooth way the operation was going. At that time, no one would have challenged the signifier. . . . The more Anna provided signifiers, the more she chattered on, the better it went. It was a case of the chimney-sweeping treatment (SXI 157).

And of course the good doctor was quite happy. But "there was no trace, in all of this, of the least embarrassing thing. Look again. No sexuality." Now Freud always claimed that the essential point in the unconscious, however much it might be linked to symbolization, was sexual. But as Anna dutifully provided signifiers ("for the sake of him who takes the place of the father"), no trace of sexuality appeared.

"Yet sexuality was nevertheless introduced by Breuer" (SXI 157), who had begun to wonder about his preoccupation with this interesting patient: "Thereupon, the dear man, somewhat alarmed, good husband that he was, decided that things had gone quite far enough," and set off for a vacation in Italy with his wife—

> in response to which, as you know, [Anna] O. displayed the magnificent and dramatic manifestations of what, in scientific language, is called *pseudo-cyesis* or, more familiarly, she blew up with what is called a nervous pregnancy (SXI 157).

The question Lacan poses at this point concerns the transference. The symptom in this case, tied to sexuality, is not one that brought the patient into analysis, but is produced in the relation to the analyst. In different language we might say that it is not her memory, that it would not seem to be a reminiscence. But how, exactly, are we to understand this symptom, as it opens beyond biology onto the relation to the Other? One thing is clear: in the "Rome Discourse" (and elsewhere), Lacan had said that the symptom can be understood in terms of the symbolic order, and resolved by means of symbolization; but now, there is something beyond the symbolic, a factor that links the symptom to sexuality, which is not reducible to the happy days of chimney-sweeping, when one remembered "right down to the dregs"; it is this factor, moreover, that disrupts the concept of the transference. The symptom is no longer understood as a signifier "written in the sand of the flesh" (E 69): "the nervous pregnancy is a symptom, and, according to the definition of the sign, something intended for someone. The signifier, being something quite different, represents a subject for another signifier" (SXI 157).

Parallel to this transformation of the symptom (from signifier to sign), one finds a second shift, in keeping with the peculiar twist that has taken us from the symbolic to the real. Following Freud, Lacan has stressed the voodoo of the "talking cure," the magical effects that detached the symptom from its place in organic medicine, adding that since the symptom is symbolic, so also the operation of the talking cure is symbolic. Lacan says, citing *The Interpretation of Dreams:* "nothing can be grasped, destroyed, or burnt, except in a symbolic way, as one says, *in effigy, in absentia*" (SXI 50). But the symbolic order is "not the whole truth." And Freud says in "The Dynamics of Transference" that "when all is said and done, it is impossible to destroy anyone *in absentia* or *in effigy*" (12:108; Lacan cites this remark as well, SI 38). Are we simply faced with a contradiction, or is it not rather that, as Russell Grigg says, "something beyond the signifier is at work in the transference," something Freud will elaborate as "transference-love," an *identification* that binds the subject to some "thing," outside the network of signifiers?[17]

Faced with this remarkable turn of events, Freud speaks to his colleague about the case. "Let us observe what Freud says to Breuer—*What! The transference is the spontaneity of the said Bertha's unconscious. It's not yours, not your desire,*" Lacan writes, adding "I think Freud treats Breuer as a hysteric here" (SXI 158). Now for Lacan, this is the beginning of the end, the first foothold of a movement that *forgets* the Freudian discovery, a movement that has its source in Freud himself. Freud exonerates Breuer, certain that this is really a manifestation of Bertha's desire, since after all it is *her* symptom. We must notice the distribution of responsibility here: Breuer's action, after all, was entirely philanthropic, and surely merits no guilt. "The curious thing is," Lacan observes, that Freud's response "does not make him feel less guilty, but he certainly makes him feel less anxious" (a decisive opposition: less anxiety, but more guilt). "This brings us to the question of what Freud's desire decided, in diverting the whole apprehension of the transference in a direction that has now reached its final term of absurdity" (SXI 158).

Still later in *Seminar XI,* as it reaches its end, Lacan returns to this issue once more, claiming that Freud appealed to "a kind of rapid sleight of hand when he said—*after all, it is only the desire of the patient*—this should reassure one's colleagues" (SXI 254). But "why not consider Bertha's pregnancy rather, according to my formula *man's desire is the desire of the Other,*" that is to say, recognizing that Bertha's symptom was "the manifestation of Breuer's desire . . . that it was Breuer who had a desire for a child?" (SXI 158). It might be confirmed if we remembered that Breuer, on vacation with his wife, "lost no time in giving her a child"—a child who, at the very time Jones ("the imperturbable Welshman") was writing this history, had just committed suicide, thereby demonstrating the profound and unnatural force of unconscious desire, and the indestructibility that preserves it from one generation to the next.

We cannot stop here, with the platitude that would conclude "it is not her desire, but his." Such a view would only end up with a mere reversal, by which we would be encouraged to admit the "counter-transference," the fact that the analyst, too, has feelings. Lacan writes: "You must follow my thinking here. It's not simply a matter of turning things upside down" (SXI 158). For if Breuer was unable to sustain the position of the Other, if he abandoned the position that would support the elaboration of her unconscious, if he was reduced to finding *himself* caught up in the "intersubjective relation" with his patient, and if this failure to maintain the position of the analyst leads to "the final term of absurdity" and modish remarks about the "counter-transference" (simply turning things upside down, along the imaginary axis), we must nevertheless acknowledge that, whatever may have been Breuer's desire, Bertha ("Anna O.") herself *identified* with this desire, put herself in the role of *completing* the other, as if throwing herself, dutiful daughter, into the void that showed itself in the disconcerted doctor. Thus, behind whatever may be expressed as "Breuer's counter-transference," we must acknowledge what is at stake in Bertha's desire, or more precisely in the *abdication of desire* which she suffers in *identifying* herself as the object that will complete what is lacking in the Other. In this sense, something in the symptom would indeed appear to belong to the patient, not so much as a reminiscence, but as a repetition.

It is this identification that the analysis ought to encounter. The desire of the analyst is radically distinguished from that of "the other person," which Breuer manifested, thereby abdicating the position of the Other which allows the patient to play her cards. If something is nevertheless revealed about Bertha's own desire, or more precisely her *identification with the object* of the Other's desire, this should allow us to recognize that the position the analyst occupies, the "place" of the analyst, is not ultimately reduced to that of the Other, supporting the discursive formations of the unconscious, but is a position that obliges the subject to relinquish this identification with the Other. The twist that concerns us is to be found here: if the analyst assumes the position of the Other, the one whose silence or supposed knowledge supports the discourse of the unconscious, the unfolding of the signifying chain in its alterity, this symbolic operation is not the end of analysis. For this Other is not the whole truth, and must emerge as lacking, in order that the lack in the subject be *given its place* in turn.

Lacan is therefore not ultimately concerned with Breuer and *his* desire, relevant as it may be in demonstrating that Breuer's desire was precisely *not* what Lacan calls "the desire of the analyst." Lacan's focus is rather on what we may learn about the direction of the treatment. If the analysis were taken further, then, it would have to show, not only that the pregnancy is the expression of Breuer's desire (contrary to Freud's sleight of hand), and not only that

Bertha was herself prepared to answer this desire, to dedicate herself to this unconscious labor of love, a symptomatic, incestuous labor "for him who takes the place of the father," a labor in which her desire is lost; if the analysis continued, it would have to proceed to the point where this identification with the object lacking in the Other could be broken. As long as this identification is maintained, the question of her desire will remain closed.[18] As long as the lack in the Other is not given its place, the lack that brings her own desire into being will be refused, *in the name of love*. "It is from this idealization that the analyst has to fall in order to be the support of the separating *a*." Thus, the analytic action would proceed from the labor of symbolization supported by the analyst's position as Other, to the point at which the analyst occupies the position of the object, by virtue of which the Other comes to be lacking. In this way, the analysis would be brought to bear on the identification which Anna O. maintains, in which her desire disappears. "The fundamental mainspring of the analytic operation is the maintenance of the distance between the I—identification—and the *a*" (SXI 273).

In "crossing the plane of identification" (273), the analyst emerges as helpless to do anything on behalf of his dear patient. The analyst is finally useless, a castoff, a reject. In the end, analysis has this depressive aspect, a dimension of mourning and even death. Human emotions tend in the other direction. They hope for a homeland that the community could share in common, recognizing themselves in one another, in keeping with the "best part" of human nature, love and philanthropy, those passions by which our moral being would be guided. Such a community has a dark side that its promises conceal, according to Lacan, "something profoundly masked" (274), a sacrificial character which rears its head "in the most monstrous and supposedly superceded forms of the holocaust," the "drama of Nazism" being the culmination of a long history of sacrificial identification in which the People were formed—and formed, we must acknowledge, in just this dutiful labor of love on behalf of "the desire of this Other that I call here *the dark God*" (275). Perhaps we can see here the intervention "that analysis makes possible in relation to the many efforts, even the most noble ones, of traditional ethics" (276). If the position of the analyst, at the limit of communication, at the limit of science and law, is an ethical position, this is not because it culminates in a moral law (prohibition, taboo) that would bind us all within the symbolic unity of the human community, a law by which desire might be given its limit, but because it confronts the pathology of such a law, insofar as this law always entails an "offering to obscure gods" (275).

Abbreviations

Lacan
E   *Ecrits: A Selection,* trans. Alan Sheridan (New York: Norton, 1977). Translations are occasionally modified; see *Écrits* (Paris: Seuil, 1966).

SI   *The Seminar of Jacques Lacan, Book I: Freud's Papers on Technique,*
      1953–54, ed. Jacques-Alain Miller, trans. with notes by John For-
      rester (New York: Norton, 1988).

SII   *The Seminar of Jacques Lacan, Book II: The Ego in Freud's Theory and in*
      the Technique of Psychoanalysis, 1954–55, ed. Jacques-Alain Miller,
      trans. Sylvana Tomaselli, with notes by John Forrester (New York:
      Norton, 1988).

SXI   *The Four Fundamental Concepts of Psychoanalysis,* trans. Alan Sheridan
      (New York: Norton, 1978). Translations are occasionally modified;
      see *Le Séminaire, livre XI: Les quatres concepts fondamentaux de la psych-
      analyse,* ed. Jacques-Alain Miller (Paris: Seuil, 1973).

T   "Television," trans. Denis Hollier, Rosalind Krauss, and Annette
      Michelson in *Television: A Challenge to the Psychoanalytic Establishment,*
      ed. Joan Copjec (New York: Norton, 1990).

Freud
SE   *The Standard Edition of the Complete Psychological Works of Sigmund Freud,*
      trans. and ed. James Strachey et al. (London: The Hogarth Press,
      1953). 24 volumes. Works will be cited by volume and page number.

Notes

1.   Jacques Derrida, "Let Us Not Forget—Psychoanalysis," *Oxford Literary Review,* vol. 12, nos. 1–2 (1990), pp. 3–7, citation p. 3.

2.   *Parva Naturalia,* Loeb Classical Library edition, vol. VIII, trans. W. S. Hett (Cambridge: Harvard University Press, 1975). pp. 285–313. This text contains the pieces which have been titled "On Memory and Recollection," and "On Sense and Sensible Objects." The same Loeb volume also contains *On the Soul.* References to all these will be given in the text according to the Bekker numbers, in this case, 449b9–10. Translations are occasionally modified.

3.   The "Rome Discourse" is an abbreviated name for "The Function and Field of Speech and Language in Psychoanalysis," published in the *Ecrits.*

4.   These remarks in the "Rome Discourse" are developed in Lacan's "Le temps logique et l'assertion de certitude anticipée," *Ecrits,* pp. 197–213 ["Logical Time and the Assertion of Anticipated Certainty: A New Sophism," trans. Bruce Fink, *The Newsletter of the Freudian Field,* 2, 2 (fall, 1988), pp. 4–22]. The text, as well as some later remarks on time from *Seminar XI,* are discussed by John Forrester, *The Seductions of Psychoanalysis: Freud, Lacan and Derrida* (Cambridge: Cambridge University Press, 1990), pp. 168–218.

5.   I am indebted to David Krell's discussion of Aristotle in *Of Memory, Reminiscence, and Writing: On the Verge* (Bloomington: Indiana University Press, 1990).

6.   William Wordsworth, "Preface" to *Lyrical Ballads* (1850 edition), in *The Prose Works of William Wordsworth,* ed. W. J. B. Owen and J. W. Smyser (Oxford: Oxford University Press, 1974), vol 1, p. 138.

7.   We find here the constitutive ambiguity of memory, the original bifurcation by which imagination, buried in the past, opens towards both empiricism and idealism. The poet cannot see, in the most wild frenzy of speculation, something that has not been seen *before;* the

child cannot learn, Plato says, something that it does not *already* know in some way; it is impossible, Locke remarks, for the most extravagant fancy to compose anything new, since even the monstrous Gorgon or Manticore are composed of elements all of which have been encountered somewhere *previously*. This gesture has a long history. But does this doctrine that binds the imagination to recollection amount to a Platonism of transcendent Forms, in which the "most real" objects of recollection would reside Elsewhere, or is it a doctrine of empiricism in which, as Locke seems to suggest, the senses provide all our information? To which "reality" is the imagination bound, in being bound to recollection?

8.   A splendid example of this magical interpretation can be found in Peter Dews, *The Logics of Disintegration: Post-Structuralist Thought and the Claims of Critical Theory* (London: Verso, 1987).

9.   The remarks Derrida has made about chance and law should be referred to this passage in *Seminar XI*, where Lacan claims that "according to Freud nothing is left to chance," though as we shall see there is a limit to the law in Lacan, a limit, it should be said, that poses problems for the "scientific" status of psychoanalysis. This problem is explicit in *Seminar XI*, though it is given less attention in Derrida's analysis than it warrants. See Jacques Derrida, "My Chances/Mes Chances: A Rendezvous with Some Epicurean Stereophonies," *Taking Chances: Derrida, Psychoanalysis, Literature,* ed. Joseph Smith and William Kerrigan (Baltimore: The Johns Hopkins University Press, 1984), pp. 1–32.

10.   See Jean Laplanche, *Life and Death in Psychoanalysis,* trans. Jeffrey Mehlman (Baltimore: The Johns Hopkins University Press, 1976), p. 23.

11.   Friedrich Nietzsche, *Untimely Meditations,* trans. R. J. Hollingdale (Cambridge: Cambridge University Press, 1983), pp. 60–61. Translation slightly altered. The German text is in the *Kritische Gesamtausgabe,* ed. Georgio Colli and Mazzino Montinari (Berlin: Walter de Gruyter, 1972), pp. 244–5.

12.   See Krell, *Of Memory,* p. 16.

13.   William Wordsworth, "Note" to "The Thorn" in *Wordsworth: Poetical Works,* ed. Thomas Hutchinson, revised edition by Ernest de Selincourt (Oxford: Oxford University Press, 1936), p. 701.

14.   Jean Laplanche and J-B Pontalis, *The Language of Psychoanalysis,* trans. Donald Nicholson-Smith (New York: Norton, 1973), p. 245.

15.   Marie-Hélène Brousse, "La formule du fantasme?" in *Lacan,* ed. Gérard Miller (Paris: Bordas, 1987), pp. 107–22, cited from 112, translation mine.

16.   See Slavoj Zizek, "The Truth Arises from Misrecognition," *Lacan and the Subject of Language,* ed. Ellie Ragland-Sullivan and Mark Bracher (New York: Routledge, 1991), p. 206.

17.   See Grigg, "Signifier, Object, and the Transference," *Lacan and the Subject of Language,* ed. Ellie Ragland-Sullivan and Mark Bracher (New York: Norton, 1991), p. 110.

18.   Hamlet of course poses the "life or death" question from the side of the obsessional, in the speech beginning "To be or not to be." But we should recognize that this question, in which Hamlet appears "partly outside life," has a clear origin, for it is in response to the demand of the Other, the mandate of the father's ghost, that Hamlet, bound by love, dedicates nothing less than himself:

> Remember thee!
> Yea, from the very table of my memory
> I'll wipe away all trivial and fond records,
> All saws of books, all forms, all pressures past
> That youth and observation copied there:
> And thy commandment all alone shall live
> Within the book and volume of my brain (Act I, scene v.).

It is worth noting the lines on "woman" that result from this.

Literature as Symptom

COLETTE SOLER

When Lacan gave a year-long Seminar on "Joyce as Symptom" in 1975–76, he wrote the word symptom as it used to be written in French—"*sinthome*"—introducing thereby the enigma of a translinguistic equivocation. We hear in it the English words "sin" and "home," as well as the French words *saint* (saint) and *homme* (man). This playing with the mother tongue sets the tone. We must try to intimate the importance of the possible effects of this way of handling the letter. But don't think that this is a literary question. Rather, we will see that it is an analytic question. Moreover, it will come as no surprise to you that this question concerns the psychoanalyst, for the agency of the letter can be found in the unconscious, as Lacan put it back in 1956. Here, in fact, we have a question: how is psychoanalysis allowed to speak of a work of art, here of literature?

Freud, for his part, would not have been likely to say "Joyce the symptom," but rather, "Goethe [or Jansen] the fantasy." Do these phrases imply a belittling of the work of art? We are aware of what Freud did with literature. In artists he saw his precursors, and in literary texts he saw an opportunity to verify the analytic method. From Sophocles to Goethe, via Jansen and Dostoyevsky, he found in literary fiction an anticipation of the discovery of the unconscious; and thus for Freud it is the neurotic who seems to be copying the fable in telling his family history, which he calls the "family novel" to say that his fantasy is structured like a novel. In any case, Freud lapsed into applied psychoanalysis, treating the artist's know-how as equivalent to what he himself called the work of the unconscious, putting artistic and literary works on the same level as dreams, slips of tongue, bungled actions, and symptoms, all of which are interpretable.

Lacan reverses Freud's position concerning this point: it is not that the written text must be psychoanalyzed; rather, it is that the psychoanalyst must be well read. Psychoanalysis does not apply to literature. Its attempts in doing so have always manifested their futility, their unfitness to lay the grounds for even the most meager literary judgment. Why? Because artistic works are not products of the unconscious. You can well interpret a novel or

From *Lacan and the Subject of Language,* ed. by Ellie Ragland-Sullivan and Mark Bracher (New York: Routledge, 1991), pp. 213–19.

poem—i.e., make sense of it—but this sense has nothing to do with the creation of the work itself. This sense has no common measure with the work's existence, and an enigma remains on the side of the existence of the work of art. This would even be a possible definition of the work in its relation to sense: it resists interpretation as much as it lends itself to interpretation. Nevertheless, if psychoanalysis does not apply to literature, psychoanalysis can learn a lesson from literature, taking a page out of its book, as it were. More precisely, the teaching of Lacan displays that we can learn either from the writer's work or from his person, from his life, but without deducing one from the other. Thus a psychobiography is possible, but it does not explain the work of art, which is impossible to deduce from the author's life. Anyway, following Lacan's numerous literary references we could say: "Hamlet, desire"; "Antigone, beauty"; "Gide, the fetish"; "Sade and Kant, the will to *jouissance*"; "Edgar Allan Poe, the letter"; and finally "Joyce and his literature, the symptom."

Lacan's recourse to literature follows in the line of his recourse to linguistics. You know that people—not everyone, but the people of the IPA (International Psychoanalytic Association)—have wanted to denounce therein a tendency towards intellectualism and verbalism. But this early recourse of Lacan's was necessary and inevitable for a simple reason: linguistics delivers the "material" of analysis, and even the "apparatus with which one operates in analysis," which is nothing other than the statements proffered either by the analysand or the analyst.

But the analytic operation itself is not a linguistic one, for it attests to language's hold on the symptom, the symptom as it presents itself in analysis. For the moment I am thinking of the symptom in its clinical sense, as it is presented to the analyst as that which does not stop from imposing itself on you. It is not being able to refrain from thinking, or from feeling in the body, or from experiencing affects, and it is only through speaking that you can change the thought, the feeling in the body, and the affect.

Let us return to literature. In psychoanalysis, language operates on the symptom, and the question at hand is to know how the literary use of language can be said to be a symptom. Is it enough to drop speech in favor of writing? And how can literary creation—the spice, as it is often thought, of civilization—be placed on the same level as the symptom, when, by its very definition, a symptom is what is a bit "fishy," or doesn't quite "fit in"? First let me point out the general direction of the solution: literary creation can be a symptom because a symptom is itself an invention. What does it mean to create? The answer is: to bring something into being where there was nothing before. But saying "where there was nothing," I already imply a place. And there is no such thing as a place without the symbolic and its marks, and every symbolic mark engenders as empty the place that it creates.

Allow me on a lighter tone to recount a personal memory which comes from my years of supposed religious education. I must have been about nine or ten years old when an old canon came up to me during an examination, with great pomp and ceremony, and asked me a banal question of catechism: "What was there before God created the earth?" What would you answer? For my part, I answered with the greatest self-assurance: nothing. Note that "nothing" is nothing other than what remains when the signifier "earth" is barred. But my answer was not correct, to my astonishment and sanction. The answer was "nothingness." That had a great effect on me. I even stirred up the people around me, trying out the problem on them, but the old canon turned out to be right. Nothingness in not nothing. It is the word which was invented to speak about the unthinkable pre-symbolic void, which, compared with "nothing"—the result of the elision of something—is a horse of a different color, though that in no way dispels the aporias of divine creation! What is clear is that all creation supposes that the Symbolic has brought forth a lack in the real, where by definition nothing can lack.

I can complete my first statement: creation brings something into being, where there was nothing before, nothing but a hole, which is not nothing. This void is found in analytic experience at every level—first of all as the subject's lack, the first effect of speech being to transform the living being into the subject of the want-to-be, which we symbolize with the minus phi ($-\varphi$) of castration. It is also found, as a consequence of this first level, as the lack of the object which would plug up this crack or fissure. This is what Freud closes in on with his theory of an object which is always substituting for an originally lost object. We recognize in this formulation that it is simply the subject's lack which gives the object its importance.

This is what Lacan takes up, grounding it with his logic of the signifier in the statement: "there is no such thing as a sexual relationship." What does it mean? There are certainly bodies, biological bodies of different genders, and signifiers related to sex: man and woman, father and mother, as well as all those which erect sexual ideals, such as "virgin," "whore," "wife," and so on. None of these inscribes the object which would annul the sexual lack, and they all fail to compensate for the hole, for "the partner of *jouissance* is unapproachable in language." The result is that one seeks; that's why one speaks and why there is even satisfaction in blah blah blah, unless one finds a . . . replacement.

That is what the symptom does: it plugs up the "there is no such a thing" of the no-relationship with the erection of a "there is." Given that the appropriate partner for *jouissance* is lacking, a symptom puts in place something else, a substitute, an element proper to incarnate *jouissance*. The first consequence is that there is not subject without a symptom. Its function is to fix the mode of the privileged *jouissance* of the subject. It is the symptom that makes the singularity of the subject, subjected otherwise to the great law of the want-to-be. The symptom is a function—a logical function—of the unconscious. A symptom snows in, nails in, *jouissance,* while the unconscious displaces *jouissance.*

Now how did we get from the Freudian discovery to these last formulas about symptom? In Freud's terms the deciphering of the symptom reveals the fantasm and the libidinal satisfaction that it engenders. The Freudian notion of compromise formation implies that the symptom constitutes the return of repressed *jouissance*. It is not simply a memory of *jouissance*. It is *jouissance* forever current, unchangeable in its core. Now if it can be deciphered, and its transformation brought about, for us Lacanians it can be deduced that it is of the same nature as language—which accounts for the thesis that the unconscious is structured as language. But on the other hand, its inertia contrasts with what is proper to language, namely the substitution of signs, substitutions by which meaning is engendered. This contradiction is resolved by Lacan in the following way: in the symptom, the signifier is married, so to speak, to something else, and finds itself transformed accordingly.

And what would this something else be, if not what is manifested in suffering, and dwells in fantasy, namely what we call *jouissance*? Cathecting a term, a signifier, which is subtracted from signifying substitution, from the incessant ciphering of the unconscious *jouissance,* turns it into a letter which is outside of meaning and therefore real, a letter which alone is able to always fix or tie down the same being of *jouissance*. This is why Lacan says that the signifier returns in experience like a letter.

But then how could literature be a symptom? Literature serves, of course, as a vehicle of *jouissance*. But which *jouissance*? It is most often the *jouissance* of meaning, especially in the case where literature is novelistic and makes use of fiction, in other words, of the imaginary. Is not this a contradiction? Here let us consider Lacan's examples of symptomatic invention. It is not only Joyce's literature which can be called a symptom according to Lacan. A symptom is also a Woman, or to take another example, the masochistic scenario, or even the Lacanian invention of the real. When a man is compliant with the paternal model, a wom<u>a</u>n (with the "a" underlined) can be his symptomatic invention, because Woman (with a capital "W") does not exist. Which is to say that supposed normality, heterosexuality—which Lacan writes *"norm-mâle,"* or *"père-version"* (since in French "père" means father—in English you could say "version of the father")—is itself a symptom. A symptom which Freud renders in the Oedipus myth.

Here we can see that perhaps invention is not creation. The symptom invents—that is to say, chooses, selects—the singular term which is not programmed by the Other, and which fixes *jouissance*. But this term is not necessarily an original one. In this sense, if creation—true creation, which produces a radical novelty—is a symptom, it is a special one, and we could say that the artist/creator is always without a father. Even if always dated, his work does not have filiation. He is always the "son of his work," as Cervantes said. And therefore it is always foolish to look for the key to a work of art in its sources. The masochistic scenario as a symptom is something else. But its case is an instructive one for us, since it indicates that a scenario—i.e., the imaginary—

can be the variable of the symptom. Therefore why not speak in the same way of the novelistic symptom? Clinical experience provides examples among readers, but also among artists/creators. Read again for example the account of Jean-Jacques Rousseau regarding the composition of the *Nouvelle Héloïse,* the novel that made all Europe tremble. Certainly a novel is dedicated to meaning, while a symptom is real, outside of meaning. But this is a paradox only in appearance, since nothing opposes a unity of meaning as a novel does the one of the symptom.

It is in this context that Lacan invokes Joyce, using *Finnegans Wake* to illustrate Edgar Allan Poe's message about the letter-object, the litter. What was, according to Lacan, the message of Poe when he wrote "The Purloined Letter"? A letter is not only a vehicle of a message; a letter is also an object. Joyce took equivocation, which is the essence of poetry, to an exponential power excluding meaning, pushing it to the power of the unintelligible. Before Joyce, one could not say that poets, even at the height of their art of the letter, demonstrated anything more than the efficacy of the letter in the genesis of meaning. The poet makes clear the joint or seam at which the audacity of the letter engenders something new in meaning. That is the operation by which the poet subverts so-called common sense. His operation certainly produces a *jouissance* to which the Kantian antinomy of taste/judgment is no objection, for this *jouissance* need not be universal for it to be attested to. Nonetheless, this *jouissance* is not pure *jouissance* of the letter. It does not go beyond the *jouissance* of the pun, which in playing on literality, produces an effect of meaning, sometimes brought as far as non-meaning. Its *jouissance* emerges at the joint at which meaning wells up out of the literal, going far beyond, and thus short-circuiting, the subject's intention.

Poetry and puns thus use a know-how of the letter, but it is to move the unconscious. Joyce takes an additional step with *Finnegans Wake.* He manages to use language—where unconscious knowledge rests—without making the meaning vibrate. This is why Lacan says of Joyce that he is *"désabonné à l'inconscient"*—i.e., not registered in the unconscious. This work, characterized by something like elation, something very close to what in psychiatry is called mania, unburdened of the weight of meaning, belongs to the scientific era. It fascinates by the *jouissance* to which it attests, and has a greater affinity with the *jouissance* that the mathematician finds in figures than with that of the classical novelist. And maybe he even signals the end of the classical literary symptom. But note that Joyce does not shut himself within the unintelligible: another of Joyce's accomplishments is to have succeeded in imposing on his commentators, for centuries to come, the weight of meaning that his work forecloses.

Now what in the symptom of Joyce interests the analyst? More precisely, what in his know-how interests the analyst? What interests the analyst is the limit of the analytic action. The symptom of Joyce is the unanalyzable symptom; it is in its own *jouissance* closed to the effects of sense, let us say outside of transference. And psychoanalysis is precisely a practice which operates by sense. It assumes that the subject lets itself be seduced and captivated by meaning, as an effect of the signifying articulation. Well, this limit, which probably explains why Joyce did not undergo analysis, appears to Lacan as the model for the end of a psychoanalysis. Joyce went straight to the best that could be expected at the end of a psychoanalysis, says Lacan. Why? What is the analytic problem at play here? It is the problem of putting a term to the transferential relationship with the analyst, which is itself a new symptom. It is a problem of disengaging the analysand from the *jouis-sens* of the unconscious. On this point Joyce is an example. This is what Lacan teaches us with Joyce. Here, you can see, that each one learns to the extent of his own knowledge. And I believe that we are far from catching up with Lacan.

Works Cited

Lacan, Jacques. *Le Séminaire de Jacques Lacan. Livre XXIII: Le Sinthome* (1975–1976). Unpublished text.
———. "The Agency of the Letter in the Unconscious or Reason since Freud" (1954). Trans. Alan Sheridan. *Ecrits: A Selection.* New York: W. W. Norton & Co., 1977.
Poe, Edgar Allen. "The Purloined Letter," in *The Purloined Poe: Lacan, Derrida, and Psychoanalytic Reading.* Eds. John P. Muller and William J. Richardson. Baltimore: Johns Hopkins University Press, 1988.
Rousseau, Jean-Jacques. *La Nouvelle Héloïse.* Paris: Librairie Larousse, 1937.

Freud's Jewish Science and Lacan's *Sinthome*

DAVID METZGER

In chapter nine of *Seminar XVII,* Lacan writes that the position of the analyst cannot be separated from Jewish history (158). More particularly, the invention of analytic discourse is part and parcel of a Hebraic tradition—represented by the *Book of Hosea*—in which one's god underscores the fact that even if everyone is speaking (let's say about sexual knowledge) this does not mean everyone is saying something. One of the defining moves of a Jewish Science, in this specific frame of reference, would be to situate the knowledge, "There is no Other," precisely where other intellectual and religious traditions establish their rapport with the divine as "I am your Other." In the first section of this essay, "Belief and the Clinical Structures," we will observe how Lacan situates this "There is no Other" in terms of hysteria, obsession, psychosis, and perversion. We will also see how the confirmation of these clinical structures leads Lacan to conceive of unconscious fantasy as something constrained not by the Other but by what he called the "sinthome." Sections two and three of the essay ("God and Discourse, the example of Aquinas"; "God and Sinthome, the example of Descartes") chart a similar development in the theological arguments of Thomas Aquinas and René Descartes. In *"Moses and Monotheism:* Is there a Jewish *cogito?"* (the final section of the essay), we will see how Lacan's specific delineation of the sinthome can be traced to Freud's own hope for a "Jewish Science," his desire to construct "something" that might shoulder the weight of Jewish fantasy.

I. BELIEF AND THE CLINICAL STRUCTURES

In terms of analytic practice, we might more specifically render Other as Other Sex, leaving us to consider the position of analyst as the "There is no Other Sex," where other discourses might find "I am your Other Sex."[1] For this reason, Ellie Ragland, in her most recent book, *Essays on the Pleasures of*

From *American Imago,* Vol. 54, No. 2, 149–164. © 1997 by The Johns Hopkins University Press.

Death (1995), proposes a precise relation between "belief" and the "structures" delineated in the Lacanian clinic:

> The neurotic [is] an atheist or an agnostic, a disbeliever in God who tries to evade the problems of the Other while holding on to the Other's desire. The pervert [is] a true atheist, one who has no symbolic father at all, only the gaze of the real father. The psychotic, the only true believer, believes in the gods who inhabit the field of the real, speaking in omniscient voices and casting looks that scald. Belief shows that we necessarily think we have innate language or innate knowledge precisely because we 'have' a structural deficiency we must deny (220).

What precisely is this structural deficiency? Is it what one might term "the unconscious"? Not really. The unconscious, in this light, might be viewed as an answer to questions the human subject does not altogether understand. In their most overt forms, these questions concern one's particular orientation within a field of signifiers Lacan termed "The Other." For the hysteric this question is "Am I a Man or Am I a Woman?" and for the obsessional it is "Am I Alive or Am I Dead?" The unconscious tirelessly responds to these questions:

> The Name(s) of the Father _ _ _ _ _ _ _ *a*
> The desire of the Mother

In some sense, this response is not much of an answer. In fact, the response of the unconscious might only be another question. Much like the computer from the Douglas Adams' *Hitchhiker's Guide to the Galaxy* (1989)—if I may use an example from popular culture—the unconscious provides an answer that is in need of interpretation. "What is the meaning of life, the universe and everything," one of Adams' characters asks. "42" the computer responds (120). The major difference between the unconscious, as Lacan understood it, and Adams' fictional computer is that the unconscious has something up its sleeve; it wears our hearts on its sleeve, one might say. In other words, the unconscious proposes that the object *a,* the "There is no Other" sustained by the laws of interpretation, is itself an answer. If we are not satisfied with the object *a* offered by the unconscious, there is always *jouissance* understood, at the level of the unconscious, as (1) the equation of the Names of the Father with the Desire of the Mother, (2) the assumption that the "I" of one's own particular *cogito* (I think; therefore, I am _____) is either a mother or one of the three fathers (the symbolic, imaginary, or real).

Without the object *a*—which we might term "a third position" that is neither the mother nor the father—the unconscious becomes real for the individual. The unconscious becomes not something to be interpreted, but exactly who one is at the level of the "I am (the I) think." This "I" is psychotic, subject to the law/*jouissance* of the Real Father for whom nothing is prohibited, since the object *a* is no longer remaindered. The object *a,* one might say, is precisely what even the Real Father cannot make use of—except for the psychotic.

For this reason, Ellie Ragland called the psychotic, "the only true believer." This statement will make more sense if we observe that, in *Seminar XX,* Lacan spoke of *jouissance* as the only substance for the unconscious subject. To suggest the implications of such a statement, Lacan called this seminar *Encore:* the unconscious deals out the same card (*a*)—the possibility of identifying with one's *sinthome*—and as unconscious subjects, we have only one Other response, an imperative that repeats our *jouissance* (*Encore!?* Again!? Hit Me!?).

One might understand this imperative as the *sinthome* (of hysteria, of obsession, of psychosis, of perversion). And one might understand the interrogative as (the) discourse (of hysteria, obsession, and so on). This is not to say that discourse and symptom are the same—only that in light of some such thing as the unconscious, one might assume the following: (1) both discourse and symptom impose themselves on the human subject; (2) *jouissance* is the sister to truth.

Statement (2) is a chapter heading taken from Lacan's *Seminar XVII: L'envers de la psychanalyse,* where Lacan presents his most thorough presentation of a psychoanalytic theory of discourse. What is more, if one recognizes that, for Lacan, truth is a position taken in one's discourse and *jouissance* is something guaranteed by one's *sinthome,* one can see how the relationship between symptom and discourse delineated above might lead Lacan to just such a statement about truth and *jouissance. Jouissance* (the choice of either the desire of the mother or one of the three fathers) is that which substantifies the human subject (as an "I") in the "discourse of the Other" understood here as "the unconscious."

But how is this "discourse of the Other" possible? Where does it come from and in what matter might it presume to speak? The first step to understanding Lacan's designation of the unconscious as the "discourse of the Other" is to recall Lacan's description of alienation and separation. After all, the logical operations gathered under the headings of alienation and separation result in the $, S1, S2, and *a* that Lacan identifies with the subject, other, production, and truth positions of the discourse structures:[2]

Alienation: the subject of the unconscious ($) discovers that there is a whole (S1) in her being in relation to the Other (S2). This is not to say that the human subject can be represented entirely in the Other. Quite the contrary, the effect of this S1 is to ground the human subject's lack in terms of the Other.

Separation: the subject of the unconscious ($) discovers that there is a hole (*a*) in her being in relation to the Other: "There is no unconscious I." For this reason, human subjects cannot be represented entirely in the Other

(S1——>S2). The effect of this *a* is to ground, in terms of the Other, the human subject's lack of a signifier for an "I" at the level of the unconscious.

In the above description of alienation and separation, lack seems to be a lack-in-identity. One asks of the Other, "who am I?" And the answer is either alienation, "S1: If not the S1 or master signifier, then I don't know" or separation, "*a*: There is an 'I,' but I don't know where" (separation).[3] Lacan takes this formulation a step further when he speaks of *jouissance* as a substance. The question "Who am I?" is more specifically the question, "Who am I to enjoy?" The latter question might be understood in two ways: "who am I to enjoy?" or "Who am i to enjoy?" In this manner, the question of one's identity and the question of one's identity as a subject of enjoyment are related in Lacan's conception of the Other. It is no surprise, then, that the unconscious has only one answer to any question of identity, "object a." The problem is that the object a doesn't mean anything. Someone hosting a party might insist that we enjoy ourselves, but that does not mean we have any idea about how to go about doing that in public or in private. Now, let's see how *jouissance* (the mere choice of either the desire of the mother or one of the three fathers) necessitates that the unconscious assume the status of a discourse.

II. Discourse and God: The Example of Aquinas

Lacan defines "discourse" in terms of four positions:

subject   *other*
truth   production

Furthermore, Lacan tells us that these four positions are themselves the result of something called "the signifier" and that these discourse positions are reflected in Aristotle's four-part sketch of causality. Lacan, unfortunately, does not go on to explain how these four positions in discourse specifically relate to material, final, efficient, and formal causalities delineated by Aristotle. However, we might begin to understand Lacan's point if we consider, as he did, that Aristotle's notion of causality addresses four possible responses to the human subject's "birth into language": 1) Subject: I am something for the Other understood as efficient cause, 2) Other: But my actions are not wholly constrained by this Other as formal cause, 3) Production: Something else (a material cause) assumes the duties I presumed were the Other's, 4) Truth: I can know what Other (a final cause) constrains my actions. Or more simply put, for Lacan, discourse promises that we might know our Other. However, in this possibility of knowing one's Other, one assumes that the truth does not set a person free from her or his Other (the order of symbolic constraint), but the truth can, under certain conditions, make a person free to enjoy his/her Other.

The alternative to this enjoyment is to be enjoyed by one's Other. Earlier, I had indicated that, for Lacan, truth is the little sister of *jouissance*. At this point, we might recognize that, for Lacan, truth is a choice of or by *jouissance:* to enjoy or be enjoyed by one's Other. Notice, however, that this *jouissance,* this enjoying or being enjoyed, is predicated on the existence of the Other, which may or may not exist or may only exist as an image or as a symbol for an individual's particular preference for order (I like it; I don't like it; It behaves; It misbehaves). For this reason, one might speak of discourse—within a Lacanian orientation—as, in some fashion, constraining us to speak in a particular way, but it does not impede us; it does not keep us from saying something embarrassing: "if the Other does not exist, there is no such thing as discourse (the making of a social relation in language); therefore, if there is discourse, then the Other exists." This statement is embarrassing not because it is incorrect, but because it leads one to consider that the Other might be understood as a fiction. In theological terms, this embarrassment characterizes the development of medieval Christian thought from Anselm (whose tautological argument inspired Gaunilo the Fool to equate the existence of God with the existence of a fictional island) through Augustine (who asked if one could really live as a Christian in a non-Christian state) and Aquinas in whose work this theological embarrassment blossoms into an anxiety fostered by the very presence of a Christian state. Clearly this genealogy of medieval Christian theology is inadequate. I only can hope to present the general contours of a Lacanian orientation to Christian theology, here—outlining, in the broadest terms, the general problem of treating God as Other, or treating God as discourse.

Aquinas' discussion of "Offices and States" from the *Summa* provides one example of how the existence of the deity as Other might translate itself into a theory of discourse while, at the same time, weakening the existential necessity of the deity. If one is to understand discourse as a way to construct a social link, as Lacan did, how might the fact of a "state" be related to the particular requirements for the deity's existence?

Aquinas addresses this difficulty from the very beginning. "It seems," he writes, "that the concept of state does not denote a condition of freedom or slavery. 'State' comes from the verb 'to stand,' and one is said to stand by reason of his upright position" (3). First of all, we must consider why someone would at first think that a state has something to do with freedom or slavery, that a state is the effective working out of another person's dominion over another. One might assume that an individual human subject who stands upright does so according to his or her own wishes. A state, assumed here as a congress of those that might stand, would then simply be a series of individual states (or standings). Undoubtedly this way of speaking will seem curious to the modern reader. It will be argued that what Aquinas is making reference to is not "state" as nation but "state" as "condition"—just as one hears these days of someone who is in a "state" of confusion, for example. In fact, this assumption about "state" is very much what Aquinas is responding to. Aquinas feels compelled to say that the concept of a state is not a condition, not even a condition that might qualify one person as a slave and another as a master. Such a state would only be a way of speaking about one person's relationship with another—not a way of speaking about one's relationship to the deity. That is, how is it that one discovers that there is a state given the one to One relationship required by a god? Through obedience, one discovers the state as the image of the One.[4]

The second problem that Aquinas addresses is the apparent "stability" or "immovability" of the state as "standing." If a person remains steadfast as the one, if a person does not deviate from his/her standing as the one of God, how does this lead to something that we might recognize as social? It doesn't. Aquinas tells us, at this point, that steadfastness in one's standing is an effect of virtue, and virtuous activity is one of the building blocks of the state as a social entity. In other words, what we are able to see of the state as a social entity is the state as an individual standing. Through obedience, an individual discovers that her/his individual standing might persist as something social, here conceived as an image unobstructed by an individual's desire.

But if all of this is true, how is it possible to account for the differences among individuals except as a master discourse founded on the construction of a most curious theoretical entity, "everybody's fantasy"? Desire might be that which distinguishes the human subject from the divine, but without desire how is it possible to distinguish among human subjects? For this reason, the existence of grades, orders, and offices might seem to be a problem. Further, if obedience, virtuous activity, steadfastness, and standing lead to a state, doesn't it appear that a state is very much concerned with freedom qua freedom from desire? In that case, the state is a condition of freedom and slavery from desire or sin.

Aquinas observes, as well, that one is required to represent oneself in court. There are to be no advocates. It is possible to see here the basis for a presumption of guilt. In one's sin, in one's desire, one is individual; therefore, when accused of sin or wrongdoing, one must stand alone because, in sin, one is alone; only in public discourse (one might go so far as to say in the impossibility of representing one's sin to another) one discovers that all discourse is good discourse. All discourse is social; all discourse is godly. The only problem with this notion is that if all discourse is godly, how is it possible to account for the possibility that one person might have a more pleasant life than another. Surely God's whim is not what makes one person a slave and another a master.

Aquinas replies by saying that differences in position are reflections of how other people are disposed toward one's nature. He then indicates that one's position cannot be easily changed; one is not first poor, then rich.

Rather, one's position has a certain steadfastness of character. One gets what one deserves. And what one deserves is a measure or condition of what one gets. Thus, a state does have something to do with how one dominates or is dominated by others, for how one dominates or is dominated is a mark of one's relation (through grace or sin) to a permanent cause (one's particular relation to the deity).

From this discussion, Aquinas draws three points: (1) Being upright as such does not pertain to the notion of a state; no matter how upright one might be, this means nothing in terms of the state unless one "stands fast and steady"; (2) Being steadfast is a necessary but not a sufficient cause for the state; (3) Differences among individuals are themselves individual. In other words, one's dominion over another cannot constitute a state; a state is no one person's work or power. As Aquinas (1973) put it, "a state requires stability in that which regards the condition of the person himself" (7). The stability requisite of a state is founded on the individual's particular relationship with the deity; this relationship is the very condition for the state.

This position is not without its problems. One major problem is that, curiously enough, a person's particular relationship to the deity is sin. Remember, as we discussed above, Aquinas argued that human subjects are alone and particular to themselves only in sin. In this manner, Aquinas' discussion of God as a social relation opens up an entire heretical field where some might assume (as the Knight's Templar were accused of doing) that only through sin (our fundamental difference from God) might a Christian state be established. The reality of a so-called Christian state might then be a sign of difference or original difference from God (sin/original sin) or a master discourse presuming to address "everybody's fantasy" (a.k.a. obedience). If one recalls the schema for the unconscious that I presented in section 1 (the names of the father over the desire of the mother, then object *a*), one might understand that both of these alternatives seek to constitute the unconscious as Real (a place where the Other might be said to ex-ist) by ignoring the position of the object *a* as something unavailable for use even by the Real Father, the Incestuous Father. Aquinas leaves us with the following dilemma: Either nothing is available to this God-The-Father (sin/original sin) or everything is (obedience). With both of these alternatives, the deity's relationship to the state (which I have used as a metonymy for "discourse," as Lacan understood it) is contingent rather than necessary. And for good reason. The deity's existence must be contingent to discourse, or we might need to consider the possibility that the deity is evil—either because God assumes both the position of "nothing is available for [his] enjoyment" and "everything, including sin, is available for [his] enjoyment" (as we see among the Manicheans) or for God "everything is" (what Descartes projected and rejected much later in the character of an "evil genie who deceives" and what de Sade proposed and embraced as "Nature"). The confirmation of the deity will require something other than discourse, just as confirmation in the psychoanalytic clinic requires something other than discourse, something that Lacan called the *sinthome.*

III. SINTHOME AND GOD: THE EXAMPLE OF DESCARTES

The very possibility of a psychoanalytic discourse responds to the problem of confirmation adumbrated in philosophical critiques of the statement, "God exists." For the purposes of this discussion, I will focus on two general philosophical criteria for evaluating the presumed existence of a deity: (1) "The existence of God" makes sense of something outside of language (*a*); (2) "The existence of God" makes possible something that is inside of language (Φ). The little letters provided in parenthesis are what Lacan called mathemes; Lacan used these symbols to reorient philosophical and scientific discoveries in terms of something that emerges in the psychoanalytic session, Freud's so-called "discovery" of the "unconscious." This is not to say that these little letters are the unconscious; rather these little letters allow us to speak—without irony—about the unconscious. I say "speak without irony" to underscore what Freud (1900) himself recognized as "problem of confirmation" for anyone who presumes to speak about the unconscious: when one speaks about the unconscious, doesn't it seem that it is no longer unconscious (147). These mathemes, although carefully defined by Lacan, afford the psychoanalyst the possibility of speaking about it (as a place or position in language), while—at the same time, recognizing that we are not speaking about it (as meaning). In other words, Lacan uses these mathemes to demonstrate how it is that human subjects might know or understand something ever present in what they say but never present in what they mean.

For example, when one asserts that God must exist in order for a person (understood here as the I of the Cartesian "*cogito*") to know what it means to know something, a Lacanian might write in the argument's margins, *a,* the *objet petit a,* the object cause of desire, something more than *jouissance.* A Lacanian orientation of Descartes' *cogito,* then, would be that there are no words for what it means to know oneself as being or not being, but words are nevertheless compelled to do this awesome work of confirmation. What is more, the fact that language is not quite up to the task requires that people pitch in, by way of interpretation, to help language along. These interpretive efforts (whether constative or performative), these ways that people help language along are what Lacan called *objet petit a.* Descartes, one might say, helped language along by asserting that thought was not wholly subject to language, leading him then to assume that human subjects exist outside of language only insofar as they think. There is something outside of language (I am) that can be confirmed insofar as one identifies with something outside of language (I think). In this regard, one might say that the "I think" is the phallus, as Lacan understood it (the all that is in language or *jouissance*), and the "I am" is the object *a* (the not-all that is in language or *jouissance*).

A Lacanian might then write Descartes' *cogito* in the same manner that Lacan wrote down the fantasy of the obsessional: $\Phi \rightarrow$ a, a, a, a. . . . But there is one proviso. Descartes believed in the existence of God, and for this reason, he is not caught in the potentially infinite regress/progress afforded by moving from one not-it to another. That is, Descartes did not assume that a series of not-its (object *a*) would ever lead us to the following whole: all that is in language, all that is not. In this manner, his cogito (unlike Anselm's argument) avoids speaking about God as a tautology. Descartes positions God as something that functions like a language but is not language itself. This is what Lacan called the *sinthome,* the guarantee that there is at least one word, one "thing" (a master signifier) which language allows us to identify as a human subject (either an all or a not-all in language).

From this rather brief discussion of Descartes, one might make some general statements about Lacan's use of mathemes: 1) mathemes are a psychoanalytic short-hand; 2) Lacan uses mathemes in order to write unconscious fantasy, so that he might posit the *sinthome* as the possibility of confirmation for psychoanalytic inquiry. The first, rather superficial observation describes the obvious: explaining, or making sense, of a matheme takes more time than writing it. The second observation will require more explanation. We will need to see how the *sinthome,* as Lacan understood it, allows him to show how one matheme can be held together with another.

This is not to say the phenomena of obsessional neurosis is the same as the phenomena of hysteria or psychosis; these phenomena are related not by something apparent to the eye, let's say, but something apparent to the eye of analysis. Obsession, hysteria, and psychosis are not definable, within a Lacanian orientation, according to a preset catalogue of characteristics. Nosological characteristics are what something other than the "I" (understood here as object *a* and not as master-signifier) of psychoanalysis might want; nosological characteristics are the generic/logical exigencies that sustain a particular individual's *sinthome* as obsessional, hysteric, perverse, normative, or psychotic. Let me explain further.

Those familiar with Lacan's early work (some of which is presented in his *Ecrits*) will remember that Lacan advised analysts to solve crossword puzzles. Why would he do that? Even in the early 1950s Lacan had conceived of symptoms as a particular chain of signifiers (things to which one might identify because of language). And just as one might say that if 5-across is lymph, then 5-down must begin with an l, the presence of one signifier delimits the signifiers that might be even "free-associated" with it. The particular moments, at which the 5-across is lymph and 5-down appears to be house, are the psychoanalyst's hint that something other than the symbolic order is at work in the analysand's speech. Lacan called this "something other," fantasy. And he developed a precise way of identifying these moments when something other than the symbolic order (or the subject constrained by the exigencies of the symbolic order) was speaking: a, 8, $S(A)$, Φ. Thus, to write Descartes's cogito as "$\Phi \to a$" means that one has written down what was said (what *it* said) in Descartes' argument, but not simply what Descartes said. Now, what does this "what *it* said" mean? And how might one be in a position to confirm this "what *it* said"?

With reference to Descartes, we are not really in the position to make such a determination—although we might recognize, in light of psychoanalysis, the particular discourse structure that Lacan called the "discourse of the master." With reference to an analysand, however, we might be able to say something else—if we assume that the analyst is not in the business of putting words into the analysand's mouth. Where then do these words come from? One might say the Other, from the set of all signifiers or words. And if the symbolic order does not always constrain or order this big-O Other, what does? We're back, again to the *sinthome,* which Lacan tells us is the guarantee—other than the Real—that some Other exists for us at the level of fantasy. What is more, not every *sinthome* makes the same guarantee. Understanding hysteria as a *sinthome* means knowing what kind of Other is guaranteed by the hysteric's fantasy; understanding obsession means knowing what kind of Other is guaranteed for the obsessional, and so on with the other clinical structures. In this manner, one's *sinthome* might be connected with one's ability to believe—one's fantasy of believing—in a particular Other as opposed to any Other.

IV. Moses and Monotheism: Is There a Jewish Cogito?

Has Lacanian psychoanalysis, then, proposed that God might be what we have been calling "the *sinthome*" rather than a discourse? Or, does Lacan leave theology precisely where Aquinas and Freud left it, at the very point where the object of desire (the Mother State, we might call it) is proximate or realizable? Indeed, how strong is the confirmation of psychoanalysis tied to theological confirmation?

A Lacanian response might be to say that both Freud and Aquinas thought neurosis and its attenuations of guilt and anxiety were a better deal than psychosis, and that Descartes did not. So, Lacanians pick up theology right where Descartes left it, at the point where the unconscious is Real, where Lacan identified psychosis. But rather than accept the terrible price of psychotic certainty, analysis offers the possibility of identifying with one's *sinthome*—by placing the object *a,* which is beyond the reach of any demand, precisely in the position of the master signifier (You are this!), which is wholly available to the Real Father. One of the initial results of this analytic move is the analysand's identification with the object a (I am this non-signifier for the Other). We might wonder if this is precisely the space which Freud opened up for the Jewish faith in *Moses and Monotheism,* "People of the Jewish faith believe they are the chosen ones [for the Other]" (1939, 143).

If one were to map this statement onto the Cartesian schema previously delineated, the psychoanalytic goal of Freud's *Moses and Monotheism* becomes a possible answer to the question, "How might Jewish faith and religious practices avoid the infinite regress/progress fostered by a *cogito*: I think; therefore, I am (this), I am (that), I am (the other thing), and so on, until the world of beings (possible I am's) has been evacuated? In other words, "How might Jewish faith and religious practices accommodate 'symptoms,' as they have been delineated in psychoanalytic practice?" If the Jewish faith cannot make such an accommodation, perhaps, psychoanalysis will develop as something other than a Jewish science.

Freud even goes so far as to suggest that Christianity might be viewed as Egypt's "vengeance on the heirs of Akhnaton" (1939, 136). Perhaps, he did not wish that psychoanalysis should do the same. Freud tells us that "there is no place in the framework of the religion of Moses for a direct expression of the murderous hatred of the father" (1939, 134). For that reason, he attempted to write the Jewish fantasy. Just as we observed that an "it" speaks in Descartes' *cogito,* so Freud observed that an "it" speaks in the Exodus: Moses was an Egyptian; Moses was killed in the wilderness (142). Using Lacanian mathemes, one might write Freud's statements as follows, $a/\sim \emptyset \rightarrow \Phi$, in order to indicate that what Freud is addressing here isn't historical but is, rather, history understood as fantasy operating according to the logic of the *sinthome* and not the logic of the symbolic order. History is a choice: "being this (a) for some Other rather than not meaning anything ($\sim \emptyset$) for some Other leads one to access a *jouissance* remaindered by our failed attempts to verify the existence of an Other/God. Whether the historical Moses was an Egyptian or not is hardly the point; the point is that given all of the possible evidentiary constraints of history, faith, and interpretation, *it* wants to say Moses was an Egyptian, and *it* wants to say Moses was killed in the wilderness. The focus of a Jewish science, then, would be to see how a *sinthome* might shoulder the weight of this fantasy and not the other way around.[5]

Notes

1.   Now, does this mean that Lacan thought that, as an analyst, he assumed the position of a god charted in Hebraic thought? No. But Lacan is warning us that for some psychotic patients the analyst might appear as such. For that reason, there may be no end to an analysis for a psychotic patient except her/his death. An analysis may only be able to temper the psychotic's *sinthome,* since there is no such thing as a psychotic discourse; the psychotic does not speak in order to make a social link. The psychotic speaks so that others might bear the burden

of interpreting what he or she experiences as Real. The psychotic has foreclosed the master signifier that keeps him/herself from ex-isting as the Other in the Real. The psychotic, for that reason, would not be able to make a move into the discourse of analysis, since analysis—as I suggested above—involves placing the object *a* in the position of the analysand's master signifier, which again is foreclosed for the psychotic.

2.   In *Seminar XVII* and *Seminar XX,* Lacan delineates four discourse structures; each is constructed by placing one of four mathemes in one of the four positions in each discourse structure.

The four mathemes: S1, the master signifier; S2, knowledge; $\mathbf{\mathcal{S}}$, the unconscious subject; *a*, the object *a*, cause of desire, also known as the more-than-*jouissance.*

The four discourse structures:

U	M	H	A
$\dfrac{S_2 \longrightarrow a}{S_1 \quad \mathcal{S}}$	$\dfrac{S_1 \longrightarrow S_2}{\mathcal{S} \quad a}$	$\dfrac{\mathcal{S} \longrightarrow S_1}{a \quad S_2}$	$\dfrac{S_2 \longrightarrow \mathcal{S}}{S_2 \quad S_1}$

For further discussion of Lacan's discourse structures, see my book, *The Lost Cause of Rhetoric: The Relation between Rhetoric and Geometry in Aristotle and Lacan* (Carbondale: Southern Illinois University Press, 1995).

3.   Lacan's discussion of separation might be understood as his particular reading of the Freudian dictum, *"Wo es war, soll ich werden."*

4.   Aquinas presents, here, the logical basis for the foundation of monasteries: put the S1 (the master signifier of the law) precisely where there was desire (*a*) and a community will be formed. Place obedience where the master signifier of the law was, so that a person might not relate his/her desire to the law. In fact, one can observe just such a procedure in chapters 4 and 5 of St. Benedict's Rules of Order. In chapter 4, St. Benedict lists what it is a member of the order should and should not do—for example, "not to murder, not to commit adultery, not to become attached to pleasures." Then, in chapter 5, entitled "Obedience," Benedict suggests that members of the order need not worry about only seeming to follow the law of the order if they so hastily commit themselves to work that they forget about whether or not they wish to do it or not: "The first degree of humility is obedience without delay. . . . Such as these, therefore, immediately leaving their own affairs and forsaking their own will, dropping the work they were engaged in and leaving it unfinished, with the ready step of obedience follow up with their deed the voice of him who commands. . . . [T]he Lord says, 'Narrow is the way that leads to life,' so that not living according to their own choice nor obeying their own desire and pleasure but walking by another's judgment and command, they dwell in monasteries and desire to have an Abbot over them. Assuredly such as these are living up to that maxim of the Lord in which he says, 'I have come not to do My own will, but the will of Him who sent me' " (St. Benedict 186).

5.   Freud makes the same point in a much more specific fashion: "The seed of monotheism failed to ripen in Egypt. The same thing might have happened in Israel after the people had thrown off the burdensome and exacting religion. But there constantly arose from the Jewish people men who revived the fading tradition, who renewed the admonitions and demands made by Moses, and who did not rest till what was lost had been established once again. In the course of constant efforts over centuries, and finally owing to two great reforms one before and one after the Babylonian exile, the transformation was accomplished of the popular god [ ] into the God whose worship had been forced upon the Jews by Moses. And evidence of the presence of a peculiar psychical aptitude in the masses who had become the Jewish people is revealed by the fact that they were able to produce so many individuals *prepared to take on the burdens of the religion of Moses in return for the reward of being the chosen people and perhaps for some other prizes of a similar degree"* (emphasis mine, 111).

References

Adams, Douglas. 1989. *The More Than Complete Hitchhiker's Guide*. New York: Wings Books.
Freud, Sigmund. 1900. *The Interpretation of Dreams*. S.E. 4: 1–388.
———. 1939. *Moses and Monotheism*. S.E. 23: 7–137.
Lacan, Jacques. 1991. *Le Séminaire, Livre XVII: L'envers de la psychanalyse*. Texte établi par Jacques-Alain Miller. Paris: Seuil.
Metzger, David. 1995. *The Lost Cause of Rhetoric: The Relation between Rhetoric and Geometry in Aristotle and Lacan*. Carbondale: Southern Illinois University Press.
Ragland, Ellie. 1995. *Essays on the Pleasures of Death*. London: Routledge.
St. Benedict. *Rule for Monasteries. Readings in Medieval History*. Edited by Patrick J. Geary. Petersborough, Ontario: Broadview P. 180–214.
St. Thomas. 1973. *Summa Theologiae*. Vol. 47. New York: McGraw-Hill.

Fictions

STUART SCHNEIDERMAN

In formulating a commentary on Poe's account of the purloined letter, Lacan was led to invent a fiction. His intention was to allow the truth to speak to you, to address you from a written text through veils of critical inquiry. If Lacan succeeded in allowing something to speak to you through the gaps in a written text, the subsequent issue must be how and whether it was heard and by whom?

Lacan's fiction concerns the point at which Dupin prepares to purloin the letter from the Minister D——. The act that finally accomplishes this will lead eventually to the removal of the letter from its deviant circulation, return it to the Queen, and thus to its true destination, obliteration. This final return will put an end to the seemingly endless cycle of repeated purloinings. Only the narration will remain to torment the faithful.

Lacan's fiction focuses on the crucial moment of the story when Dupin sees and identifies the purloined letter; it describes a scene that is other than the actual scene. The fiction makes sense of Dupin's identification of the letter and also of his act. His act appears to be an *acte manqué,* a parapraxis, but it is thoroughly intentional. The action takes place in the offices of the famous Minister D——, and Dupin's act is an act of intelligence. It is Dupin's act, not that of his unconscious, and it is not his last act.

Here is the story. Having been apprised of the theft of a letter from the royal apartments by the Minister D——, and having heard the Prefect of Police explain in detail his futile efforts to find said missive, C. Auguste Dupin decides to pay a visit to the Minister. His eyes covered by green sunglasses, Dupin enters the office of the Minister. His concealed look scans the room until it lights upon the purloined letter. He continues his conversation, and, upon leaving, forgets his snuff box, thereby having a reason to return to abscond with the letter. He has devised a strategy, roughly as the Minister had in purloining the letter in the first place. His act is part of his own strategy.

Lacan's version of the story introduces what we will call a fictitious entity. Again Dupin enters the room wearing green sunglasses. But now spread out before him is an immense female body, waiting to be undressed.

From *Lacan and the Subject of Language,* ed. by Ellie Ragland-Sullivan and Mark Bracher (New York: Routledge, 1991), pp. 152–66.

Lacan avers that Dupin did not need to listen at Dr. Freud's door to know where to look for the object this body is made to conceal. It is there, between the legs of the fireplace, within reach, waiting to be ravished. But Dupin restrains himself, recognizing that if the Minister knows that the letter has been ravished and that the ravisher is under his control, Dupin will not leave the house alive. Thus Dupin prepares an act that fictionally will be the ravishing of a female body, one where the subject of that body will not know immediately that the body has been ravished or by whom.

Dupin knew that he could not take possession of this signifier, of an inscribed signifier, a localized signifier (not all signifiers are inscribed), without leaving in its place a fac-simile, a substitute, an object, a worthless piece of paper whose destiny will be to be rolled up into a ball and tossed out with the trash.

As you know, Dupin did not believe that his fac-simile was worthless, but Lacan emphasized the unlikelihood of this substitute producing the effect Dupin expected. There, of course, Dupin did commit a lapse of judgment; due, as Lacan said, to the fact that those who take possession of the letter are possessed by it. Dupin repeated the scene in which the Minister purloined the letter in the first place, because when the Minister substituted a worthless piece of paper for the precious letter, there was, Lacan said, a remainder whose importance no analyst will fail to recognize.

So we have two letters of which only one is a signifier and which are certainly not doubles. The second letter, the fac-simile, is the object *a* and its connection with the letter as barred signifier constitutes the structure of a phantasy. Lacan's fiction was generated out of the phantasy he read in the text.

Such is, with variations, Lacan's telling of the story of Dupin's theft of the purloined letter. The female body in question is properly a fiction and it is because Dupin knows this and disregards the real space that he engages his desire and succeeds in taking the letter. His desire leads him to modify the real. The truth found in the fiction concerns desire and Lacan consistently made the point that to turn away from this truth was not just a function of an excessive fascination with facts, to say nothing of texts, but was also a symptom of the overestimation of the importance and usefulness of working with the ego. This is not to say that facts are not significant or relevant, nor that they do not have a place. Desire is not the facts, but to translate your desire into reality, you had best know the facts. As Wittgenstein said, it is one thing to know whether the window is open or shut, quite another to know whether you want it open or shut.

Lacan saw Dupin as having revealed the naked truth of a fictitious entity. The sight of the nakedness of truth has led Jacques Derrida to essay to cover it up, all of it, to cover its entire surface. Whether he wrote out of compassion or prudishness, I will not venture to guess. "That the inscription [or scription] in its entirety—the fiction named 'The Purloined Letter'—is covered, over its entire surface, by a narration by a narrator who says 'I' does not let us confuse the fiction with the narration" (Muller and Richardson, 180).

Basing his approach on the phenomenon of the script, of the activity of writing, Derrida inadvertently and with passion engages himself in a massive cover-up. Many, if not most, of his errors have been revealed by Barbara Johnson in her excellent article "The Frame of Reference: Poe, Lacan, Derrida" (See Muller and Richardson). However accomplished his writing, Derrida's criticism of Lacan has a familiar ring. To refute Lacan Derrida falls back on the points Lacan has always been criticized for: the failure to give sufficient weight to the imaginary, to the ego, to narcissism, to the horrors of corporeal fragmentation. In a sense one might rightly say that Lacan could have given more weight to these points, though one should in the interest of fairness note that Lacan did devote considerable theoretical effort to them. The point is that Lacan asserted the primacy of the symbolic over the imaginary, and that Derrida sees the imaginary as swallowing the symbolic.

And so we find Derrida accusing Lacan of everything his psychoanalytic adversaries have criticized him for: the overvaluation of the Oedipus complex, the overestimation of the phallus, overintellectualizing, being too interested in philosophy, failing to take into account the pre-oedipal fears of corporeal fragmentation, failing to give place and importance to the ego; there is even a sense that Lacan is being accused of giving insufficient place to affects.

To empower the narrating ego, the psychic censor leads first to the glorification of the imaginary problematic of narcissism, aggressiveness, and the fragmented body (a problematic analyzed first by Lacan, incidentally), but it leads more ominously to the collapse of an imaginary identification into the real. Instead of having to deal with the ego and its counterpart you are faced with the phenomenon of the double, a phenomenon which is properly delusional.

To say that the narration, commanded by the narrator's I, covers the fiction entirely supports a tendency to avoid seeing, but more especially to avoid hearing the truth when it speaks. As though the unconscious, i.e. the letter, could be entirely censored by the ego, irrevocably blocked, so that its message may perhaps not reach its destination, which is of course to be spoken. To be brief, Derrida's argument rationalizes disinterest in the unconscious, by asserting that if you never stop writing or if the writing never stops, you will not have to hear its message. At the same time this argument pretends to express great interest in the unconscious, in the play of writings, but the unconscious thus in play is collective, not personal.

What is Derrida's scriptural strategy and to what is he opposed? This is not a very difficult question. Certainly, "Le Facteur de la Vérité" is an overwritten and overwrought text that reads like an indictment. It constantly repeats the same charges, piling up evidence of tendencies that appear to be worthy of condemnation. The tone is moral, and the text is animated throughout by the mostly seemingly indubitably correct moral passion. Ultimately, that is the secret appeal of deconstruction.

Derrida's condemnation of Lacan's discourse is based on the fact that Lacan emphasized the division of the sexes. Nothing else. The opening attack on Lacan's use of the concept of truth in its connection with femininity will eventually yield to another attack on the importance Lacan accorded to the phallus and speech, especially as these are linked to the structure of masculinity. As I have pointed out in my book *An Angel Passes*, there is nothing new or radically subversive in such a strategy.

Was Derrida then denouncing Lacan's theory of sexual difference, or Freud's, or was he denouncing sexual difference as originally defined by pagan writers like Plato and Aristotle? Presumably, the answer is the latter. I have said that in his zeal Derrida is led to make many mistakes in reading Lacan. One basic misreading should however be underscored; I am not certain that is has been remarked before.

Derrida insists that Lacan's reading is about the castration of the mother, a topic not unworthy of a psychoanalyst. He sees Lacan as saying that the proper place of the letter is between the mother's legs (*La Carte Postale,* 489). Thus he declares that Lacan is saying the same thing that Marie Bonaparte had already argued, namely that the destination of the letter is the place of the Queen (480). However, Lacan said clearly that the destination of the letter is the place previously occupied by the Law, thus the King. According to Lacan this place comports blindness, and the point is that blindness not only prevents one from reading, it also assures that the letter will be spoken, that what is to be spoken will eventually be spoken.

What did Lacan mean? Quite simply that the final destination of the purloined letter, as of all letters, is to be destroyed, thus that the physical presence of the letter will necessarily yield to speech. This point is well understood by Derrida and he understands it clearly as a significant threat to his enterprise. Thus the importance Lacan placed on the remainder left by the Minister in the royal apartments, left to be rolled up in a ball and thrown away. Similarly for the fate of the fac-simile Dupin left in the Minister's apartment. It is only when the letter embarks on its detour through the agency of the Minister and Dupin that its place is between the legs of "an immense female body."

Let us, in any case, begin to evaluate the argument for the central importance of the narrating ego. In everyday practice if you have a case where you have a patient who, for the sake of the argument, has an ego that covers entirely all fictions, then the thing to do is to disregard the communication, or in other words, to refuse to respond to the demand to take the productions of that ego as a road to the unconscious. We have nothing against telling a story; after all, Dupin does just that after he has exchanged the letter for a considerably financial payment. But he tells of an act in which he was engaged while the narrator tells a story of an act in which he was not engaged. In the first case the narrating is part of an engagement of desire while in the second the narrating represents a way to continue to avoid acting upon any desire.

If you are listening to what the ego would like you to believe, you will miss the message, a message which in these cases is spoken only in a lapse, or better, unintentionally. If the message is not heard, it has effectively not been spoken, and if it is not spoken, what happens to it is that it becomes inscribed and not on paper. At that point the analyst suffers it, just as the patient's symptom, represented by his own suffering, is the inscription of an unaccomplished speech act. Once the letter is inscribed as a symptom, efforts to write oneself out of it will simply double the inscription and confuse the issue.

Why does the narrator do such a thing? To avoid anxiety, you might say, and this failure is repeated in the writer who takes his writing to be a repetition of what the narrator has done. There is anxiety that something might be spoken, then it might be addressed to the subject and that the subject might have to do something about it. To ward off this anxiety, to make sure that nothing is spoken, all you have to do is to keep writing.

One of Derrida's accusations against Lacan is that he fails to consider the importance of anxiety over bodily fragmentation. In effect, there is some truth to this since Lacan's Freudian view sees the structure of anxiety in the context of castration. To understand this we refer to a point Lacan made in a discussion of Little Hans. In his (unpublished) seminar on anxiety Lacan stated that the boy's anxiety was not produced by castration threats. Rather, he suggested, it was when the boy saw his own genitals in his mother's hands, thus, in a place he knew to be lacking a phallic attribute of its own, that he experienced anxiety.

He does not experience anxiety because it looks like his mother has a phallus, but rather because the boy knows that she does not have one, thus that the existence of something that looks like male genitals on her body can only be uncanny—especially when he recognizes them as his own. Anxiety, Lacan said, is not without an object. This object, cause of anxiety in this case, is not a new phallus for mother, but rather something that designates a lack.

The structure in question here involves on the one side of the object *a* in his mother's hands, the cause of the subject's desire, and on the other, the cut of the subject's body that has separated him from a most precious object. In my view this cut is produced by the proper name and the function of naming thus will become crucial.

To say that the cut corresponds to the purloined letter is to say that it is the barred signifier, the signifier that undergoes a detour by being inscribed in the unconscious.

This does not tell us the meaning of the letter or the meaning in the letter. Of course Lacan was not and never claimed to be a hermeneut. Names do not have meanings and they do not say anything about the person named. Their function has everything to do with the structure of the signifier. It is only in the absence of a functioning proper name that the problematic of hermeneutics opens up. Where the proper name does not function to hook language into speaking subjects, the search after the meaning of words becomes of critical importance.

Proper names identify the subject and place him within a symbolic structure. The impulse to deconstruct the "proper," often indulged by Derrida, would normally have a bearing on the function of proper names. If we are no longer to use proper names to identify people, what is left but descriptions of personality traits and activities. And however much these descriptions appear to identify a person uniquely, there is no way of knowing whether the person so identified is the person or his double. Thus the deconstruction of the proper, thus of proper naming, creates the problematic of the double.

To return to Dupin and the narrator, we ask what differentiates them, and even why Lacan privileges the place of Dupin? Here the pertinent fact is that Dupin is the only character in the story with a proper name. By contrast the narrator is unnamed, thus anonymous. This anonymity seems to provide the advantage of making him identical to whatever is written about him in the text, but it also obliges us to identify him only in relation to his narrating activity, through a nominalized verb.

It is almost as though Lacan is advising that one ought not listen to someone who presents himself as nameless. Either you speak in your name or you are not speaking. Other characters are designated by letters, as though their names had been censored, or by titles or even epithets. C. Auguste Dupin is the only character whose name has not been censored, and clearly the story is his story. He is the subject. He is the only character who truly speaks as an I. While the narrator's I is a substitute for a proper name, Dupin's is the only I that is in apposition to a proper name. Within the context of the story the purloined letter will become the referent of the proper name to Dupin. The object he lost in receiving this cut is the fac-simile he leaves in the Minister's apartment. And there is no doubt that Dupin leaves something of himself in the place left vacant by his purloining of the purloined letter.

So, Dupin speaks in his own name and acts in his own name. He transports himself into a space of desire and his successful act is in accord with a desire that he assumes as his own—at a price to his person. He is the one who confronts the fiction of the immense female body, just as the Minister had confronted it before him. Such a confrontation is in no way a part of the activity of the narrator, as Derrida correctly states, because the narrator is attempting to cover over the fiction, to cover up the action, and to lead the reader astray. You may feel compassion for the narrator; and you may wish to assert that his acting to retrieve the purloined letter was never in question. He was never called upon to act. This is true enough, but the narrator makes no suggestions, has no ideas about what to do. He is content enough to allow his friend to act. He never sees himself as acting, but rather he sees himself as serving his friend.

Dupin's act is effective and its effect is not diminished fundamentally by the vengeful message he leaves behind. But note that when Dupin becomes impassioned and leaves a vengeful message in the fac-simile he does not sign his name. He expects that he will be identified by his distinctive handwriting—well known to the Minister. This does not prevent Dupin from narrating the events that transpired in the Minister's apartment, if only to demonstrate that he, as we, have nothing against narrators or narrating in general. This is in stark contrast to the position of the narrator, to say nothing of the writer. The narrator does not act, he does not tell his story, and one might even say that it matters little to the narrator that Dupin succeed or fail; a good narrator can narrate either with equal skill. It is interesting to note a literary parallel here. The problematic of making someone else's story your own when you have failed to perform a prescribed act is precisely what happens in *Hamlet*.

If Derrida's text "illustrates" anything, it shows the false sense of superiority gained by those who fail to act, for whom acting in accord with their desire is never in question. The ability to find a flaw in the acts of others gives a conviction of the moral virtue of their own position—that of compassionate and ultimately innocent bystanders.

The narrator is a fictional device, a pretense, an invention of the author. It places a buffer between Dupin and the reader. Dupin does not address the reader, does not write his story for public consumption, and if we know the story it is because the narrator and writer have taken it from him to present it to us. This appears to many readers to be parallel to the other acts of purloining recounted in the story. It is not. It represents a gaining of ego mastery, understanding, awareness, and insight into acts that one is not capable of performing.

The position of the narrator seems to provide for the reader an entry into the story, but this entry is a ruse. It is not because the reader identifies with the narrator, or takes the narrator to be his double, that he is interested in or by the story. To the extent that he identifies with the narrator he avoids being interested in the story, he avoids seeing his desire in a fiction.

The narrator's I does not designate him, does not identify him, but is an indexical which in fact could be used by anyone engaged in the activity of telling the story or writing the text. An indexical does not designate a subject, but rather an activity, speaking or writing, or else, if it is something like "here" and "now," it establishes a place or a scene.

Not only will the reader be identified, but he will have to have an interest in what happens in the story. The reader's interest in the fiction derives first from the fact that something of his, an object, is to be found therein. Roughly as Little Hans might have seen something of his in his mother's hand. As Lacan elaborated in his discussion of art in *The Four Fundamental*

Concepts of Psychoanalysis the viewer of a work of art finds his own look dissimulated in the painting. It is only through this structure that the work of art can be said to regard the viewer or audience.

But ought we not say that Dupin himself is a fiction, an invention of the author? There are many theories of fiction which begin with just such a premise. My response is that if the proper name is, as Kripke said, a rigid designator, then it designates rigidly even where the reader does not know whether a person has ever received that designation. My hypothesis is that a fictional proper name seeks a person to designate, and that the reader, while he is reading the story, allows himself to be identified by that name. You read the story as if you were Dupin, as if the story were about you, not as if you were the narrator.

To pay attention to the nameless narrator is to eliminate the function of proper naming as designating the same referent rigidly in all possible worlds, even in fictional worlds. It is also to place oneself on the side of the almighty Verb, loved especially for its capacity to avoid reference. This is done with the greatest clarity in the privilege accorded to an activity like writing, or better the scene of the writing.

The privilege of the scene of the writing annuls the subject, referent of the proper name, and throws things entirely on to the side of the verb and its predicates. In the absence of a reference the scene of the writing harkens to another scene of writing and yet another; each text is joined to another text in a multiplication of meanings or even a multiplication of unmeaning, each of which is superceded as soon as it is established. The process, as you can experience while reading texts produced according to such principles, continues ad nauseam.

So the Writer writes that it is all an affair of writing, of writing about writing about writing, leading to some ultimate fall into the abyss of non-referentiality. What you have here is a contemporary translation of a form of mystical ecstasy, of an enjoyment that responds to the demand of a superego who prescribes that the command *"Jouis"* or "Enjoy" is best satisfied by writing. Compulsively writing or compulsively seeing everything as a function of writing responds to that Law. And it is that Law that is satisfied by this approach.

Let us elaborate what we have said about proper names. As far as the name Dupin is concerned, it was the real name of a real detective, though the real detective had a different first name. And it happens often enough that a fiction will concern a real person, a point noted by Aristotle in relation to tragedies and repeated recently by Thomas Pavel in *Fictional Worlds*. A play about Julius Caesar may well be a fiction but the Julius Caesar in the play is not a fictional Caesar, a counterpart of the real Caesar. Whether or not the author is telling the truth about Caesar, the play is still about the historical Caesar. But the referent, being the same, may certainly, like the purloined letter, be moved to different places, to be detained by different people. Thereby the reader can identify or be identified by the name of an historical character by appropriating the mark or cut that is the referent of that name.

The fiction is in the telling or in the saying, even the prediction, and this is not the same as the naming. While it appears that a character in a fiction is simply the cluster of characteristics and actions that are said to be his in the fiction, I would argue that these characteristics and actions are no more determinate of a reference than they are for a real person. It is just that in a fiction you are allowed to believe that they are.

This does not resolve the difficulty of proper naming of fictional characters; rather it defines it. It leads quite naturally to fictional characters with proper names who are not real. In other words, what about Sherlock Holmes? And here I think that the same applies. If a fictional character has a proper name, then that name designates rigidly, except that you do not know whom it designates. Here the act of naming is not public, but is private, known perhaps only to the author. My supposition is that the character of Sherlock Holmes was based on a model, someone with another name, who was given the name Sherlock Holmes for the purposes of fiction. One of those purposes is that since the reader is not supposed to know who the model is, the author is not obliged to accord what he says about his character with what is known about the model. If the reader is not called upon to know whether the statements made are true or false in relation to a person, he is more likely to be drawn into the story. The reader's ignorance of the identity of the model functions in this case to open the path for the reader to allow himself to be identified by the name of Sherlock Holmes. This would supersede any identification by resemblance.

So long as you do not know who the person in question is, then your usual tendency to judge the truth of the statements about a person in relation to your knowledge of the real person is subverted. You cannot when reading a fiction map the fictional predicates onto a real person, even when the character's name is that of a real person. The person designated or identified by the name is not the cluster of recognizable or verifiable characteristics we see in the person. The name designates no matter what you say about the person.

How then do we determine the truth value of statements made about someone about whom you effectively know nothing, about whom there is no history? How do you determine truth value when the saying or the telling is radically non-referential, but where the naming is? Obviously we are not talking about something being true to the facts, because there are no facts, nor are we talking about the theoretical situation described by David Lewis where the events of a fiction are facts for the characters in the fiction. How, in other words, do you know what your desire is? Assuming that desire does not correspond to the facts and that it is not something that you feel in your gut, how do you know what it is? And even if you arrive at grasping a desire, how do you know that it is yours and not that of someone else? Or else, how do you verify a statement of that desire? What is the truth value of a fiction?

A relevant question here is why should you take yourself to be designated by the name of Sherlock Holmes and not that of Dr. Watson or of Prof. Moriarty? It may well be that your own personality corresponds more closely to that of Watson or of Moriarty. As someone who has no talent for detection and strong impulses to write you may find yourself more in sympathy with the position of Watson. You may even attempt to rationalize that choice by writing a study of the Sherlock Holmes stories demonstrating that Watson is really the central character, the hero of the affair. If you tend toward the character of Moriarty, of course, you would be less likely to be sitting at home at your desk writing down your exploits.

Intuitively we would like to say that the reason lies in the fact that Sherlock Holmes is more intriguing, more interesting, more sympathetic, more engaging; he is the agent, the one who acts in the world after engaging in a series of more or less complex mental acts. Sherlock Holmes is the hero of the fiction, the one who is most fully engaged in the world of the fiction. He is always the subject. All of this to say that it is Holmes's desire that is in play in the fictional reality described by the stories. Or better, that the desire manifest in the stories is one that the character named Sherlock Holmes takes to be his own. To refuse to be identified by that name reveals a failure on the part of the reader.

The author's act is a renaming, a repetition of the first act of naming, and this renaming is essential to the formation of an unconscious. The new name, which I have called an improper name, is considered to be meaningful in a way that the proper name is not, to define a being rather than a lack of being, to be adequate to descriptions of the person, to be in a direct relation with whatever can be said about the child. As philosophers like to say about fictional characters, they are whatever their authors say that they are. Finally, of course, this is not the case; the new name, as a signifying structure, is no more meaningful than the proper name. It is just that the reader is allowed to believe that it is, thus the appeal of fictional characters. The reader is allowed to believe that within this new world of fiction, not only will he be renamed, thus, be permitted to break out of the symbolic constraints imposed by his proper name, but that this new name, received by the grace of the author of the fiction, will absolve him of the obligation to act and to speak in his own name. This is the lure of the literariness of some fictions; it provides a disinterested aesthetic enjoyment. The question is whether this is all that it provides.

We will return here to Lacan's fiction of Dupin's encounter with the immense female body waiting to be undressed. In fact, what Dupin encounters upon entering the room is the Minister in a room. To say that he encounters a female body is counterfactual. So Dupin surveys the room as if it were a female body, and it is only by shifting himself into this "as if" perspective that he can identify the placement of the letter.

The "as if" construction translates well into a counterfactual conditional: If this were a female body, the letter would be in such and such a place. And in fact the letter is in precisely that place, which does not mean that the room is a female body. So you have a reality that can be exactly measured and on another level you have another world which is a fictional body.

But the truth in the fiction is not to be confused with the facts, even with what the characters take to be the facts. And I would add the following conjecture, which I derive more or less from the theorization of Thomas Pavel in *Fictional Worlds*.

The idea of undressing and ravishing a female body, while it may certainly be part of a fiction, has, when compared to the events of the story, a quality that is closer to myth. Pavel argues in his book that fictions are the residues of myths that have failed, that have ceased to function socially, to be part of a discourse as a social link. Or you might say that a myth is a particular kind of fiction that has a social function. As Pavel states: "When a mythological system gradually loses its grip on a society, the ancient gods and heroes start to be perceived as fictional characters" (41).

Pavel asserts that the function of myth is to provide the truth of whatever happens in everyday situations. If a person living in a culture where myths are functional has a certain experience and if he compares it to the story of Diana and Acteon, that story serves as providing the truth of the experience. The myth is the truth of the desire in play, and if desire should be taken literally, it does not admit of interpretation.

Fictional entities exist at a remove from real ones, they are in relation with real ones, and perhaps this is true of characters in fiction. Perhaps the truth of the fiction or even the coherence of the fiction will only function if the fiction is at a certain remove from the real entity. The question is what is the kind of relation in play here? We could say simply enough that there is a resemblance between character and model, that something like a form has migrated from the one to the other. This is simple, it suggests mirroring, but it is not consistent with what we have been saying up to now.

My assertion is that a fictional character is always based on a model, a real person, who has been renamed. Needless to say, whatever story is told about the character does not necessarily have to be accurate about the model. If the reader does not know who the model is, the question will often not even arise. This leads to the question of whether anything of the model makes its way into the fiction, not as an identifying characteristic, but as a remainder of the process of renaming.

A more radical argument is that an object is cut off from the model to find its way into the fiction, roughly as Little Hans sees his severed genitals in his mother's hands. Another example Lacan offered was a fiction of his invention in which the eyes of Oedipus, torn from their sockets are now lying on the ground looking back at Oedipus. Or else, in Holbein's *The Ambassadors* the death's head in the foreground has a look that is the place from which the painting is looking back at the spectator while the spectator does not see the look. We should mention that the object in question here has other than uncanny manifestations. Little Hans might be horrified to see his genitals in his mother's hands, but later on, after his psychoanalysis, he might find a pair of diamond earrings hanging from a woman's ears to be extremely attractive.

Of course, if we are talking about a literary fiction, it is not sufficient that something from the model is in the fiction; for if the fiction is to interest an audience, then the object must function as a severed part of the body of each spectator. This is hardly a simple task. Certainly, it would preclude making a mirror identification of spectator and character the rationale for the spectator's interest in the fiction.

You may consider this to be an impossible object, one that is not within the realm of the possibilities of possible worlds, one that even is in contradiction with the rest of the world, whether it is the look in the death's head in the Holbein or the figurines, the *agalmata,* that Alcibiades glimpses one day in Socrates. On the one hand this object comes from the model, and on the other hand it is to the spectator something of his own that he now sees or hears in the work of art.

How do you find out what your desire is? Freud responded to this question by saying that a dream always contains a realization of one's desire. The problem is that in most cases the desire is inscribed in code; it is available only after it has been deciphered. The deciphering is an intellectual act; whatever desire is encoded in a dream is necessarily one that the dreamer has avoided recognizing. But if the desire is grasped intellectually only at the cost of suspending sentiment, how does one know that the deciphering has been performed correctly? And if, for example, you should decipher a desire, how do you know that the desire in play is yours and not that of a parent or friend? How do you know that the desire and its truth are yours? And how does the speech act which articulates the desire function in relation to the desire and in relation to the ethical obligation to act upon the desire? Is desire something that cannot be grasped outside of spoken dialogue?

Such are the questions at issue here. To attempt to offer responses to all of them in a short paper would be to diminish their seriousness. My position is that the scene of desire cannot be grasped outside of a spoken dialogue and that the judgment of the correct performance of the intellectual act of deciphering will lie in the response of the person to whom it is spoken. Thus a written "proof" of the correctness of the reasoning will never suffice to establish the desire as the one deciphered in the dream. Not only must it be spoken by the speaking subject in his own name but it must also be addressed to the listener in his own name. Finally, I propose that the subject knows that it is his because there is within that scene a lost part of his body.

Works Cited

Averroes. *Averroes' Middle Commentaries on Aristotle's Categories and De Interpretatione.* Princeton: Princeton University Press, 1983.

Bentham, Jeremy. *The Works of Jeremy Bentham.* Vol. 8. New York: Russell and Russell, 1962.

Derrida, Jacques. *La Carte Postale.* Paris: Flammarion, 1980. See also *The Post Card.* Trans. Alan Bass: Chicago: University of Chicago Press, 1987.

Knuuttila, Simo and Jaakko Hintikka, Eds. *The Logic of Being.* Dordrecht, Holland: Academic Publishers, 1968.

Kripke, Saul. *Naming and Necessity.* Cambridge, Mass: Harvard University Press, 1980.

Lacan, Jacques. *Ecrits.* Paris: Seuil, 1966.

Lacan, Jacques. *Le Séminaire, Livre 2: Le moi dans la théorie de Freud et dans la technique de la psychanalyse.* Texte établi par Jacques-Alain Miller. Paris: Seuil, 1978. [See especially the chapters on "The Purloined Letter."] See also *The Seminar of Jacques Lacan, Book II: The Ego in Freud's Theory and in the Technique of Psychoanalysis* (1954–1955). Ed. Jacques-Alain Miller. Trans. Sylvana Tomaselli. Notes by John Forrester. New York: W. W. Norton, 1988.

Lewis, David. "Truth in Fiction," *Philosophical Papers.* Vol. 1. New York: Oxford University Press, 1983.

Loux, Michael, *"Significatio* and *Suppositio:* Reflections on Ockham's Semantics." *The New Scholasticism,* 51. (Autumn 1979), 407–427.

Muller, John and William Richardson, Eds. *The Purloined Poe: Lacan, Derrida, and Psychoanalytic Reading.* Baltimore: The Johns Hopkins University Press, 1988.

Ogden, C.K. *Bentham's Theory of Fictions.* London: AMS Press, 1932.

Pavel, Thomas. *Fictional Worlds.* Cambridge, Mass: Harvard University Press, 1986.

Schneiderman, Stuart. *An Angel Passes: How the Sexes Became Undivided.* New York University Press, 1988.

Walton, Kendall. "Fearing Fictions." *The Journal of Philosophy,* 75 (January, 1978), 5–27.

Wittgenstein, Ludwig. *Philosophical Investigations.* Trans. G.E.M. Anscombe. New York: Macmillan, 1958.

Lacan's Theory of Sublimation:
A New Look at Sophocles's *Antigone*

Ellie Ragland

In *Seminar* VII: *The Ethics of Psychoanalysis* (1959–1960), Lacan emphasizes that the genre of tragedy shows that the root of human experience is tragic, even prior to the effects of the Oedipus complex: "*Antigone* is a tragedy, and tragedy is in the forefront of our experiences as analysts—something that is confirmed by the references Freud found in *Oedipus Rex* as well as in other tragedies."[1] The seeds of dissatisfaction are sown even before sexual difference is constituted in the Oedipal trajectory. In 1959 in "Desire and the Interpretation of Desire in *Hamlet*" Lacan put forth the idea that the literary genre of tragedy finds its dialectical cause in desire.[2]

Not only is tragedy not constituted through mimetic identification with emotions as Aristotle thought, tragedy reveals what is lacking in identification itself. By rethinking the process of identification away from its standard psychoanalytic meanings, Lacan redefined catharsis in terms of desire. In so doing, he evolved a theory that will interest literary critics and aestheticians, as well as psychoanalysts. In his Seminar on ethics, he states, for example: "It seems to me to be what it was for Hegel . . ., namely, the Sophoclean tragedy that is of special significance. In an even more fundamental way than through the connection to the Oedipus complex, tragedy is at the root of our experience, as the key word 'catharsis' implies" (S 7, *Ethics,* 243–244).

While Aristotle thought catharsis classified a work as tragic, its goal being to purge the spectators of pity and fear, Lacan found the quest for a desired object or effect at the point where Aristotle thought to have discovered an imitation of emotional experience. Not only does Lacan put forth a new theory of catharsis, moreover, his interpretation of Sophocles's *Antigone* elaborates a new aesthetic theory of the beautiful. Taking up sublimation in different terms than did Kant or Freud, Lacan's contribution to aesthetic theory lies in his explanation of how literature quintessentializes an ethical dilemma fundamental to all human life. Pinpointing *desire* as the cause of the

Revised by the author from "La Teoria de la sublimacion de Lacan: Una nueva vision de la *Antigone* de Sofocles" (trans. into Spanish by Shula Eldar), *Freudiana: Escuela Europa de Psicoanalisis* (Catalunya), no. 7 (1993), pp. 58–72.

ethical dimension in tragedy, he opposes both Hegel's and Goethe's interpretations of *Antigone* to argue that no event occurs in tragedy except in relation to the *aim* of desire.[3] For Hegel, the tragic dilemma lay in the dialectical opposition of State (represented by Créon) and family (represented by Antigone). The conflict between public versus private creates two principles of the law of discourse. And both sides are doomed to lose because each dialectic contains the seeds of its own collapse within the opposition itself. Goethe blamed the tragedy on Créon's excessive desire, his wish to kill Polynice a second time, thus interpreting Créon as a Faustian kind of figure.

The play is not built out of dialectical opposition as Hegel thought, Lacan argued: neither two rights, nor two wrongs. Rather, Créon is wrong to oppose Antigone's effort which *is* ethical. The need for an ethics of psychoanalysis that Lacan elaborates in *Seminar* VII arises from the impasse of the real—the unbearable, the impossible to think or remember—that demands a new ethics for mankind. Any person who upholds the law of a particular local-universal convention, equatable with reality, upholds the law of superego morality that Lacan found "ferocious and obscene," placing the law of Thanatos over the law of Eros or life. Moreover, superego moralities create the immoralities that characterize today's bureaucratic organization of society, based as it is on the love of rules over and above any concern for individual life and joy. Antigone is trying to sustain herself *in life*, despite the fact that her destiny has made her life impossible to bear. Having been born of Oedipus and Jocasta, cursed by the gods, having lost two brothers who killed each other, she cannot accept the final indignity pronounced by Créon. By thwarting her *desire* to offer a minimal respect to the name of the family that bore her, he strikes at the identificatory root of being where one can say only I AM WHAT I AM.

By the *aim* or path of desire Lacan means that the hero or heroine of a true tragedy is the one who never caves in on desire, never gives up on desire. The tragic heroine is not essentially different from her fellow beings. They can recognize their plight in hers. Lacan states what no one before him had: a reason why the tragic heroine *suffers* and a reason why the audience is moved by the spectacle of that suffering, that perdition. By linking desire to the real—the place of impasses that bespeak traumatic material—Lacan formulates a theory of sublimation that requires us to rethink the process of how identification functions beyond the imaginary. The first identifications of humans occur by incorporation of unary traits or features at the level of the primary object that Lacan locates in the pre-specular real as the Good that is the mother. He presents us with this paradox. The first trait or mark (S_1) inscribed on the body is the nothing—*rien*—of the mark itself. It only appears as a negative universal (0 or -1 of real numbers); that is, as a mark indicating that something is lacking in its particularity.[4] Lacan's point is that nothing can be inscribed unless it has *already* been "written" in a different time and place before the moment of its first appearance. The subject appears, then, as a lack in the signifying chain, a nothing which causes the infinitization or multiplied repetitions of the all ("Matrix," 48). As such, the nothing is the mark of difference that places a limit on the positive universal one might describe as the void of absolute *jouissance*.[5]

The step from the empty void of the real to the mark begins the stratification of the symbolic and imaginary orders by identifications with unary traits that replace whatever was lost at the level of experience and the body. Filling in the void place left by the *loss* of primary object(s), these first identifications make of the subject a paradox: a dialectical closed surface, made of its own criss-crossing, concrete identifications that all refer to a central void. Because the subject was first constituted as an Ideal ego unconscious formation by others (ego ideals), in a transference relation, his or her earliest associations of meaning are signifying responses to the other, the partner, in any relation. Thus, the second identification of humans is to the pure signifier, while the first identification is to the unary traits of identification that fulfilled desire in connection with the other (S 9, *Identification*).[6]

In 330 B.C., Aristotle wrote in the *Poetics* that the poet's skill is analogous to the creative forces of nature.[7] Thus, the poet succeeds in creating characters who will appeal to spectators at the level of profound human emotion *because* he or she *imitates* nature. In other words, the spectacle of pity and fear on the stage elicits pity and fear in the viewers via the transformation of natural forms already given in the rhetorical medium. And critics throughout the centuries have sought to explain this phenomenon. In Aristotle's theory of mimesis, the inner structure of action imitates the inner structure of nature, while the transformation of forms by language and art aids in creating the effects that link spectators to actors through an identification of emotions between actors and audience.

Not adhering to this correspondence theory of mimesis, Lacan stressed that not only is meaning made diacritically, it is constituted in the first place by a dialectical process, by which terms it subsequently functions. Except in the case of psychosis. Lacan's theory of mimetic identification carries with it what Aristotle's lacks: a theory of causality. We identify with others because we have lost the objects and identificatory traits that connected us to them and, thus, desire to be called to by them again, to be (re)-reified as an identity in relation to what we know, which is what we are. And we desire this because being identified by the other confers the necessary *jouissance* of feeling one's being as consistent. Taken as a filler of the void that confers a sense of unity on being and body, the object *a* is Lacan's name for what appears at the point where *das Ding*—a primary object—has been lost. We try to fill the holes in being with objects which condense the enjoyments and signifiers taken on in our own family stories.

Lacan called the process by which any person works with the object *a* sublimation. While sublimation is not repression—that is, it is not unconscious—it, nonetheless, responds to the drive which is essentially the demand to *be,* at the level where *being,* for instance, means being heard (the invocatory drive), being seen (the scopic drive), being nurtured (the oral drive), being given things to prove our value as creatures of lack and reciprocity (the anal drive).

By conferring on individuals response(s) of recognition, the Other enables speaking beings to escape a confrontation with the void that begets aggressiveness, mourning or pure anxiety. Thus, one's most basic identifications are sublimations of traits of the real object—the primary object—that *causes* desire in the first place. In other words, the subject emerges as an *effect,* not a *cause.* Lacan points out that the French translation of "catharsis" as "purgation" lets us attend to this other dimension of the meaning of *cathexsis.* One meaning of purgation is medical. One is purged of an illness, a disease. Freud used the word *Besetzsung* to mean occupied or inhabited as by a military force. Strachey translated the word as "abreaction," meaning discharge of a suspended emotion. And discharge means purging or cleansing. One can even find the meaning of purification in the etymology of "catharsis." The Cathars were a twelfth-century group of Catholic heretics who tried to become *pure* spirit by not reproducing themselves, by not begetting more flesh. Lacan maintained that this effort to eradicate the conflictual effects of desire—not to mention the sexual difference—was doomed to failure. Having excluded sexual intercourse with women from their religious practices, the Cathars took the issue of sexual pleasure into the realm of perverse sex acts with men and women (S 7, *Ethics,* 123–124). I understand Lacan to mean that the effects of the primary object become all the more insistent, the more the sexual difference is excluded from social sexual practices. The Catharist heretics demonstrated the same thing as the Marquis de Sade, in one sense: That there is an impotence in "natural" desire, that there is no innate or harmonious sexual relation of Oneness between man and woman.[8] Everyone is related, rather, to the primary object-*cause*-of-desire, *das Ding* that Lacan named the object *a.*

It is in this sense that Antigone's *éclat,* her beauty, is dialectically related to her perdition, to her being lost in grief. Her own sorrow redoubles the *always already* lost object at the center of all meaning and being. Antigone's perdition, like the Marquis de Sade's, locates the truth of human despair at the level of the forbidden. At the point of blindness one finds a *jouissance* relation to the primary object that causes suffering at its limit (*Nomos*/law) (S 7, *Ethics,* 262–263). In "Kant with Sade" (1963) Lacan argued that Sade was more honest than Immanuel Kant about the *cause* of the human condition. One finds this cause in the only constant there is, the constant on which drive energy is based: The impasse of the sexual relation which makes it impossible that two ever be One. While Kant denies the pain of the lack-in-being with his mask of morality, neither Antigone nor de Sade can accept conventional notions of the Good. De Sade destroyed himself in trying to eradicate the very object that gave him pleasure. Antigone rejected Créon's morality of quotidian happiness. Like de Sade, she transgressed the natural order of things, placing herself, rather, on the side of crime, that which a given society locates beyond their laws of convention. When given the chance for love, marriage and children, she could not tear herself away from the profound pull of the pathos and *jouissance* of her childhood family novel. Indeed, her effort to redeem her brother's name, and by extension the name of her damned father—Oedipus—resembles the hysteric's idealizing efforts to restore dignity to a denigrated father.

Antigone's grandeur, Lacan argued, lay in her ability to refuse the unbearable denigration of the laws of man, even though the price of her act is death. But how does such a paradox define heroism? In Lacan's estimation, Créon is an ordinary man, weak in thinking of his good as nothing more than an empty representation of laws made by others. He does not know what *he* wants, but serves as a mere figurehead who refuses to think beyond the requisites of state law. By definition, state law does not deal with the real of passion, desire, or the humiliation of the children within a family lineage. But Antigone, unlike Créon, can assume her desire. While Créon stays at the level of psychology—the science of happiness, the place of denial and ignorance—, Antigone confronts the ethical dilemma that defines the sorrow of the human condition: the stakes of this plight are nothing less than life and death. Because her predicament places her in an impasse—of the real—where the *impossible to bear* of suffering is at stake, Antigone is a proper motivating force for tragedy. It is not only that she wishes justice rendered at the level of a symbolic debt. When she answers Créon regarding whether she has heard his proclamation against her burying her brother she says: "Could I help hearing it? / [Créon] And yet you dared defy the law. [Antigone] I dared. It was not God's proclamation. That final Justice / That rules the world below makes no such laws. . . . / But all your strength is weakness itself against / The immortal unrecorded laws of God. / They are not merely now: they were, and shall be, / Operative for ever, beyond man utterly."[9] She invokes the insult to the primary object—to the good that is her mother; the love she bears her family—perpetrated by Créon. In human affairs there is a higher law than the law of the state, laws known by the gods who deal with the passion and pain of the real.

By introducing the real as a *cause* into aesthetic response, Lacan implies that Aristotle's aesthetic theory lags behind in the imaginary: By imaginary I mean that order of identifications in human relations that makes being seem whole and adequate to itself. Characterized by the visible, by representation, by the mask, the imaginary takes appearances to be *das Ding,* which I shall explain further on. In such a phenomenological view of the world, neither spectator nor actor has a *cause.* Their emotions are self-regulating and self-explanatory in terms of the historical conventions of their surroundings. Placing Antigone's cause beyond the visible, beyond social codes, in the impossible real, Lacan says she does not experience either pity or fear until her entombment. Until she actually undergoes the lack and loss that give rise to the emotions of pity and fear, Antigone follows another set of laws; one that knows nothing of the gods of the real. Antigone's "act" is not "mad"; she simply has never encountered the void of the real and does not know what she is choosing.

Taking *Antigone* as an example, Eric Laurent proposed that there is a point prior to catharsis as particular to tragedy; and a point after catharsis where pleasure is found. Proposing that the structure—pre-catharsis, catharsis, post-catharsis—follows the same path as the unfolding of an analysis, which consists of taking a subject who is happy in a pre-analytic moment,[10] he argues that in this moment, the subject lives a blind happiness. The happiness is blind because it is based on the lies of narcissism: Repression and ignorance govern speech and thought. The paradox Lacan uncovered, and that Sophocles dramatized centuries before, is the price a person pays for such happiness. One might say that such happiness is easily bought: Antigone should have obeyed Créon, or Créon should have heeded her plea. But tragedy in literature, as in life, has the structure of the impossible: The "doesn't stop not being written . . . is the impossible as I define it on the basis of the fact that it cannot in any case be written" (S 20, *Encore,* 94). Because it goes hand in hand with a profound covered-up suffering, the price concerns the conditions of Eros and Thanatos in each individual's life. Every life situation contains an Antigone and a Créon in microcosm or macrocosm. Duty and desire are in conflict, not only among individuals, but within each person as well.

The experience of catharsis—passing through a crisis—produces pity and fear in those Aristotle called the "pathetics." But after the moment of *purgation,* a purging, or dropping, of the object *a* to which *jouissance* is attached, an analysand goes ever deeper into desire. Lacan says psychoanalysis permits us to understand what Aristotle meant in his *Metaphysics* (*The Complete Works*/cf. note 7) when he spoke of tragedy as a *catharsis* of the *pathémata* of suffering: "In effect, *Antigone* reveals to us the line of sight that defines desire. This line of sight focuses on an image that possesses a mystery which up till now has never been articulated, since it forces you to close your eyes at the very moment you look at it. Yet that image is at the center of tragedy, since it is the fascinating image of Antigone herself . . . in her unbearable splendor" (S 7, *Ethics,* 247).

At the climax of the trajectory towards her desire, Antigone enters a new realm—the realm of the second death—where she commands the audience as a fascinating image, blinding the spectators by the devastating message carried by that image. But why would *one* image in a series of images purge the spectators? And of what? Lacan says in "The subversion of the subject and the dialectic of desire, or reason in the unconscious since Freud" that desire aims at a fantasy.[11] In the post-cathartic moment proposed by Laurent, when one can truly look oneself in the face beyond the illusions and lies that sustained a life in the Ideal, one has seized himself or herself in the core of his or her "being for death." But by "being for death," Lacan does not mean some existential or phenomenological philosophical project. He claims, rather, that psychoanalysis delivers us from the imaginary which is "the rubric of all the objects produced by the world . . . all the enchanting objects which are traversed by death's head. . . . All the objects are there to distract us from this, that there is death" [my translation] (Laurent, *Vers un savoir nouveau,* April 10, 1991).

When one passes outside the imaginary realm of narcissistic lies, one is stunned *in the real.* In such an instant, the analysand or spectator is delivered from the all-pervasive imaginary with its lethal power of inertia, of entrapment in images. As Antigone goes toward her tomb, Sophocles allows her to confront us with the truth of what the image hides: It is the object *a* of fantasy of which we must purge ourselves if we are to realize any freedom of desire, wherever it may (or may not) lead. But even more basic than the object *a* subsequently sought in fantasy is the real of the primary objects which *cause* desire in the first place. Lacan seems to invoke the fixation to a given primary object in the attention he pays to Aristotle's argument that some*Thing* in being needs to be tamed, if not cleansed out. In *The Politics (The Complete Works*/cf. note 7), Aristotle described catharsis as taking on the Dionysiac quality that allows music to appease it, paradoxically, by creating enthusiasm. On the one hand, Laurent points out that the tragedy of Antigone lies in the fact that she situates herself at the limit of language (*Vers un nouveau savoir,* April 10, 1991). But if language were the whole of the story, if our breaking with language were curative, there would be no tragic dimension to life, no need for Antigone's death. Of what do we need to purge ourselves *beyond* our words?

Of whatever remains as noxious in the primary object which Lacan describes as *das Ding,* the only Good, the mother as the matrix of everything: Our attachments to the gaze, the voice, the phoneme, the breast are the first *jouissance* qualities which anchor one, first in relation to the mother's body as present, and later in relation to being with an other and with others. We later try to represent and repeat these effects by naming them at one remove from the real of having first experienced and then lost them. But Lacan does not equate the mother with the whole person, nor does he depict her as the bearer of part objects, or as the carrier of virtue or any other essence. Rather, the primary object refers to the constitution of libido or *jouissance* as derived from the actual presence of the symbolic mother. The mother's physical proximity—experienced at the level of the real of the breast, the feces, the gaze, the voice, the nothing—gives her progeny a sense of bodily consistency in the world. It is this imaginary consistency one might confuse with Being as a given, or pregiven, rather than as a constructed order. Second, the primary object refers to the first quality of the primary other's presence. If the primary other was intrusive, omnipresent or abusive, this presence will introduce a negativistic experience of the Ur-objects-*cause*-of-desire which will remain as a bedrock determinative effect of the subject's relation to objects in the world. One might characterize such effects as affects of the real. This would imply that primordial concrete experiences not only lie behind but also give rise to the real element underlying concepts such as the evil eye, haunting, and even the ever-watchful eye of God.

The experience of the cut is constituted by the loss of a sense of oneness at the edge or rim or surface of the imaginary body or real of the flesh. An object a that initially caused desire returns not only to slice into corporal comfort but also to reintroduce the logic of separation experienced by the mirror-stage infant. These primordial moments situate the subject in later life in reference to a nonspecular object that caused desire, but which, paradoxically, is knowable only insofar as it is lost. Insofar as the object a is one of the two referents included in the phallic signifier's injunction to interpret the sexual difference as a representation of law or reality (Φ), and castration implicitly demands that one interpret the difference as a lack-in-being ($\mathcal{S}$), the two operations giving rise to the four kinds of logic Lacan called normative, perverse, psychotic or neurotic, one understands why Lacan placed the sub-structure of separation on the side of metonymy at the site of the object a-cause-of-desire. Orienting this sub-structure in the direction of the transference, Lacan stressed that the product of separation (or intersection) contains like elements from two ensembles, or two intersecting circles.[12] While alienation derives from the eclipsing of the object behind representations, separation will always bear on the fundamental characteristics of loss, be they of lack ($\mathcal{S}$), the void ($\varnothing$), or the in-existence of the essential WOMAN. The primary object a will always harken back to how the mother constituted the primary layer of an infant's being-for-lack by which Lacan redefined castration. Not surprisingly, the continual movement of fantasy is made up of the myriad objects that progressively fill in the lack-in-being, negotiating their way around the obstacles of alienation and separation: $\mathcal{S} \diamond a$. Only the psychotic does not undergo castration, does not lose the primary object(s), but retains the mother *as if* she were whole. The other differential categories negotiate the primary object(s) *as if* they were there, thus showing metaphorical substitution as possible because, although the primary object is lost to memory, it leaves behind some unary traits that constitute memory associatively—but non-linearly—in single strokes, one by one.

The events that constitute tragedy lie in the *aim* of desire, Lacan taught. Desire aims for the pleasure of homeostasis—supported by the lure images of fantasy—via the object a, insofar as this symbol denotes any thing, person or event that produces a feeling/memory of consistency. In reality, the object qua thing or event only gives a fleeting pleasure. The *real* object we seek lies outside the fantasy and beyond the drive, at the point where the subject was first constituted as a subject of bodily *jouissance* and an object of the Other's desire. The Good we desire is not the mother, then, but the pleasure of Oneness and timeless certainty that make desire aim at a point just beyond the masked object; an impossible point. In this context, Lacan describes tragedy as the highest imitation of a complete action: The complete action lies in the human effort to create unity and Oneness over and above the realities of division, the cut, loss, discontinuity and inconsistency. And Antigone's tragedy represents the quintessence of such desire.

Antigone is not physically beautiful. Sophocles calls her a *sale gosse* (a dirty girl). Yet, she achieves what Jean Genet claimed for his maids in *Les Bonnes:* She vacillates and shimmers in an *éclat* of luminous beauty, increasingly to the end of the play.[13] Lacan's theory of sublimation is, in part, an interpretation of this phenomenon. Incarnating a place beyond the human, Antigone represents a great, unresolvable life MYSTERY. She has left mankind and gone *with* the gods. Having acted on her desire, she is the antithesis of the hysterical *belle âme* who is a consciously *willing* victim. Antigone has accepted something closer to the meaning of Jesus Christ's sacrifice; to die for the sins of her fellow man. One could argue that her passionate commitment to her family constitutes the masochistic love of suffering. But that is not the lesson of this play. Rather, Antigone represents the possibility of acting from desire, rather than from egoistic or narcissistic being. She steps outside the game of social lies, imaginary spectacles, and grief games, thereby revealing their underside: victims and holocausts.

Lacan's stunning thesis ties desire and identification to the Kantian beautiful and to sublimation. The beautiful is bounded, familiar, whereas the sublime is unbounded and potentially horrifying. The desire to protect one's own at the level of the primary object—the Good of the mother—can be taken as an anchoring point at the base of all tragedy. Antigone's brother belongs to her *matrix*. This desire to protect the familiar object—the *agalma* that is her brother's body—foregrounds the real, whether it goes in the direction of Antigone's sacrifice of her life, or the destructive voracious acts the Marquis de Sade perpetrated on others. Antigone tells Créon that there is a law beyond the laws of man. And insofar as the passion of the real—defined here as trying to break out of the confines of an impossible contradiction—is the cause of every person, whether the effort to exit the double bind takes the form of artistic expression, religious worship, criminal desecration of others, or sacrifice of one's own being and body, any tragic spectacle that dramatizes the conflict between the social order and the real will move the audience.

Audience participation, thought of in Aristotle's sense, is not something Lacan believed in. In fact, spectators think about many things, Lacan stressed,—the detritus of everyday life—other than what is happening on stage. Thus, when Antigone *moves* the audience, she does so in a particular way and in a particular place Lacan calls the beautiful. In *The Ethics,* Lacan says: "I was talking to you just now of excitement. And I will take a moment to have you reflect on the inappropriate use that is made of this word in the usual translation into French of *Triebregung*, namely, '*émoi pulsionnel*,' 'instinctual excitement.'. . . *'Emoi'* (excitement) has nothing to do with emotion nor with being moved. *'Emoi'* is a French word that is linked to a very old verb, namely, *'émoyer'* or *'esmayer'* which, to be precise, means . . . 'to make someone lose' not 'his head,' but something closer to the middle of the body, 'his means.' In any case, a question of power is involved" (S 7, *Ethics,* 249).

In his discussion of *Antigone,* Eric Laurent notes that *"esmayer"* gives the Spanish verb *"desmayer"* which means *"s'évanouir"* ("to faint" in English). An *émoi,* says Laurent, following Lacan, is what makes you lose your power relations. Clarifying Lacan's discussion of *Antigone* here, Laurent points out that he inscribes this commentary in a dialectic between emotion and *émoi,* emotion being what pushes you forward and *émoi* what stops you. And here we come to Lacan's theory of sublimation which gives a new meaning to the beautiful, following the work of Kant and other aestheticians in his wake: "The beautiful is what stops a subject. . . . It is what produces the *émoi"* (Laurent, *Vers un nouveau,* April 10, 1991).

Quoting Baudelaire's "La beauté sera convulsive ou ne sera pas," Laurent points to what is new in Lacan's theory of sublimation: the beautiful is the *moment* when the dynamic of desire stops, is stunned in its path (April 10, 1991). Beauty dwells at a distance from desire. When desire stops, loss of power (*émoi*) means the loss of eros that opens onto death. In this sense, catharsis has the function of purging ugliness at the point where the hero—or analysand—is at the limit of the possible. When suffering encounters itself in its impotence, one enters what Lacan called the realm of the second death. This is actually a *place*—in time—between life and actual death.

Freud did not understand what causes suffering, Lacan says. In Lacan's teaching, the real returns *from behind,* in suffering, as terrible and beautiful. In "On Mourning and Melancholia" (1917), Freud had, nonetheless, introduced the idea that suffering was a masochistic mask, a monumental narcissistic mourning.[14] Viewing art as that which gives form to the forbidden, Freud pinpointed a realm of *jouissance* in the forbidden that bears on (not) wanting the other's good that he called *Lebensneid,* or envy of the other's very life (S 7, *Ethics,* 237). In "Character and Anal Eroticism," he attributed artistic sublimation to "dirt [as] matter in the wrong place," dirt replacing feces for the anal erotic.[15] In the Wolfman case in 1905 he described sublimation as an instinctual leftover whose goal was a *passage* from the active to the passive, the desire behind it being the wish to retain the *jouissance* attached to fascination with an object.[16]

In his study of Leonardo da Vinci (1910), Freud argued that sublimation was not repression.[17] It arises *instead* of a breakthrough from the unconscious which marks repression. Moreover, Freud maintained that the quality of neurosis is absent in sublimation, there being no attachment to the original complexes of infantile sexual activity. Thus, the drive can operate freely, he says, in the service of intellectual interest (*SE,* 11: 79–80). Put another way, Freud writes in many different instances that sublimation does not have the structure of a substitutive formation of the unconscious. It is neither a repressed symptom, nor an *acte manqué,* nor a dream or fantasy (*SE,* 11: 130).

Freud developed his theory of sublimation even further in "Drives and Their Vicissitudes" (1915) where he viewed sublimation and repression as synchronized and reciprocal correlatives.[18] *Sublimierung* is the name he gives one of the four fates or vicissitudes of the drives (*Trieben*) he describes as the "mythology of psychoanalysis" (*SE,* 14: 94; 11; 132). Psychoanalysis is anything but a mythology, Lacan counters. The *unbearable* weight of the real dragged into the analyst's office refutes Freud's idea of a mythology over and over. Tragedy, in life and art, refutes Freud's theory as well. Moreover, Lacan was against Freud's efforts to prove the unconscious by art.[19] Rather, sublimation is a non-concept, he said, an *unbegriff.* It concerns what is cut and the object *a* that comes to take the place of the missing part.

But Freud gave Lacan the theoretical base for linking desire to identification via the drive. Defining sublimation as the name given a lack when it overlaps with another lack, Lacan said sublimation describes the experience of the body—caught up in the drive—at its borders or edges. In this it is negative and liminal:

> Sublimation, Freud tells us, involves a certain form of satisfaction of the *Triebe,* a word that is improperly translated as "instincts," but that one should translate strictly as "drives" (*pulsion*)—or as "drifts" (*dérives*), so as to mark the fact that the *Trieb* is deflected from what he calls its *Ziel,* its aim.
>
> Sublimation is represented as distinct from the economy of substitution in which the repressed drive is usually satisfied. A symptom is the return by means of signifying substitution of that which is at the end of the drive in the form of an aim.
>
> It is here that the function of the signifier takes on its full meaning, for it is impossible without reference to that function to distinguish the return of the repressed from sublimation as a potential mode of satisfaction of the drive. It is a paradoxical fact that the drive is able to find its aim elsewhere than in that which is its aim—without its being a question of the signifying substitution that constitutes the overdetermined structure, the ambiguity, and the double causality, of the symptom as compromise formation (S 7, *Ethics,* 110).

Lacan retains Freud's four terms for the drive: Source (*Quelle*), tension or pressure (*Drang*), aim and goal (*Ziel*) and object (*Objekt*). Tension appears at the surface of the regulated openings and closings of bodily rims, showing the void to be the source. The aim of the drive constitutes its own goal through a detour or impasse. That is, in sublimation the aim of the drive is satisfied at the same time its goal is inhibited (*zielgehemmt*). Thus, sublimation brings satisfaction to the drive outside the sexual or reproductive act, and without repression. That is, the *aim* of the drive is quite different from its *goal* which is satisfaction, actual satisfaction—the disappearance of tension—which is the tip of the iceberg in what concerns the partial drives. One might wish to be invited to a *choisi* dinner party, for example, that being the *aim* underlying a certain tension. But the goal of that pressure in one's thoughts is the desire for recognition within the scopic field of the gaze where one sees oneself being seen in relation to ideal others. The aim is to be invited, to be desired. The goal is the *jouissance* of Oneness that sustains the illusion of a consistency in being. Indeed, the aim is to eradicate the loss at the center of being (S. 11, *FFC,* ch. 14). If the drive is a montage and sublimation marks a limit or border, it makes sense that the hole at the center of being and knowledge be literal and concrete. These are topological notions of the way space links body to being.

Freud called the drive a limit or border between fields of biological force and representation. Lacan modifies Freud by insisting that a drive is not a myth, but a fictional entity that ex-sists in language as a real presence. One cannot stress strongly enough that its cause is neither organic nor a non-sexual force, but a *Vorstellungsreprasentanz* (S 11, *FFC,* ch. 5). The drive is put in place in two logical moments, Lacan taught. Jacques-Alain Miller clarified this as occurring in a primary identification with oneself at the level of *das Ding* that he has called the *jouissance Une.*[20] In a second logical moment, Lacan found a linking of sublimation to the Oedipal structure at the time a secondary identification with the same sex parent is made.[21] Put another way, the displaceability of the sexual drive into representations gives rise to sublimation in one direction, and to repression in another. Sublimation has the unique power of bringing to drive a different satisfaction from its goal, always defined as its natural goal. But the natural goal, on inspection, shows us that drive is not purely instinct (S 7, *Ethics,* 111). Rather, the drive is inscribed on the body, where it is first constituted as the *Real-Ich* in rim-like structures that mark off empty places or sets (the mouth, the eyes, the ears, the anus). The *jouissance* that comes to mark these organs in a first moment is created by the incorporation of a desired object that produces a remainder. Only later is this *jouissance* given concrete meaning by the signifier; in the moment of castration (Miller, *Les divins détails,* May 17, 1989).

Antigone is a creature of pure desire, Lacan maintains. One might say that *pure* desire means the absolute lack or loss of the dialectical power of desire. As such, pure desire would open onto the void, onto death, onto beauty. In that such desire is absolute, it transcends the lack that ordinarily makes it human, showing the beauty in despair: Any absolute quality will be flawless. When the object of satisfaction is unattainable, one sees the underside of what supports the common illusion that some object will make us whole. One sees the object for what it is: "Simply the presence of a hollow, a void, which can be occupied . . . by any object, and whose agency we know only in the form of the lost object, the *petit a.* The *objet petit a* is not the origin of the oral drive, . . . the original food. It is introduced from the fact that no food will ever satisfy the oral drive, except by circumventing the eternally lacking object" (S 11, *FFC,* 179–80).

In "Kant with Sade" Lacan surprised his interlocutors by arguing that there is an effect of beauty in *Philosophy in the Bedroom,* but it is not the Sadean sexual acts or the Revolution that create this effect. It is, rather, the elevation of a sublime and indestructible object to its ultimate limit in life.[22] What de Sade keeps intact in his sadistic scenarios, Lacan proposes, is an absent place, a monument to the loss of *das Ding*—in itself, sublime. Sade's efforts to destroy objects *in the world* imprison him in his own tomb, awaiting an object worthy of being called mother—even as he makes Eugénie sew up her own mother's vagina and anus at the end of his novel. In this image, he tries, in my estimation, to banish forever the ghost of his own castration which is given the lie, in a Freudian reading, by his mother's missing penis.

Lacan teaches us that beauty is not what we think it is. It is beyond the Good, even a barrier to the Good. Eric Laurent, analyzing how beauty could be a barrier to the Good, says it suspends desire, disarms it, intimidates it, mocks the lack inherent in it. And so beauty is linked to desire in the guise of outrage, appearing in the form of some agony that forces each subject into an encounter with the primary object that delineates him or her as an extimate object (S 7, *Ethics,* 238).

Antigone's beauty arises, Lacan argues, from the *image* of her destitution, as underlined by the Chorus's pity. Her brother's corpse tells the story of the refusal of the symbolic order to constitute him as a being in language. His body is an excess in language that must be destroyed so the state can continue viewing its laws and beliefs as a whole, a consistency. And Antigone responds to this insult to her brother by sacrificing her own body, thus refusing the lies of the language of law. She refuses language at its limits, showing that at the limits of the Other, there is a hole. So she takes the spectators right up to the point where the real appears as an impasse, on the side of the gods. By covering her brother with dirt and herself with a stone, she shows the excess *hors sens* that opens onto the knowledge that is *jouissance.* The body, covered in death, unveils the lies that language hides, revealing that language hides emptiness as a void place.

In "The subversion of the subject and the dialectic of desire in the Freudian unconscious" (1960), Lacan describes an object that is the very material of the subject, its *doublure.* Moreover, the insistence of the real on identifying with being produces the cadre of the fantasy. But, the object *a*—the symbol for the object that marks the void place—that emerges with separation and speech, to represent the absent object, is not only imaginary in the fantasy. It is also real, for the real of anxiety clings to it. Although we try to deny lack, to give ourselves an imaginary consistency, the object *a* disrupts language and appears as an excess in *jouissance.* And this is not a mythical object, for it has the mathematical properties of a topological object: passage, perspective (image), and geometrical optic (dimensions of space) which come from the mirror-stage structure. Prior to and during the mirror stage, the gaze begins to be constituted in the words and effects of social judgement and in the "language" of ideals, thereby forming the kernel of the tension common to the drive aimed at reifying the Ideal ego. Put another way, the optic of the field of the gaze—object-cause-of-desire and partial drive—is so powerful in consciousness that reciprocity all but disappears at the level of object relations.

In *Antigone* we see a young woman moving around in psychic space, trying to turn the social gaze around, trying to move between the words that define her in the social order (the Other) and we witness her horror at the image constituted by those words. But Antigone cannot make a detour around the impasse of the real in her story. Clinging to her identity as Oedipus's daughter, she hopes, nonetheless, to escape her destiny. Not finding new signifiers, Antigone cannot create a new object to which to attach her *jouissance*. Lacan points to the one speech Antigone made that Goethe said shocked him, rattled him. When the final condemnation has been made, and even her lamentations said, she stands at the edge of her tomb and tries to justify herself. She says: "Understand this: I would not have defied the law of the city for a husband or a child to whom a tomb had been denied, because after all, if I had lost a husband in this way, I could have taken another, and even if I had lost a child with my husband, I could have made another child with another husband. But it concerned my brother . . ., born of the same father and the same mother" (S 7, *Ethics,* 254–255). "Such was the law whereby I held thee first in honor," she told Créon.[23]

The law of society is the law of metaphor: exchange and substitutability. But metonymy defines the law of the family on the slope of *jouissance,* at a point where goods are not replaceable. Mother, father, sister, brother—these are fixed values. Thus, Antigone holds onto the only good she knows: *das Ding* that Lacan calls the mother as primary object; even the mother's desire as unconscious. That is, Antigone's cause is her mother's cause: That of the family. The Sophoclean text alludes, he says, "to the fact that the desire of the mother is the origin of everything, . . . the one that brought into the world the unique offspring that are Eteocles, Polynices, Antigone and Ismène; but it is also a criminal desire. Thus, at the origin of tragedy and of humanism we find once again an impasse that is the same as Hamlet's, except strangely enough it is even more radical. . . . Antigone chooses to be purely and simply the guardian of the criminal as such. . . . It is because the community refuses this [to pardon] that Antigone is required to sacrifice her own being in order to maintain that essential being which is the family *Atè,* and that is the theme or true axis on which the whole tragedy turns" (S 7, *Ethics,* 283).

In this sense *das Ding* does not refer to the mother as an actual object or to the object (*a*) that animates Antigone in the real. Lacan taught that the drive's aim can never reach its goal. Thus, desire can never correspond with itself, with a mirror object in the world. But Lacan finds an intuition of his theory of a primary object—first the mother; then, the partial objects associated with the mother—that causes desire in Freud's "Project" (1895). At the point where the memory trace misses an object in its identificatory work of judging new objects in their most primitive organization, Freud found objects he described as *fremde objekten*.[24]

In Lacan's critique, sublimation is not identification, for sublimation arises from the drive, from its own impossibility of merging with a primary object. That is, the aim and goal always miss each other. Most people circumvent this impasse by identifying themselves at the level of ego. And the ego, by definition, excludes the *fremde*—the foreign or strange. The object *a* each person seeks to fill their lack-in-being ($) constitutes itself in reference to a particular, concrete ideal. Meanwhile, the ego ignores the fact that there is an empty place that buoys the drive, a place which pushes thought to the action of always seeking something else to stand in for what is missing. Antigone cannot continue to live at the level of ego. Trapped in the void place in the Other (Ø), she finds herself overwhelmed by the evil in the Other's *jouissance*. Sophocles imbues her with the power to make his spectators sense the concreteness of the *nihil* that presents itself as a hole to be surrounded or bordered (S 7, *Ethics,* 121). The power of sublimation made manifest in *Antigone* lies in its *not* eliding the cut, Lacan maintains. Antigone portrays the true goal of sublimation—to re-present what has been missed—by elevating the void object to the level of the drive, thereby placing it in relation to *das Ding* as sublime.

The *aim* of sublimation, then, is to reproduce the lack from which it comes. And Antigone, by refusing to let sleeping dogs lie, by refusing the comfort of the social lie, creates in the spectators this very emptiness that lies at the heart of being and language. Her refusal makes of her the sublime object of nothingness that lies at the heart of all quests, there where the object sought turns to ashes: "It" is never itself, is never the real thing. And so the human condition turns on the tedious axis of the death drive, of inane repetitions. In Lacan's new way of thinking about sublimation, neither content nor history is at issue. Rather, he wants to teach his interlocutors something about sublimation that can only be addressed at the level of structure, there where the Other desires, precisely because something is always lacking.

Beauty as defined by Lacan, in terms of the second death, means an eternal suffering that one finds at the point where an archaic good is defended as if it were a veritable object. "Involved in what I had to say to you about catharsis is the beauty effect . . . [which] derives from the relationship of the hero to the limit . . . defined on this occasion by a certain *Atè*" (S 7, *Ethics,* 286). The pathos one finds magnified in the drama, and dramatized in individual lives, is the propensity to defend this nothingness of familiarity over and above all specificity of its lethal powers and properties. Lacan's theory here is not incompatible with Kant's aesthetic theory of the beautiful, wherein any judgment of an object as beautiful must be disinterested and independent of the actual object. Insofar as Lacan does not mean objects or things in the world, but absolute—even objective, albeit invisible—objects that constitute an Ur-lining of the real that fixes being to body via identifications, one could describe the object *a* as independent of the actual object, representing it only as lost. Yet, since the representing object constitutes our souls at the level of the intimate—from which the extimate arises in a continuity of surfaces—one can never be disinterested in the object of the signifying cut that language introduces into being (S 7, *Ethics*, 282).

Antigone, viewed as an incarnation of a sublime object, is de-idealized to the point of such an object's realness where one finds pain and nothingness. Kant speaks of this aspect of the sublime as its unboundedness. At this point, the tragic effect and the production of beauty intersect. Antigone's image vacillates as her words unveil the real dimension of the impossible. Desire cannot realize itself—no matter what its cause—if the social stands opposed. This true nature of tragedy concerns the radical impasses in language where one encounters the impossible to bear. And the effect this produces on the spectators is that of pity and fear: Pity for the poor creature that is man and fear of the loss that lies at the heart of being (S 7, *Ethics*, 247–248 & 257–258). But can spectators be purified by watching the demise of a fellow being? Is this *Schadenfreude*? No. The *absolute* quality of beauty is reflected in *Antigone* in the depiction of the absolute alienation of Otherness. When one cannot bend the Other towards one's desire, then one is truly bereft among friends.

Antigone dramatizes the transformation operated by sublimation, at the point where a simple object of desire is transformed into a being, loved (or hated). Against Aristotle's argument that beauty arises from an orderly arrangement of the parts of a whole into a formally beautiful work, Lacan shows another order: That of objects where nothing less than life or death is at stake. This order disrupts the smooth surface of rhetorical skill and stylistic harmony. It takes its interlocutors to the point of anxiety which Lacan defines as a sensation of the presence of an Other's desire in us. Blind Tiresias appears at the end of *Antigone,* verifying the power of grief games in the house of Oedipus, in the Oedipal house that inhabits each of us at the level where the demands of the primary object that structures our desire are absolute, even as Lacan refers such demands back to the mother's desire as unconscious.

The moral of Sophocles's *Antigone* is this: Man lives by staying away from the limits, by accommodating lies—big and small. Occasionally one can bear to look at the underside of the price paid for BEING in the social. The genre of tragedy in all its guises stands as a monument to the subversive and private power of human desire, to the Antigone that lives in each of us.

Notes

1. Jacques Lacan, *The Seminar, Book VII: The Ethics of Psychoanalysis* (1959–1960), ed. by Jacques-Alain Miller, trans. by Dennis Porter (New York: W. W. Norton & Co., 1992), 243.

2. Jacques Lacan, "Desire and the Interpretation of Desire in *Hamlet,*" *Yale French Studies: Reading Otherwise* (April 29, 1959), Nos. 55/56 (1977), 11–52. Special issue edited by Shoshana Felman, French text edited by Jacques-Alain Miller, trans. by James Hulbert. *Le séminaire, livre VI* (1958–59): *Le désir et son interprétation* is unedited officially.

3. Georg Hegel, "On Tragedy" in *Hegel on Tragedy* (New York: Harper & Row, 1962); Cf. also Johann Wolfgang von Goethe, *Conversations with Eckermann* (1850), trans. by John Oxenford (San Francisco, CA.: North Point Press, 1984).

4. Jacques-Alain Miller, "Matrix," trans. by Daniel G. Collins, *lacanian ink,* no. 12 (Fall 1997), 45–51.

5. Jacques-Alain Miller, "Language: Much Ado About What?," *Lacan and the Subject of Language,* ed. by Ellie Ragland-Sullivan and Mark Bracher (New York: Routledge, 1991), 21–35.

6. Jacques Lacan, *Le séminaire, livre IX* (1961–1962): *L'identification,* vol. II (of III), unedited.

7. Aristotle, *The Poetics, The Complete Works,* Rev. Oxford trans., ed. by Jonathan Barnes in 2 vols. (Princeton, NJ: Princeton Univ. Press, 1984).

8. Jacques Lacan, *The Seminar, Book XX: Encore, On Feminine Sexuality, The Limits of Love and Knowledge* (1972–1973), ed. by Jacques-Alain Miller, trans. by Bruce Fink (New York: W. W. Norton & Co., 1998), 73–89.

9. Sophocles, *Antigone* in *Literature,* ed. by Hans P. Guth (Belmont, CA.: Wadsworth Publ. Co., 1968), 317–318.

10. Eric Laurent, *Vers un savoir nouveau en psychanalyse?,* Course, 1991–1992, University of Paris VIII, Department of Psychoanalysis, Clinical section. Course of April 10, 1991.

11. Jacques Lacan, "The subversion of the subject and the dialectic of desire, or reason in the unconscious since Freud" (1960), trans. by Alan Sheridan, *Ecrits: A Selection* (New York: W. W. Norton & Co., 1977).

12. Jacques Lacan, *The Four Fundamental Concepts of Psycho-Analysis: The Seminar, Book XI,* ed. by Jacques-Alain Miller, trans. by Alan Sheridan (New York: W. W. Norton & Co., 1977), cf. ch. 16.

13. Jean Genet, *The Maids* and *Deathwatch,* intro. by Jean-Paul Sartre, trans. by Bernard Frechtman (New York: Grove Press, 1961).

14. Sigmund Freud, "On Mourning and Melancolia" (1917), *SE,* 14; 239–260.

15. Sigmund Freud, "Character and Anal Eroticism" (1908), *SE,* 9: 168–175.

16. Sigmund Freud, "From the History of an Infantile Neurosis" (1918), *SE,* 17: 103–122.

17. Sigmund Freud, *Leonardo da Vinci* (1910), *SE,* 11: 59–137.

18. Sigmund Freud, "The Instincts and Their Vicissitudes" (1915), *SE,* 14: 111–140.

19. Jacques Lacan, "Kanzer Seminar," Yale University lecture, November 24, 1975; published in *Scilicet* 6/7 (1976), 25.

20. Jacques-Alain Miller, *Les divins détails.* Course of 1989, May 17, 1989, unedited.

21. Jacques Lacan, *Aggressivity in Psychoanalysis* (1948), *Ecrits: A Selection,* trans. by Alan Sheridan (New York: W. W. Norton & Co., 1977), 8–29.

22. Jacques Lacan, "Kant with Sade" (1963), *October,* no. 51 (Winter 1989), trans. with annotation by James B. Swenson, Jr, 53–104.

23. Sophocles, The Antigone of Sophocles in Greek and English, trans. by R. C. Gebb (Boston: Ginn & Co., 1897), p. 81.

24. Sigmund Freud, *Project for a Scientific Psychology* (1887–1902), *SE,* 1: 283–397.

The Palace of Thought

John Holland

During the afternoon of a day spent at Newmarch, the country house where most of *The Sacred Fount* is set, the unnamed narrator contemplates for a moment the "perfect palace of thought" that his mental exertions have built for him.[1] In his childhood, as he recalls, "I used to circle round enchanted castles, for then I moved in a world in which the strange 'came true,' " and recent events have allowed him to recapture this feeling (128). By means of this highly caricatured character, *The Sacred Fount* explores the relations among thought, *jouissance,* and obsession, the neurotic form of masculinity. Examining the ramifications of a theory concerning his fellow guests, the narrator will locate femininity as a force that threatens his calculations; his response to the disruption that it creates will lead him to undertake the symptomatic act of writing, through which he can prolong his relation with an enjoyment that disturbs him, but which he cannot escape.

I

A Relation of Transmission

At the beginning of the novel, the narrator generates a theory in order to make sense of three puzzling and embarrassing incidents, which, when taken together, wound his sense of his own high intelligence. Upon boarding a train that will take him to a party at Newmarch, he encounters a distant acquaintance, a man named Gilbert Long, whom he has met at other gatherings. He chooses not to greet Long, who had "always, in the interval" between their meetings at house parties, "so failed to know me that I could only hold him as stupid unless I held him as impertinent"; to his surprise, however, Long welcomes him promptly, and seems to behave with an intelligence far greater than he has ever exhibited before (2). A moment later, the narrator encounters another surprise; a woman who will be sharing their compartment

From *bien dire: A Journal of Lacanian Orientation,* edited by David Metzger, Vols. 2–3 (1995–1996), pp. 29–118.

enters, and when she sees that he does not recognize her, she "turn(ed) to me with a reproach: 'I don't think it very nice of you not to speak to me.' " Catching "at her identity through her voice," he realizes that "she was simply . . . Grace Brissenden," a middle-aged woman who has suddenly and inexplicably recovered her youth, and who has thereby become almost unrecognizable; embarrassed by his failure to realize immediately who she is, he suspects that "she might easily have thought me the same sort of ass as I had thought Long" (3). His sense of perplexity is soon compounded when he arrives at Newmarch and almost immediately encounters and fails to recognize Grace's new husband Guy, who has also undergone a metamorphosis. A man who is not yet thirty, Guy Brissenden has become middle-aged, and the narrator, shocked by this third change, can only marvel at "the oddity of my having been as stupid about the husband as I had been about the wife" (30).

These incidents have a strong effect upon the narrator, because they not only seem to result from a force that may inherently be disturbing, but also because they wound what Leon Edel has called his "extraordinar[y] va[nity] about his powers of observation."[2] Having elevated his sense of his intelligence into a master signifier, and having therefore, consistently defined himself as the "cleverest man" at Newmarch or anywhere else he may happen to be, he sees in these seemingly minor failures of recognition a subversion of his status, and he reacts to these surprises in a way that is characteristic of obsession (37). All of his references to the possibility of seeming stupid betray a concern that his appearance of cleverness may be little more than a mask, beyond which lies a mind as ignorant as any other of the forces that change people whom he believes that he knows. In a manner typical of obsessional neurosis, he does not care to acknowledge for more than a moment the emptiness that his usual pretensions may conceal; therefore, partly in order to escape these lapses, but also for more complex reasons, he develops a theory which he will spend the rest of the book trying first to establish, and then to defend.[3] This theory, however, will go far beyond being a mere attempt to cover over his failures, for it will also testify to his sense that, if his powers of cognition have failed momentarily, they may have done so because of his encounter with a bizarre force. They have perhaps been disturbed because he has come face to face with a mysterious libidinal power, which his theory will be an attempt to locate. As he now suggests, he has witnessed the effects of secret and supernatural events, for somehow, by means of an act that defies any easy explanation, Guy's youth has been transmitted to Grace, and the intelligence of an unknown person has been given to Gilbert.

The donors' primary motive for taking part in this process lies in their attempt to achieve an enjoyment that manifests itself through one of the strongest ambitions of love: the wish to participate in an act of "fusion" that will, in Lacan's words, "make one out of two."[4] Guy Brissenden "loves [Grace] passionately, sublimely," and through the process that transforms her into a young woman, he allows a portion of his youth to flow into and suffuse her, thereby uniting them as possessors of a common substance (30).[5] This dream of union is thus part of an attempt to achieve a *jouissance* of the body, a sense of Oneness that will allow him to leave behind the divisive power of discourse and the social world; all other interests are sacrificed to this single overriding fascination. Having taken part in a relation that Grace herself, when discussing Gilbert Long, will characterize as "so awfully intimate," the donor will have little interest in social exchange; s/he can only regard society as an alien element that will, at best, fail to comprehend this union, and at worst, be hostile to it (33). This attitude becomes explicit later in the novel, when the narrator is in the presence of a woman whom he believes to be the source of Gilbert's intelligence. This woman, he surmises, derives no pleasure from the festivities at Newmarch. Instead, her purpose in attending the party is to be near her lover and to use a "complex diplomacy," which will prevent anyone from suspecting that her covert relation has changed her; in this way, she hopes to protect her secret from those outsiders who would disapprove of this union (139).

In his own formulation of this theory, however, the narrator does not refuse to acknowledge the action of discourse; instead, he immediately realizes the impossibility of making one out of two, and therefore portrays these characters as having been marked by a cut. His earliest attempts to make sense of the mysterious changes among these people assumes the existence of a "phallic function," which has expelled from the realm of possibility these hopes for a *jouissance* uncontaminated by division.[6] This function has its origin in the young boy's sense of a threat that he will be deprived of his penis if he does not relinquish his infantile "autoeroticism," a term that should be understood in its broadest sense; it extends beyond a reference merely to masturbation, and embraces instead the possibility of an enjoyment that would pervade not only his entire body but also his language. Within this state, the infant uses words not so much to create meaning, but rather as a way of experiencing *jouissance;* the isolated, meaningless signifiers issuing from his mouth have been imbued with this enjoyment, which he can experience in the very act of speaking.[7] Such a condition, however, will be almost impossible to maintain, for the changes within the boy's body can precipitate a reaction that will destroy it; the penis' movement from tumescence to detumescence will create in his own mind the fear that he can lose it altogether, and he embodies this possibility within a perceived parental threat that he abandon his *jouissance* or be deprived of the penis. In order to relinquish this enjoyment, he must begin to connect his first signifiers with other words, and to produce meaning from them; once these terms become enmeshed within articulations, the *jouissance* with which they had been saturated will be expelled from them and from the body, and they will become the early basis of an identity. The phallic function will thereby become the name of the process by which the boy rejects enjoyment, submits to the realm of language, and allows a signifier to represent him in relation to other words.

Whatever hopes that the donor may have had when entering into this process of exchange, the narrator sees that they could not be achieved; instead, he presupposes from the beginning that this relation has been defined in terms, not of a *jouissance* of the One, but of the absence that the signifier introduces. Recalling that Guy Brissenden has aged just as much as his wife has been rejuvenated, he posits the existence of a lack at the center of this process of transmission;

> the "miracle" that has allowed Grace to regain her youth is expensive. Mrs. Briss had to get her new blood, her extra allowance of time and bloom somewhere; and from whom could she so conveniently extract them as from Guy himself? She has, by an extraordinary feat of legerdemain, extracted them, and he, on his side, to supply her, has had to tap the sacred fount. But the sacred fount is like the greedy man's description of the turkey as an 'awkward' dinner dish. It may be sometimes too much for a single share, but it's not enough to go around. (29)

The narrator thus immediately rejects the ideal that the substance possessed by the donor—whether it is youth or intelligence—is inexhaustible and free of signifying division; declaring this position to be impossible, he instead defines all of the participants in these relations in terms of the two fundamental positions within the fantasy. This psychic structure, which Lacan writes as $\math$ $\diamond$ $a,$ consists of the relations between a libidinal object and the subject, which has escaped from its alienation within a signifier that usually stands in for it in the realm of language. The subject, which Lacan writes by means of an S that has been cut by a bar, is a pure absence, for it is nothing more than a hole within the set of signifiers; nevertheless, by attempting to reach and to identify with the object, it can escape its sense of blankness.[8] This object—the object (a)—is only a finite residue, for it is the small element that remains of infantile enjoyment after the subject has submitted to the signifier and has expelled this *jouissance* from his/her body; it is incarnated, in its purest form, by the breast, the feces, the gaze, or the voice.[9] The narrator's own theory, of course, does not reduce this object to its radical purity; instead, having sensed, in the events that have disturbed him, the subterranean presence of a small element of libidinal enjoyment, he is content to embody it within the substances of youth and intelligence. Since these forces are finite rather than infinite, the two donors are in a position that will eventually threaten their lives. As the process of transmission continues, all of the substance that enables them to live will eventually be drawn out of them, and therefore, as one of the narrator's interlocutors remarks, Guy, after "paying to the last drop . . . can only die of the business" (30).

The recipients of these positive qualities will be marked by a different form of lack. Throughout his early formulations of his theory, the narrator assumes that they feel a genuine affection for the donors; they cannot bear the idea that, in taking into themselves the substance with which they identify, they are gradually draining their partners of life. To enjoy the process of destruction itself would be the opposite of the donor's nostalgia for a mythical unity, but as the narrator's later reflections will make clear, he imagines that it would constitute a *jouissance* of such intensity and horror that it too would stand outside the phallic function. He therefore excludes the possibility of this enjoyment, and argues that the recipients are dominated by a determination not to know what is occurring. The donor and the recipient, instead of being united completely by their love, are thus, according to the narrator, separated even at the level of knowledge; Guy Brissenden has a "beautifu[l]" consciousness of his sacrifice, but is not joined in this awareness by Grace, who maintains her ignorance through an act of repression (31). Her perception of her husband's depletion, "if she had it, would be painful and terrible—might even be fatal to the process. So she hasn't it. She passes round it. It takes all her flood of life to meet her own chance. She has only a wonderful sense of success and well-being" (30). Grace Brissenden and Gilbert Long thus become barred subjects marked by the willed unavailability of any signifiers through which they could understand the process of which they are supposedly a part. As the embodiments of ignorance and a lack of understanding, they have become the location of the very characteristics which the narrator had been forced, after the three surprises, to situate within himself. He fears and wishes to deny that he is characterized by this subjective vacancy, a vacancy that will recall to him, ultimately, the parental threat which had led him to inscribe the signifier of cleverness upon himself; he does not, however, refuse completely to acknowledge the existence of the $\mathcal{S}$. Therefore he locates it within the two people who had first surprised and disconcerted him, and in this way, he initiates an unavowed identification with them.

Through this delineation of the relation between donor and recipient, the narrator has defined both of these figures in terms of their adherence to the structure of masculinity. In his mathemes of "sexuation," Lacan constructs masculinity in terms of a set—$\forall x \Phi x$—that gains its logical consistency by means of its opposition to an external term: $\exists x \overline{\Phi} x$.[10] According to these formulas, all elements x—all men—can be said to have submitted to the phallic function, because there is at least one term that is outside their set. This external force is the location of precisely the *jouissance* that has been expelled from these subjects by the phallic function; in *Totem and Taboo,* Freud embodies this enjoyment in the mythical figure of the father of the primal horde, who submits to no external law, and who acknowledges no impediment to his own *jouissance.*[11] By expelling the enjoyment embodied within this external term, the set of men is able to constitute itself as a closed and homogeneous class, a set that is defined by the submission of all its members to the phallic function.[12] In presenting a fantasmatic theory in which each of the elements—the barred subject and the exhaustible object—has been marked by the phallic limitation of *jouissance,* the narrator has placed everyone who belongs to the relations of transmission inside the structure of masculinity. He has therefore included even Grace Brissenden within this set, and this step will later cause him great difficulty.

Such problems will not confront him immediately, however, for at first his exploration of this theory will not force him to face issues that make him uneasy, but instead, will allow him to maintain without difficulty his sense of his own intelligence. His obsessional determination to evade any hint of subjective emptiness manifests itself not only through his use of the hypothesis to explain his early mistakes, but also in his very choice of cleverness as the signifier that will stand in for him in discourse. "Intelligence" is the perfect master signifier for a figure who feels the necessity to verify that a representation has effaced his blankness; through it, he can do so constantly, with every mental effort that he makes. In bringing forth a "knowledge" that consists of a complexly articulated network of relations—S2—he can demonstrate with each new discovery that his intellectual mastery remains as strong as it has ever been.[13]

Within the context of this emphasis on thought, the ambiguity of the text becomes important. One of the reasons that he is fascinated by these relations is that they are radically unprovable by any direct means, for they have as their basis a supernatural event occurring during an act of transmission that is to intimate that he cannot witness it. He is unable even to obtain confessions from the participants, for the recipients remain unconscious of the process, and the donors are probably "uncomfortable . . . when they suspect or fear" that any member of the outside world has intruded upon their hidden concerns (31). Instead of direct proof, the narrator is left with masses of indirect evidence, much of which, as the final chapters will suggest, can also be read in opposing ways.[14] This unprovability, rather than serving as an obstacle for the narrator, is instead an attraction, for, as Freud notes in his case history of the Rat Man, obsessionals feel a "predilection . . . for uncertainty and doubt," and therefore "turn their thoughts by preference to those subjects . . . which must necessarily remain open to doubt."[15] Because he can never prove conclusively that these relations of transmissions exist, the narrator hopes that he will be able to prolong indefinitely the period during which he can contemplate them; the seemingly endless ramifications of his theory will provide him with material by which he can never cease to re-establish his cleverness. For much of the book, indeed, this strategy seems to succeed splendidly, for wherever he ventures at Newmarch, his mind is able to transform seemingly ordinary appearances into new aspects of his magical theory; with each addition to his knowledge of these relations, he derives an "absur[d] excite[ment]," which he has not felt "since the days of fairy-tales and of the childish imagination of the impossible" (127, 128).[16] The narrator feels, therefore, that he has uncovered a marvelous means of occupying himself; if his later experiences in examining the process of transmission prove to be as rewarding for him as was his initial investigation, then he will be able to look forward to a deeply gratifying inquiry.[17]

The events that occur in the course of the book will not, however, bear out these expectations, and the narrator will be confronted more and more with elements of his theory that he would have preferred not to emphasize. His earliest pronouncements have indicated a possibility whose implications he has not yet grasped fully: the fantasmatic relations will not continue to exist in exactly the same form in which he had first detected them. Instead, the fantasy will submit to a series of transformations that will force him to confront a far more radical and harrowing manifestation of barred subjectivity than he had first contemplated; ironically, although he has not yet fully recognized its consequences, this process has already begun at the moment when he celebrates the magical quality of his research. Under the pressure of this sense of absence, the fantasy will undergo a succession of changes that will finally convert it into a very different psychic form: the symptom.

This process begins when the narrator takes his ideas about Gilbert Long to Grace Brissenden, whose reactions he will watch with interest, in part because they supposedly demonstrate how much greater his awareness is than hers. After he has elicited her interest in his theory, and has stimulated her to ask him questions concerning it, he feels able to remark patronizingly of her that "I had kindled near me a fine, if modest and timid intelligence." He then proceeds to demonstrate to himself the supposed inferiority of her conscious mind by addressing to her, and then watching her fail to grasp, a series of pointed allusions to the parallels between Long's position and her own. When she suggests that Long's donor may not be present at Newmarch, he replies that "It's my belief that he goes no more away from her than you go away from poor Briss" (40). A moment later, he again puzzles her by stating that they will be able to discover this unknown figure's identity by finding a person who "shine[s] as Brissenden shines. . . . By sacrifice" (43).

The narrator also, however, has a more significant reason for observing her response: he wishes to entrap her within his discursive mastery. She has a repressed knowledge of the relation of transmission, and therefore he hopes that, by skillful questioning, he can induce her to yield to him some of the information that, unbeknownst to herself, she possesses. In the context of this attempt, a question with which she confronts him will generate the new direction that his theory must take; she tells him that "if you'll only name" Long's donor, she will grant that the change in him is the result of a supernatural process (36). Asserting that she will help discover the identity of this figure, she names several unsatisfactory candidates before she notices that her husband is conversing with May Server, another frequent guest at Newmarch. She then proclaims triumphantly that this woman is the one whom she and the narrator have been seeking.

Although his first reaction to this suggestion is to dismiss it as being no more likely than any of the others, his attitude soon changes, and he starts to feel "a kind of chill—an odd revulsion—at the touch of her eagerness" to pry into the hidden lives of other people; only now does his own "curiosity . . .

beg[i]n to strike me as wanting in taste" (45). Taking leave of Grace Brissenden after agreeing, before he departs from Newmarch, to meet her one more time and to inform him of his own final judgment concerning May Server, he is forced to admit that this suggestion has made him "precipitately, preposterously, anxious" (60). Although he fails to recognize the source of his new uneasiness, and even asks himself, without much conviction, whether he had "suddenly fallen so much in love with Mrs. Server that the care for her reputation had become with me an obsession," the cause of his abrupt change can be found in his surprise at the success of his own theory (50–1).[18] He has hoped that her hidden knowledge would allow them to bring forth new information, but when he begins to suspect that it has actually done so, he is overcome with a sense that he has witnessed an uncanny event; having perhaps encountered the unconscious mechanisms whose existence he has posited, he reacts with an "agitation" whose source he is too disoriented to explain (60).

In the chapters that follow, as he becomes more accustomed to this suggestion, his discomfort will change into a sense of wonder, for evidence will mount that May Server is Gilbert Long's donor. Shortly after this conversation ends, he sees May speaking again to Guy and begins to suspect that she "may have a sympathy" for Grace's husband (76). Later in the day, the narrator learns from Guy that her frequent conversations with him are motivated by her misery and by her belief that he can help her preserve her "false appearance of happiness" (122). The information that will be decisive for the narrator, however, comes to him from his friend, the painter Ford Obert, who observes that her behavior at this gathering has been decidedly atypical; usually quiet, reserved, and a bit passive, she is now "all over the place," seeking frantically to engage one person after another in conversation (63). The narrator therefore begins to believe that through her animation, she is trying to prevent anyone from realizing that she has lost her brilliance. Moving with a "frantic art" from one person to another, she attempts to disguise her emptiness not only with a show of vitality, but also with the "glittering deceit of her smile, the sublime, pathetic, overdone geniality which represented. . . her share in any talk" (139).

The more the narrator investigates May Server, the stronger will his fascination with her become. Having postulated from the beginning that the depletion of the donor will finally and necessarily end in his/her death, the narrator must now begin to confront the implications of this conclusion. Standing before a person who has been "Voided and scraped" of almost all of the intelligence that she had once possessed, he can no longer think of her as the possessor of a positive substance, and therefore she ceases to be the incarnation of the object (*a*) (136). Instead, in watching her face a "small lonely fight with disintegration," he finds before him a far more radical embodiment of subjective absence than the two recipients have ever been (167). The fantasmatic structure whose existence the narrator has posited has thus begun to force him to contemplate more deeply the emptiness with which, covertly, he identifies.

This change within the fantasy will have far-reaching consequences; the first of these will be the transformation into an unconscious signifier of a word that May Server utters carelessly and which the narrator will place in a complex relation not only with her empty subjectivity, but also with his own. During his investigations of her, before he has finally become convinced that she is Gilbert Long's donor, she uses this word in the midst of an exchange of opinions concerning an ambiguous portrait at Newmarch. The picture depicts a person and an object; the human figure is

> a young man in black . . . with a pale, lean livid face and a stare, from eyes without eyebrows, like that of some whitened old-world clown. In his hand he holds an object that strikes the spectator at first simply as some obscure, some ambiguous work of art, but that on a second view becomes a representation of a human face, modelled and coloured, in wax, in enamelled metal, in some substance not human. The object thus appears a complete mask, such as might have been fantastically fitted and worn. (55)

Both the narrator and May Server feel that the relation between the face and the mask stands for the connection between life and death, but they disagree about which image portrays the former quality, and which is linked to the latter. When May suggests that the picture's title could be the "Mask of Death," the narrator disagrees, and argues that it is, instead, the "Mask of Life[.] It's the man's own face that's Death," for the mask is "blooming and beautiful." In trying to counter such an interpretation, May Server makes a statement that will have a profound effect upon him: the mask contains "an awful grimace" (55).

Later, after the narrator has become convinced that May Server is Gilbert Long's donor, "grimace" will become important to him both because of its relation to death, and because of the letters that it contains. On the afternoon of this day, while he is observing her once again, he creates an analogy between her exaggerated animation and the mask that, in his account, has been held by the embodiment of death. Noticing the condition of her fixed smile, he realizes that the day's exertions have left her so tired that even her appearance has begun to fail her. "Her lovely grimace, the light of previous hours, was as blurred as a bit of brushwork in water-colour spoiled by the upsetting of the artist's glass" (133). In this statement, the narrator, while adopting the term that she had used to describe the mask, applies to her face his own analysis of the picture: May Server resembles the deathly figure in the portrait because both have assumed a mask of life and happiness in order to hide the indications of their own extinction.

This association between death and May Server's smile is conscious; what transforms "grimace" into an unconscious signifier is the manner in which this symbolic awareness of death insinuates itself into the heart of a word that is a perfect verbal representation of the fantasmatic relation. "Grimace" is an anagram of the names of the two female members of these couples, "Grace" and "May," the "y" in whose name has been transformed here into an "i." It may not usually strike the reader immediately as an anagram, for it blends these names so skillfully that any blatant connection between them has been cut; by thus molding into a single signifier two names that refer to the separate positions of donor and recipient, it becomes the verbal equivalent of Guy Brissenden's attempt to transform two into one. "Grimace" will assume its unusual power within this text, in part, because it serves thus as the signifier where these two chains of ideas intersect; it embodies the aspiration to reach the One through love, and by its association with the narrator's sense of May Server's depletion and eventual death, it acknowledges the force that will prevent the donor and recipient from achieving a genuine union.

"Grimace," generated as an unconscious signifier by the spectacle of the absence within the donor, serves as a representation of the barred subject. Through this word, the narrator's theory becomes similar, in some ways, to the fantasy that Freud describes in "A Child Is Being Beaten." Both of these fantasies bring to the forefront the relation between two terms that can fill in the emptiness of the barred subject: the signifier that will stand in for it and the object that will allow it to experience a small enjoyment. In Freud's essay, this subject manifests itself in two ways. First, within the analysis, the analysand occupies this position because of her/his inability to remember the second phase of the fantasy; whenever s/he approaches the latter, s/he shows her/himself to be marked by a repression that cannot be lifted. This phase is encapsulated in a sentence that depicts an act of violence somewhat reminiscent of the scenes of torture in Sade: "I am being beaten by my father."[19] Within this fantasmatic scenario, the child, finding her/himself in a position of wordless suffering, serves as a second means of imagining the condition of a subject who is not represented by a signifier.

These embodiments of an empty subjectivity have precise structural equivalents within the narrator's fantasmatic theory, but the father is a different matter, for he incarnates a power that has made itself felt in the relation of transmission only through its absence. Finding enjoyment in the act of inflicting pain and laying bare the emptiness of the subject—an emptiness from which he is himself exempt—this father is the embodiment of the *jouissance* that has been expelled from the set of men by the phallic function. As such, he is analogous to Sade's "Supreme-Being-in-Evil" and to the father of the primal horde, who, while recognizing no law that would bind him, finds *jouissance* in the act of imposing castration upon his sons.[20] In beating the child, however, he is doing something more than exposing the hole of subjectivity, for he is also simultaneously affixing to the subject the signifier that will represent her/him and creating a spectacle in which the libidinal object can appear. The blows that fall upon the child's body become figures for the meaningless signifying marks with which the subject, in the first moments of the process by which s/he enters language, will identify; such marks will come to serve as S1, and will represent her/him in relation to other signifiers. This fantasy thus becomes, in part, a dramatization of the painful process in which the child is captured by the signifier; this aspect does not, however, exhaust the significance of this scenario, for if the second phase enacts the process of alienation, the third phase introduces a separation from the signifier.[21] The latter phase, which the subject describes with the simple statement, "A child is being beaten," witnesses the appearance of the object (*a*) in the form of the gaze; the analysand, when asked to locate her/himself in the scene, replies that "I am probably looking on."[22] This object enables the subject to use this enactment of alienation as a means of gaining a sense of her/his desire. By apprehending this object and identifying it as the deepest part of her/himself, the subject will be able to salvage from this scene of loss and torture a small remainder of *jouissance*.

In *The Sacred Fount*, "grimace" enters the narrator's fantasy as the equivalent of the signifier that the father has inscribed upon the subject, but the narrator approaches these relations between the subject and signifier in a peculiarly obsessional way. The obsessional, Lacan has suggested, "denies . . . desire . . . by forming the fantasy to accentuate the impossibility of the subject's vanishing."[23] Instead of using this scenario as a way of allowing the subject to fade before the object that would give him a sense of his own desire, and which would thus palliate the effects of alienation, he transforms it into yet another means of avoiding any full confrontation with the $. The signifier that is produced will serve to conceal the most radical manifestation of an empty subjectivity, which will not, thus, be experienced as a point of pure fading, and which will feel no necessity to realize its deeper identification with any libidinal object. At first, "grimace" functions in precisely this manner, and therefore allows the narrator to maintain a certain distance between himself and a condition that would make him uneasy. May Server's exaggerated and almost grotesque behavior has prevented him from having to confront directly the void that his own calculations have located within her; he has thus not been forced to come face to face with the absence that has led him, in his attempt to dissociate himself from it, to manufacture this theory. For this reason, he will feel no need to introduce into his thought any genuine refinements concerning the object (*a*); not having encountered fully an external embodiment of his own subjectivity, he will not be led to identify with an object that could allow him to elaborate more fully a sense of his own libidinal urgings. Instead, by means of his unconscious identification with the $ of the fantasy, he will, in a way that will not become evident until later in the book, pin this signifier to himself. Instead, he will identify with "grimace" so strongly that this new signifier will determine his destiny.

II
FEMININITY AND THE SYMPTOM

The transformation of the fantasy does not end with the depletion of the donors, for a short time later, the narrator makes a discovery that will affect the structure of his theory even more radically. At the end of a musical performance, he sees Grace Brissenden and Gilbert Long engaged in a "familiar colloquy," and immediately wonders, "Had *they* also wonderfully begun to know?" (182). If the recipients, through a shadowy process which his own investigations have perhaps indirectly initiated, have learned the donors' secret, then this knowledge may well, as he had suggested at the beginning, be fatal to the process of transmission. Will Gilbert Long, the narrator wonders, now return to his former condition, and "would Grace Brissenden [and her husband] change by the same law? . . . And if it took this form for the others . . . [w]ould [May Server], at a bound as marked as theirs, recover her present of mind and her lost equipment?" (191). During his long final conversation with Grace, however, the narrator discovers that this particular speculation has been incorrect, for in seeing her before him again, he realizes that she "had at no other moment since her marriage so triumphantly asserted her defeat of time"; this indication that the supernatural act is still continuing soon becomes conjoined with a determination, on her part, to repudiate any belief in it, for she declares that "I feel there's nothing in it and I've given it up" (240, 260). Expanding upon this statement, she will offer the unsupported assertion that Long, instead of having been transformed into a brilliant man, remains what he has always been: a "prize fool," who utters nothing but platitudes (292). She argues, further, that since he has not changed, there is no longer any reason to believe that he must be involved with a woman who would be willing to give up her intelligence for him; instead, according to Guy, Long is conducting an affair with a more egoistic woman—Lady John—who has often appeared in his company. Finally, Grace will make another suggestion that is supposedly based upon her husband's words: May Server, instead of being in love with Long, has set her sights elsewhere, and has been "mak[ing] up to poor Briss" (316). Faced with these unexpected arguments, the narrator must adjust his theory to account for the change in Grace's opinion. Therefore, he "divine[s]" that she is now in league with Gilbert Long, who suspects him of wishing to expose their secret and to put a stop to the process of exchange; Long has thus used his new intelligence by "direct[ing]" her to prevent the narrator from progressing any further in his investigation (254).

Throughout the alterations that he makes in response to these changes, he endeavors to preserve his most important premises: he does not want to believe that these two figures have become the repositories of a *jouissance* that goes beyond the strict phallic limitations under which he had first placed them. Just as he does not abandon his sense that these couples fail to achieve an idealized union outside the requirements of discourse, so also he refuses to accept any suggestion that the injury done to the donors creates, in itself, an horrific *jouissance* within the recipients. Grace Brissenden and Gilbert Long do not, indeed, want to reverse or even end the process; however, instead of wishing specifically to deplete their partners, they want merely to enjoy their possession of the substances with which they have been endowed. What they are trying to achieve, in their "fight" to prevent the narrator from endangering their new condition, is simply their hope for a "possible life in the state" of consciousness that "I had given them" (295). According to the narrator's latest calculations, the survival of the relation is the only surprise that the recipients' new awareness has created for him. The fundamental structure of the process has remained the same, for the participants within it have merely exchanged places: marked now by a radical incompleteness, Guy and May are in the position of S, while because of their new libidinal power, Grace and Gilbert have become the repositories of the *(a)*.

Faced with a situation in which his interlocutor wants to put an end to this theorizing, the narrator responds with aggression; having identified with "grimace," he now implants this signifier upon his own body, and covertly mobilizes it against her. In doing so, he is seeking to state, in an occult manner, that he knows her secret and understands the nature of her strategy; he hopes that he will be able thereby to draw a sense of strength from his own cleverness, even if she herself cannot fully recognize what he is doing. Therefore he injects a strong element of contempt into gestures such as smiles or laughter, for because of May's example, he associates them with "grimace," and then propels them at his opponent as if they were weapons. When, for example, she becomes confused by the complexities of their debate, and accuses him falsely of having asserted to her that May Server is involved with Gilbert Long, the narrator points out her mistake with an "indulgen[t]" and superior smile (269). Later, when Grace maintains that no single incident has caused her to lose faith in his theory, he "break[s] into laughter" in order to drive home his point that she has been unable to explain her change of mind adequately (290).

Nevertheless, as their conversation wears on, she is able to combat him with increasing effectiveness, and he begins to show that beneath his bravado, he is deeply uneasy about his own relation with her. Although he is faced merely with a series of assertions, rather than with a devastating disproof of his theory, the narrator begins to feel more and more ill at ease. Throughout the later stages of their conversation, Grace exerts a mysterious power over him, a power that becomes manifest when, for example, she utters two simple and supremely confident words to show her certainty that Long is intimate with Lady John: "I know" (304). Despite the fact that he does not genuinely accept this assertion, he nevertheless begins to feel great apprehension.

It was the oddest thing in the world for a little, the way this affected me without my at all believing it. . . . It was the mere sound of it that, as I felt even at the time, made it a little of a blow—a blow of the smart of which I was conscious just long enough inwardly to murmur: "What if she should be right?" (304–5)

The narrator's growing sense of disturbance will manifest itself most strongly in the gestures that he has adopted in order to allude to "grimace." At one point, she asserts to him, "I think you're crazy," and in order to show his amused contempt for this idea, he responds by laughing at her. Upon hearing the sound of his own laughter, however, he has an uneasy sense that her statement has had a stronger effect upon him than he will admit to her. "I risked that long laugh which might have been that of madness. . . . And whether or not it was the special sound, in my ear of my hilarity, I remember just wondering if perhaps I mightn't be" (278). This unpleasant feeling that his own unexpected weaknesses are beginning to emerge will be transformed, as his sense of her power grows, into an increasing inability to keep his wits about him; throughout the last stages of the conversation, he will find his own capacity to reply to her fading before her "supreme assurance" (318). This situation comes to a head in the final pages when Grace, who is still apparently unaware that he now believes May Server is Gilbert Long's donor, states that May is "awfully sharp." At this moment, his cleverness fails him completely, and he can only gasp and "stupidly" return her own words to her: "Awfully sharp?" (317). Surprised by this reaction, she repeats her earlier accusation, "My poor dear, you are crazy," and he can only agree that he has indeed lost something of his former manner: "I should certainly never again, on the spot, quite hang together" (318, 319).

This final and complete failure of his power to reply to her is not caused by the strength of the unsupported assertions with which she has confronted him; although they certainly demonstrate that his is not the only possible interpretation of the events at Newmarch, he can easily dismiss them as fabrications. Instead, his reaction results from a possibility which he will never articulate fully: in a manner that is utterly inconsistent with his original premises, which had posited that the relation of transmission can occur only between two people who have experienced great intimacy, the narrator and Grace have begun to form such a couple. Throughout the later stages of their conversation, her ability to respond to each new twist in the debate waxes and his wanes, just as if she were now draining his mastery from him. If such is the case, then, in initiating this change, she is seeking, in part, to bring out his own subjective emptiness. She is trying to reveal his status as S by draining him not of the object (a), but of one facet of the signifier that has represented him throughout his discussions with her: his definition of himself as clever. In the course of their final conversation, with the strengthening of her ability to impose upon him her own interpretation of events, the narrator, at least for the moment, has felt the weakening of an aspect of his own mental power, and his panic-stricken sense of this change will itself contribute to the complete disappearance of his composure in the final pages of the novel. He is not losing his theoretical faculty itself, for he still has "three times her method" (319). Rather, he is being deprived of his ability to use it as the means to make himself the master of his discourse; he has ceased to be able, in his conversation with others, to lead them confidently and surely onto the terrain of his own concerns, where he can draw from them a knowledge— S2—which they themselves have been unaware that they possessed. His conversation with Grace has taught him that "I too fatally lacked . . . her tone," and her repeated assertions that he is crazy are, in part, attempts to demonstrate the failure of his capacity to draw people into his concerns (319). As she asserts to him, his ability to make her participate in his search for knowledge has declined steadily. She ceased to believe in his theory, she now tells him, when he first left her alone this morning; "[a]s soon as I was not with you—I mean with you personally," she tells him, "you never had my sympathy." Indeed, in the course of the day, the power of his presence has weakened considerably; "it's not, thank God [so irresistible] now!" (287). By thus allowing her declaration that he is mad to "work" inside his mind, she is attempting to lay bare the subjective emptiness that his former mastery has hidden (280).

In observing the "supreme assurance" with which she deprives him of his manner, the narrator now discerns within her the very *jouissance* that he had sought so carefully to exclude from the recipients (318).[24] When he witnesses the mingled triumph and contempt with which she tells him, for a second time, that he is crazy, he links this declaration with the other source of her enjoyment: her recovered youth. "[G]ather[ing] herself up into the strength of twenty-five," she manifests, at the very moment when her accusation delineates the absence within him, the *jouissance* that suffuses her body (318). For the first time, she seems to derive enjoyment specifically from the act of laying bare the subject's emptiness.

Because of the narrator's new fear, the function of "grimace" changes and becomes an attempt to conceive of femininity as a structure that resurrects the very element that his theory has rejected. The laugh with which he responds to her first assertion that he is mad serves, like his earlier laughter, as an allusion to "grimace," but within this new context, this signifier no longer functions as a verbal equivalent of the fantasy; because the fantasy is a component of the structure of masculinity, it has ceased to be an adequate means of understanding the process of transmission. This particular reference to "grimace," instead, has become an attempt to conceive of femininity as a structure that is radically distinct from masculinity, and which can be understood in terms of the relation between two logical formulas: $x\Phi x$ and $x \overline{\Phi} x$. The first of these two statements suggests that there is not one term x that has not been marked by the phallic function.[25] The implications of this assertion are twofold: not only is there not a single woman who bears no relation whatever to it, but there is also, in femininity, no external term that would be parallel to the one that stands outside masculinity. In contrast with masculinity, which founds itself by means of its reference to at least one element that has not submitted to this function, this matheme denies the existence of any equivalent term that would be located in opposition to the feminine set; thus it signals a very different relation to phallic limitation. Unlike the male subject, any person who locates herself as female will not be confronted with the inaugural threat of an initial castration, and therefore will not feel the need to submit absolutely to this function; she will acknowledge it partially, because it is linked to the process by which she allows herself to be represented by a signifier for other signifier, but she will not conform to it entirely.[26]

For this reason, Lacan pairs this first matheme with a second one—$\overline{x}\Phi x$—which specifies that "not all" elements x have been marked by the phallic function. He refers to this condition when he states that a woman's "being not all in the phallic function does not mean that she is not in it at all. . . . She is right in it. But there is something more": the enjoyment that has been expelled can come flooding back to her, and can appear in the midst of elements that have submitted to the phallic function.[27] This "not all"—*pas toute*—also refers to set theory, where it designates the refusal of the class of women to cohere into a homogeneous whole. Masculinity has constituted a unified set of men, each constituent of which has submitted to the phallic function; the "set" of women is also defined in relation to this function, but resists enacting this process of closure. The members of this group have been marked only in a provisional manner, and the *jouissance* that exists outside this function can return to any of them without warning; therefore, it is impossible to define a uniform set of women in terms of all of its members' rigid subordination of themselves to phallic limitation, and femininity establishes itself as the realm of the *pas-toute*.[28]

At the pivotal moment of his "mad" laugh, the narrator transforms the meaning of "grimace" in an unconscious attempt to conceive of precisely this structure; in doing so, he also throws new light on his earlier use of this signifier. Even when this word referred to the fantasmatic connection between donor and recipient, it pointed to his hidden need to reassure himself about the relation between women and the phallic function. He can now be seen to have been uneasy about defining Grace Brissenden and May Server in terms of masculinity; by inscribing an anagram of their names at the heart of the fantasmatic relation, he has been attempting, through the force of his own unconscious volition, to enforce upon them an adherence to phallic limitation.

Now, however, he begins to use "grimace" in a different way because he is faced with two possibilities that contradict his earliest formulations: he has discerned within Grace the eruption of the *jouissance* that he had established to be absent from her, and he has begun to fear that, in spite of his emphasis upon the necessarily intimate relation between donor and recipient, he has,

merely through his conversations with her, become coupled with her in a relation of transmission. Responding to Grace Brissenden's first assertion that he
is mad, the narrator utters a laugh that seems to admit what he wants to
deny; in this way, it acknowledges the uneasiness that he feels when he contemplates this new possibility, a possibility that, a few hours earlier, he would
have dismissed as irrational. Through this laugh, "grimace," as a word that
combines "May" with "Grace," becomes an attempt to conceive of this new
development. Although its relation to femininity will be traversed by opposing tendencies, this signifier, in its most radical aspect, becomes a way of
understanding the coexistence of two seemingly contradictory approaches to
jouissance: as he has verified earlier, not one of these women has not submitted
to the phallic function, but as the change in Grace seems to suggest, she has
nevertheless become the place of an enjoyment that remains unmarked by it.
Through this word, the narrator locates femininity as a structure that can
maintain divergent relations with the phallic function, and which therefore
imposes inconsistencies upon his theory of a process of transformation in
which, until now, men and women have occupied interchangeable places.[29]

Although it allows him a provisional way to conceive of a femininity that
differs from masculinity, "grimace" is not completely equal to this most
recent task, for its very form is discordant with this new understanding. This
word first became important because, through its relation with a series of
associations, it served as the almost perfect signifier not only of the power of
depletion and death, but also of the impulse to achieve unity. Its anagram-
matical character embodied the aspiration toward an idealized Oneness,
because, instead simply of adding the essentially separate names of donor and
recipient, it molded them together and created from them a new "unity."
Even after the narrator's concern with the One recedes, for a time, and "grimace" has been transformed into an attempt to conceive of the structure of
femininity, it continues to suggest this sense of unification. As an anagram, it
still implies that the separate qualities of Grace Brissenden and May Server
have been combined into some genuinely new element; it therefore contains a
latent pretension to be the signifier of a unified and homogeneous set of
women. For this reason, it becomes discordant with the very understanding of
femininity that he is trying to formulate, for this structure resists any attempt
to unify its members in this manner. Once Grace has been endowed with a
new *jouissance,* she stands in radical disparity with May, who remains in steadfast conformity to the phallic function; the absence, in these two figures, of a
common relation to this term makes it impossible to mold them into a unity.
This dissonance between "grimace" and the conception of femininity with
which it has become related will mark a point of instability; unable to accommodate a structure of such radical alterity that even the unconscious signifying chain cannot quite comprehend it, the text will attempt to change it into
a form that can be dealt with more easily. "Grimace" will be transformed into
a "symptom," a term that should be understood in the sense in which Lacan

employed it during the final years of his teaching; in doing so, the narrator will place himself in a profoundly paradoxical position, for he will escape from the "threat" of feminine *jouissance* only by petrifying himself within another form of enjoyment.

In the middle of the 1970s, Jacques Lacan pinpointed the importance of the symptom within literary texts when he began to examine the works of James Joyce; intrigued by the extreme difficulty of producing a coherent meaning from almost any of the sentences in *Finnegans Wake,* he suggested that this very problem allows the reader to sense "the *jouissance* of the one who wrote it." Because this particular text employs, "not in each line but in each word," an extraordinarily complicated series of puns and equivocations, its words become so dense with allusions that they cannot cohere into meaningful sentences; therefore, "the meaning, in the sense that we habitually give it, is lost."[30] Once a word, in this fashion, becomes cut off from the other words within a chain of thoughts, its function changes. It ceases to be an element that is important primarily for the meanings that it can produce through such combinations; instead, it becomes once again what it had been in infancy: a vehicle of *jouissance.* The enjoyment that has been expelled by the phallic function comes flooding back and invades the isolated signifier, which thereby becomes a symptom.[31]

Finnegans Wake provides the most blatant instance of the eruption of enjoyment into signifiers that have been cut away from articulated meaning, but the symptom can also manifest itself in a less dramatic and obvious form. When it invades a literary text, it need not encompass the entire work, as it does in Joyce's final book, for in *The Sacred Fount,* it is located within a single word—"grimace." Indeed, in order for a signifier to be transformed into a symptom, it does not even have to be rendered unrecognizable by the introduction into it of complex puns and deformations of spelling; "grimace" will become a symptom while retaining its conventional meaning. In cases such as this one, it is only necessary that a signifier that has become crucial for the subject be cut from the associations through which it has been raised to prominence. "Grimace," having, because of its meaning, assumed such importance that the narrator has identified with it and implanted it upon his body, now ceases to be enchained with these other ideas. After this alteration, it will maintain its importance for the narrator, but it will nevertheless be transformed radically; just as *jouissance* was banished in childhood when the signifier that stands in for the subject became enmeshed in a series of meanings, so now, once these have been abolished, this enjoyment is able to return.

This metamorphosis occurs during the final stages of the discussion with Grace Brissenden, and first manifests itself when she asserts that, during her conversation with Gilbert Long after dinner, she had told him that he was a fool. She thus contradicts the narrator's belief that during this interchange, they first became conscious of their status as recipients, and he responds to this information not only with the same sense of unease that dominates the final pages of the novel, but also with yet another smile, which he now uses differently than he has ever done before. "I weighed (this assertion) with the grimace that, I found, had become almost as fixed as Mrs. Server's" (293). His grimace reappears in the final pages of the novel, when Grace contradicts another of his secretly cherished beliefs by claiming that May Server has been seeking a romantic attachment, not with Long, but with Guy Brissenden. Her assertion "brought . . . I fear, for me, another queer grimace" (317).

With these appearances, this word ceases to be either an aggressive means of alluding to his knowledge or an urgent attempt to understand how femininity differs from masculinity; "grimace" is no longer a signifier that creates a specific psychic meaning through its connections with a series of related ideas. It has been cut away from these associations as a result of the disturbance set up by the collision of two incompatible elements: a femininity that resists any effort to confine it within rigid delimitations and an unconscious signifying chain that attempts fruitlessly to enclose it inside stable boundaries. Confronted with the ungraspable quality of the feminine, the text makes a move that will have far-reaching consequences; it reverses the way in which the anagram functions. Shifting attention away from the associations that have conferred meaning upon this signifier, and have thus raised it to importance, the work concentrates instead upon the power of this word as a unique arrangement of letters. Once it is considered as a positive term in its own right, it becomes the embodiment of an enjoyment with which the narrator will be obliged to assume an intimate relation.

Forced to face a specifically feminine approach to *jouissance*, he has responded by bringing forth a symptom, which will be connected in a very different way with enjoyment. As the only signifier that has been irradiated by this *jouissance*, "grimace," unlike the symptom in *Finnegans Wake*, has been set radically apart from the other words in this novel. Its new relation to them—and especially to signifiers with which it had once been associated, such as "May" or "Grace"—will therefore be homologous to that of the x $\overline{\Phi}$ x to the xΦx, within masculine sexuation. Like the primal father—the one term untouched by the phallic function—"grimace" becomes the definitive location of an enjoyment that is as absent from the other signifiers in *The Sacred Fount* as it is from the set of men. In this way, *jouissance*, which the narrator has feared when he had merely expected its existence within Grace Brissenden, will make itself present to him for the first time, and will appear upon his own body.

His attempt to "protect" himself from feminine *jouissance* by imprinting enjoyment upon himself must seem puzzling; at first glance, it would seem more likely that this fear would lead him not to embrace a specific manifestation of enjoyment, but rather to flee from it in as direct a manner as possible. He follows this less straightforward course because, although it will not eliminate the source of his dread entirely, it seems to hold out a stronger hope for escaping some of the problems that Grace Brissenden embodies for him; confronted with an enjoyment that exists as a heterogeneous element within femininity, he attempts to find a way, in two senses of the word, to "contain" this *jouissance*. He seeks to find an enclosure for it, for in doing so, he will give it a precise location, and will thus prevent it from appearing anywhere without warning, as it has done in femininity.[32] By creating such a receptacle, he will be "containing" the threat that enjoyment supposedly carries with it; he will be cordoning it off so that it cannot affect anything else. "Grimace," the signifier of the condition that allows enjoyment to return within women, is thus transformed into the vessel in which this *jouissance* can be safely and precisely quarantined; having accommodated "May" and "Grace" too perfectly within itself, and thus having failed to be a completely satisfactory means of understanding femininity, it now begins to function purely as an enclosure. Through this maneuver, the narrator hopes to lessen his deepest fears about femininity, for if *jouissance* cannot return to it unexpectedly, then he will not have to worry that his careful calculations have been disrupted; he can therefore feel more confident in denying both that he has become Grace Brissenden's donor and that she enjoys the act of depleting him. Such tactics may not meet with complete success, for his fear will appear even in the final moment of their conversation, but they offer, nevertheless, the strongest obsessional defense against feminine *jouissance*.

The narrator must pay for this change, however, with a dramatic alteration of his own relation to *jouissance,* one that he will find himself unable to escape. In seeking to deprive Grace Brissenden of an enjoyment that he fears, he has been forced to locate a symptomatic *jouissance* in himself, and in doing so, he has witnessed the return of a force whose actual existence he had judged to be impossible. At the beginning of the book, when contemplating Guy's wish to unite himself with his wife, the narrator had immediately rejected any suggestion that this attempt would be crowned by success; he had refused to believe that anyone can become the pure embodiment of a *jouissance* that stands outside the signifying articulations of discourse. Now, however, in the form of a symptom that incarnates the enjoyment that has not conformed to the phallic function, the *jouissance* of the One has reappeared, stripped of the idealized veil that clothes it whenever the urge to escape from discourse is presented in terms of love. By the end of the book, therefore, the narrator has placed himself in a paradoxical position; his submission to the phallic function and his horror of an enjoyment that threatens the integrity of his theory have led him to imprint *jouissance* upon his own body. Such a condition, when seen from the perspective of a masculine uneasiness with enjoyment, can only be regarded as an impasse, and James's later texts, particularly *The Wings of the Dove,* will attempt to resolve this situation. This novel, in spite of its obvious differences from *The Sacred Fount,* will examine obsessional responses to symptomatic *jouissance* in somewhat similar terms; lacking a first-person narrator, it will not locate the symptom within a specific character, and therefore the enjoyment that invades language will manifest its presence in a less direct manner. Nevertheless, this later text, in taking up the concerns surrounding the symptom, will begin at precisely the point at which *The Sacred Fount* concludes: the juncture at which the symptom, having appeared in an attempt to contain the *jouissance* that is presumed to exist within femininity, becomes itself a burden to the obsessional.

For the narrator of *The Sacred Fount,* however, this symptomatic enjoyment will continue to maintain its hold over him, for it cannot be expelled from his mind, nor can its force even be lessened; instead, it will persist and invest the act of writing. While he relates the events that occurred during his final evening at Newmarch, he makes one of his few references to the period in which he is narrating his account, and in doing so, admits that the symptom still retains its power over him. He states that, at one point during the events of that evening, he experienced a strong, if fleeting revulsion against the all-consuming power of his preoccupation, and therefore, when he saw May Server one last time, he hopes that he would never again encounter her. Then, in an aside, he confesses that although he has not come face to face with her again, she has remained present to him in other ways. "I did see her again; I see her now; I shall see her always; I shall continue to feel at moments in my own facial muscles the deadly little ache of her heroic grin" (197). After the conclusion of the events that he has recounted, the narrator retains his connection with a *jouissance* that has taken its place within the palace of thought; each time that he reflects upon his splendid theory, he will also feel the presence of this enjoyment.[33] Through his act of composing his story, the enjoyment that fascinates and troubles him will ensure that it can continue to force itself upon his mind, and it will therefore never cease to write itself upon his body or upon the page.

Notes

1. Henry James, *The Sacred Fount* (New York: Grove Press, Inc., 1979) 311. Subsequent references will appear in the text.

2. Leon Edel, "Introductory Essay," in James, *The Sacred Fount,* xiii.

3. Ellie Ragland-Sullivan discusses obsession in similar terms in two essays: "*Hamlet,* Logical Time, and the Structure of Obsession," *Newsletter of the Freudian Field* 2.2 (Fall 1988): "The Limits of Discourse Structure: The Hysteric and the Analyst," *Prose Studies* 11.3 (December 1988): 66, 79. Colette Soler gives a somewhat different emphasis to this issue in "Hysteria and Obsession," in Richard Feldstein, Bruce Fink, Maire Jaanus, ed. *Reading Seminars I and II: Lacan's Return to Freud* (Albany: State University of New York Press, 1996), 263.

4. Jacques Lacan, "God and the *jouissance* of The Woman," trans. Jacqueline Rose, ed. Juliet Mitchell and Jacqueline Rose *Feminine Sexuality* (New York: Norton, 1982) 138.

5. For a brief discussion of the relationship between the narrator's theory and popular nineteenth-century conceptions of sexuality, see Susanne Kappeler, *Writing and Reading in Henry James* (New York: Columbia University Press, 1980) 116–117.

6. Bruce Fink, *The Lacanian Subject: Between Language and Jouissance* (Princeton University Press, 1995) 103–4.

7. Jacques-Alain Miller has discussed this enjoyment in his unpublished course, *Ce qui fait insigne,* during the session of May 20, 1987.

8. Jacques-Alain Miller has treated the fantasy in these terms in his unpublished course, *Du symptôme au fantasme et retour,* during the sessions of November 25 and December 1, 1982. For other discussions of the fantasy, see Marie-Hélène Brousse, "La formule du fantasme? *8 a,*" Lacan, ed. Gérard Miller (Paris: Bordas, 1987) 112–113, 116–120; Slavoj & Žižek, *The Sublime Object of Ideology* (London: Verso, 1989) 74, 114–115.

9. Jacques Lacan, "Introduction to the Names-of-the-Father Seminar," *Television/A Challenge to the Psychoanalytic Establishment,* trans. Jeffrey Mehlman, ed. Joan Copjec (New York: Norton, 1990) 85–87.

10. Lacan, "A Love Letter," *Feminine Sexuality,* 149.

11. Sigmund Freud, *Totem and Taboo, The Origins of Religion,* The Pelican Freud, vol. 13, trans. James Strachey, ed. Albert Dickson (London: Penguin, 1985) 185–6, 202.

12. The most detailed treatment in English of the mathemes of masculine sexuation can be found in Bruce Fink, *The Lacanian Subject,* 108–112. For a discussion of logical consistency, see Jacques-Alain Miller's unpublished course, *Extimité,* April 16, 1986.

13. For a different exploration of Jamesian thought, see Sharon Cameron, *Thinking in Henry James* (Chicago: The University of Chicago Press, 1989).

14. For discussions of the novel's ambiguity, see Shlomith Rimmon, *The Concept of Ambiguity: The Example of James* (Chicago: The University of Chicago Press, 1977), and Susan Winnett, "*Mise en crypte:* The Man and the Mask," *The Henry James Review* 5.3 (1984): 220–1. James W. Gargano, on the other hand, has argued that the novel is not ambiguous, and that the narrator has proven his theory. "James's *The Sacred Fount:* The Phantasmagorical Made Evidential," *The Henry James Review* 2.1 (1981): 49.

15. Sigmund Freud, "Notes upon a Case of Obsessional Neurosis," trans. Alix and James Strachey, ed. Angela Richards *Case Histories II,* The Pelican Freud Library, Vol. 9 (London: Penguin Books, 1979) 112.

16. E. C. Curtsinger, instead of seeing this statement as an indication is seeking a libidinal enjoyment from his theory, claims that in this sentence, James is "depicting the sources of his art." "James's Writer at the Sacred Fount," *The Henry James Review* 3.2 (1983): 124.

17. This fascination with a structure that demands an endless attention will serve both to differentiate the narrator from the author, and also to point to their common concerns. By implication, James criticizes the narrator's massively caricatured intellectual vanity, but this act of distancing himself from his created character also transforms the latter into his disavowed surrogate; the author, at a different level, repeats this fascination with a supposedly interminable process of thinking. If James is conceived as having fashioned a text of absolute epistemological ambiguity, one in which almost every detail can be read as both confirming and disproving the narrator's theory, then he too has constructed a "perfect palace of thought" (311). He has created an edifice whose intricacy serves as an obsessional monument to his own brilliance, and whose subtle and unresolved ambiguity can be contemplated without cease.

As the book progresses, the gap between these two figures will lessen. Once unconscious effects begin to manifest themselves within the text, they will presumably do so without the awareness of either narrator or author, who will be conjoined by their very lack of knowledge. Further, the symptomatic enjoyment with which the act of writing will become invested, and which will become crucially important for the narrator, can be assumed to be a force from which James himself is not entirely exempt.

18. Both Jean Frantz Blackall and E. A. Sklepowich, on the other hand, take seriously the narrator's suggestion that his anxiety arises from his love for May Server. See Blackall, *Jamesian Ambiguity and* The Sacred Fount (Ithaca: Cornell University Press, 1965) 64–5; Sklepowich, "Gossip and Gothicism in *The Sacred Fount.*" *The Henry James Review* 2/2 (1981): 13.

19. Sigmund Freud, " 'A Child Is Being Beaten': A Contribution to the Study of the Origin of the Sexual Perversions," *On Psychopathology,* The Pelican Freud, vol. 10, trans. Alix and James Strachey, ed. Angela Richards (London: Penguin, 1979) 170.

20.   For Lacan's discussion of the "Supreme-Being-in-Evil," see *The Seminar, Book VII: The Ethics of Psychoanalysis, 1959–1960,* trans. Dennis Porter, ed. Jacques-Alain Miller (New York: W. W. Norton, 1992), 297; "Kant with Sade," trans. James B. Swenson Jr. *October* 51 (Winter 1989): 61.

21.   Jacques-Alain Miller has approached Freud's essay in this fashion in *Du symptôme au fantasme et retour,* December 15, 1982. For another Lacanian reading of Freud's essay, see Marie-Hélène Brousse, "La formule du fantasme? *8 < > a,*" 113–116.

22.   Freud, "A Child Is Being Beaten," pp. 169, 171. See also Françoise Schreiber, "Des fantasmes à la phrase du fantasme." *Ornicar: Revue du Champ Freudien* 39 (October–December 1986): 103.

23.   Jacques Lacan, *Ecrits* (Paris: Editions du Seuil, 1966) 824. In "Hysteria and Obsession," Colette Soler provides a commentary on this statement and criticizes Alan Sheridan's rendering of it. See 269–270, 282. For Sheridan's own translation, see *Ecrits: A Selection* (New York: Norton, 1977) 321.

24.   John Carlos Rowe, in contrast to this argument, presents Grace Brissenden as an embodiment of the social order, and argues that she is "[f]rightened by [the narrator's] threat to the surface of social decorum." *Through the Custom-House: Nineteenth-Century Fiction and Modern Theory* (Baltimore: Johns Hopkins University Press, 1982) 187.

25.   Lacan, "A Love Letter," 149.

26.   Jacques Lacan, . . . *ou Pire,* unpublished seminar, January 17, 1972.

27.   Lacan, "God and the *Jouissance* of The Woman," p. 145.

28.   For discussions of the mathemes of feminine sexuation, see Marie-Hélène Brousse, "Feminism with Lacan," *Newsletter of the Freudian Field* 5.1/2 (Spring/Fall 1991): 117–127; Bruce Fink, *The Lacanian Subject,* 113–117. Jacques-Alain Miller has provided an important discussion of sexuation in terms of set theory in *Extimité,* May 21, 1986.

29.   William Veeder provides a different presentation of Jamesian relations to femininity in "Henry James and the Uses of the Feminine," *Out of Bounds: Male Writers and Gender{ed} Criticism,* ed. Laura Claridge and Elizabeth Langland (Amherst: The University of Massachusetts Press, 1990) 220–228.

30.   Jacques Lacan, "Joyce le Symptôme I," *Joyce avec Lacan,* ed. Jacques Aubert (Paris: Navarin, 1987) 25. My translation. See also Ellie Ragland-Sullivan, "Lacan's Seminars on James Joyce: Writing as Symptom and 'Singular Solution,' " *Psychoanalysis and. . .,* ed. Richard Feldstein and Henry Sussman (New York: Routledge) 71–77, 80–86.

31.   Miller, *Ce qui fait insigne,* January 28 and April 1, 1987.

32.   Jacques-Alain Miller has discussed the symptom's status as container in *Ce qui fait insigne,* May 27, 1987.

33.   In some ways, this account of the symptom rejoins Freud's own discussions of obsession, for although his emphasis is different, he also argues that thinking can become a source of enjoyment. Freud links such *jouissance* to "an early development and premature repression of the sexual instinct of looking and knowing"; he argues that in a person with these tendencies, the "thought-process itself becomes sexualized, for the sexual pleasure which is normally attached to the content of thought becomes shifted on to the act of thinking itself, and the satisfaction derived from reaching the conclusion of a line of thought is experienced as a sexual satisfaction." See "Notes upon a Case of Obsessional Neurosis," 124.

[From *Tableau* ("Painting")]

Gérard Wajcman

For psychoanalysis, topology is not a metaphor.[1] We must depart from this point, confusing at first, in speaking seriously of painting. It is the point with which Lacan himself starts the lesson of May 4, 1966, of his seminar, which that year concerned *The Object of Psychoanalysis*—an unpublished seminar, which is to say, unreadable twice over. This seminar leads by way of painting to a construction (no less than the construction of a world, which is quite different than a vision of the world) that I believe will be worth our trouble.

To Show

I will not take it in a bad way if one envisages what follows as a simple paraphrase. I have my reasons. First, if the modesty of my ambition is justified by the greatness of the discourse paraphrased, then I shall gain some from its aura, apart from any personal motive that would remain of puffing myself up, if I should truly seem to you the type for whom paraphrasing Lacan would be a simple thing.[2] Next, a paraphrase indeed appears necessary in order to find one's bearings in a lesson whose inventive, luminous upsurgence that creates its immense interest does not always progress in a rectilinear fashion but meanders from a nodal elaboration regarding the function Lacan gives to painting, to the picture precisely: let us add, [to the picture as conceived] in analytic discourse. (I say this to short-circuit, from the start, a debate that is not appropriate here on applied psychoanalysis.) Finally, it is because the first virtue, the elementary effect of the paraphrase, or its first function, if it means "a phrase along side," is, before even saying or resaying something, to designate what it paraphrases: a doubling, certainly, but not a simple one, for in doubling, it silently makes a gesture of showing.

From *La Part de L'Oeil,* no. 2, Académie Royale des Beaux-Arts, Bruxelles, 1987 [dossier: "Pensée des Sciences, Pensée des arts Plastiques"], pp. 147–67; pp. 147–51. Translated by Jack Stone; translation edited by Ellie Ragland.

Now, here, the showing (*monstration*) is important. For what does topology show? Structure. It is not a metaphor for structure, because "this structure, it is it."[3] Topology is the real of structure, insofar as it cannot be said. What cannot be said—or seen—is shown. Lacanian topology is a tacit showing of structure.[4]

TO SITUATE

"It is a question for us," writes Lacan, "of situating our topology—of situating ourselves as analysts, as acting in it."[5] *Situate* is an eminently Lacanian verb, inasmuch as, if all of his teaching consists of the project of orienting psychoanalysts, this project is shown to be absolutely homogeneous with the structure it seeks to transmit, because what constitutes its initial given is the designation of a place, the place of the Other, vis-à-vis which the subject must orient him- or herself. All this teaching is done in this place and it places—the place (*lieu*) of the Other being a common place (*lieu commun*), it places (*place*) the subject. That Lacan became a topologist is in the order of Lacan the toponymist, Lacan the topographer. It is even in the order of the unconscious itself that was topologized by Lacan because it is topological. One could say that Lacan always sustained his discourse by a *psychoanalysis situs* and placed psychoanalysis in space. A constant recourse to graphic representations bears witness to this: it shows representations that are so many spatializations of a structure that is itself spatial.

That one can consider the three Lacanian "dimensions" of the Real, Symbolic, and Imaginary as defining three spaces would make it permissible to distribute the ensemble of Lacan's graphic representations according to this trifunctionality: the *graph,* which inscribes *places,* responds to symbolic space (the point prevails here); the *schemas* figure imaginary space by stratifying the *planes* of the image (here, the surface prevails); as for real space, its representation supposes that one promote alongside the graphs or schemas the notion of a *picture,* which itself presents *sites* (which one could define as pure real places while stressing the pictorial origin of the term). (The graphic representation of the Borromean knot would then be a picture.) Thus, one could call a graph that which is meant to be read, a schema, that which lets itself be seen, and a picture, that which shows. Always supposing a knotting of the three in each case, inasmuch as one must admit that a writing is susceptible of showing (the blankness or white between the lines), in which respect it would be a picture—the schema, susceptible of being read, its graph side, or the picture, of being seen—it returns in this way to the schema, and so on.

The graph writes what can be said. The schema represents what can be seen. The picture separates itself from them: what can neither be said nor seen shows something.

To Represent

Topology, then, is not a metaphor. This could be understood simply: It does not represent the subject. It is neither signified nor figured. It presents the structure of the subject, the site at which the subject emerges, as effect. Topology presents what Lacan names "the foundations (*fundaments*) of its position": neither said nor seen—the subject combines itself there.

If for Lacan, topology ranks as a matheme of analysis, if the matheme aims at resolving the question of a transmission without loss of the analytic discourse, this transmission, then, takes on the status of an act, a mute one: to show without saying a word. Psychoanalysis would thus be overtaken by painting: an art of silence aiming at the real—that is, what is impossible to say shows itself.

Thus, one is led to mark a visual structure of topology, precisely this structure that Lacan constructed in his 1964 seminar on *The Four Fundamental Concepts of Psychoanalysis,* as a split between the gaze and vision, which is to say, a visual structure torn from the visible.[6] What topology shows, one does not see—such as Carpaccio's "Saint Etienne" in the Louvre, pointing his finger toward a patch of sky that is outside the field of the picture, a pure real.

The Foundation (*Fundament*)

"We must now come to what I have called the visual structure of this topological world, that on which the entire installation of the subject is founded," Lacan said on May 4, 1966. "Visual structure" of the topological world, as Lacan puts it in this seminar, is useful for underlining a sort of reversal, at least as to our point of departure in relation to the seminar of 1964 where it would be, rather, a question of constructing the topological structure of the visual world. Lacan gave such a structure then based on the model of the finger of a glove turned inside out (There from where it looks at me, I do not see; there where I see, it does not look at me: You never look at me there from where I see you; what I look at is never what I want to see. There from where I see, I am not; there where I am, I do not see; I see, therefore, that I am looked at, etc.). Thus, it is by topology that Lacan in 1966 returns to visual structure, while, formerly, it was visual structure that led him to a topology. This indicates at least one consequence we can anticipate. For if topology shows, exploration of visual structure and recourse to the picture will then have an aim: to construct the matheme of showing.

To this aim, a factor is attached that must be underlined. As we shall see, it is this: if Lacan makes of the picture a window in which the object comes to be lodged, a frame that shows it, this structure—in being that of the visual world and supposing at its center the object in question, that is, the gaze—is not only that of the visual world, and, furthermore, it is not only the gaze that is involved. In other words, if the picture is constructed by Lacan as the matheme of visual structure, that is to say, what transmits it, if it is a matheme of the showing of the object, it is the object itself that is at issue, declinable in its four currencies: that of the breast, the turd, the voice, the gaze— the gaze is included here, of course, but with a singularity in this series, a privileged status, because it is the matrix of the three others. Thus, one could say that, when the breast, the turd, or the voice show themselves, they do so as a function of the gaze. To explore visual structure will be, then, a matter of accounting for the relationship of subject to object insofar as it shows itself; this is called the fantasy. The picture, in addition to the object, thus proves itself to be also the framework of a question central to analytic discourse. In this respect, for Lacan, painting, when he speaks of it, is not applied psychoanalysis. It is pure psychoanalysis.

THE ELEMENTARY

Let us return now to where we were: a visual structure of the topological world founds the subject. Lacan is seeking the foundations of the subject. That, without a doubt, could constitute the heading beneath which the integrality of his teaching would be ranked. It applies itself, however, with a particular appropriateness to the lesson of May 4, 1966. For beyond the meanderings of a profuse elaboration, of a continued upsurgence, Lacan followed a path of surprising originality. He, in fact, drew on three distinct threads, beginning with three references: Descartes, cave painting, and quattrocentro perspective. One might emphasize that these three references have a point in common: Each aims for a point of origin, a time of emergence—of the classical subject, the speaking being, and modern space: three "births" in all. One knows that this has hardly any historical value for Lacan but that in the first moments of time, it is the elementary that is aimed at. Moreover, we might consider that each of these three threads leads back to an element that must be held to as to the foundation of each of the dimensions, the Imaginary, Symbolic, and Real, respectively. Thus, the Cartesian thread leads to the body, the thread of the wall paintings to the logical matrix of the signifier, and the thread of perspective to a hole—the chosen recess of the object. There is another way to present the issue of the three threads Lacan follows here. It is to consider that each hole implies a different structure supposed for the subject: geometrical in the first case, logical in the second, and topological in the third. I hope one sees what this is all about.

It is possible that, under too much pressure to make you depart as quickly as you can from the three furrows perceived in this lesson, seemingly an overworked field, I have only succeeded in your eyes in making this field a dense forest—full of riches, you might think, but quite impenetrable. However, it is not necessary that this forest hide the tree of simplicity Lacan is trying to grow. For all of these references, diverse as they are in nature, are only brought together to answer one question: What is there exactly of the subject, in this place necessitated by the constitution of the objective world? The subject is defined by its relationship to the world. This is the naive question—in the sense of "native"—that is posed. Lacan will offer three possible answers. If certain difficulties come to light, if a little complexity is in order, if Lacan takes some trouble—and if we do the same in following him—it is, overall, only due to his exasperating care for saying "what there is 'exactly.' " And no one can blame him for this rigor.

SCREEN

Let there be two terms, then: the world and the subject. How does the subject accede to a representation of the world? By the senses, beginning with sight. This necessitates posing, or interposing, a third term: the screen. Let it be what supports everything of the world that presents itself for the subject. The screen is an elementary term: elementary but complex, or ambiguous. For if its function is to support, even before presenting whatever it hides, it is then constructed on two opposing ideas—it presents and it hides. One would thus have trouble speaking of the "concept" of the screen (if concept means "what one can grasp"). If the screen is elementary, it is because it is a support: support of the image, of the letter, of the object (if one can speak in this last case of a support). In these three cases, the status of the screen can be stated in different ways: as support of the image, it is the surface, as essential to what an image is; as support of the letter, it is the blank background of the page, the empty background on which the letter emerges, and which arises itself from the inscription—the letter shows the background, makes it ex-sist; as support of the object, it is first the support of a hole where the object is situated—as the edge of the one, it gives its frame to the other. Inversely, to the three elements it supports, one can make three modes of the screen's presence correspond: as support of the image, of what is seen, it is hidden by the image—thus, revealing that the image veils the screen as that which hides, it veils the veil; as support of the letter, it is shown as what hides an empty opacity; as support of the object, it shows what it hides—it is holed.

In that way, then, one could say that the three threads I have indicated, beginning with the three references made by Lacan, establish themselves definitively as the exploration of the three statuses or three modes of the screen. In the movie *The World, the Subject, and the Screen,* a Lacanian film, if the subject of the film is the subject—barred ($\mathcal{S}$)—if the action is situated in the world of objects, it is surely the screen that takes the starring role; Lacan makes the screen a movie star.

Nonetheless, we must not lose sight of one thing: The screen is also an object in the world—let us not be in too much of a hurry therefore to relate the three terms of the movie to the Lacanian trifunctionality. If, however, the screen distinguishes itself from other objects, it is because it is the material on which the world is deposed; the world is drawn on its surface, the signifier inscribed itself there, the object itself pierces it, in painting itself there. Support of the image, the signifier, or of the object, the screen is, in a sense, the world itself, envisaged according to the fact that it be seen (it is its own surface): insofar as it is written (although the writing will never be able to write the world completely, to reabsorb it, all in all, into the written [*écrit*], into the surface on which it is written; also, this impossible, this real, shows. It does not stop showing the world), and as a real presence (the world that is shown, not represented, is the world that represents itself *itself*).

SURFACE

In his seminar of May 4, 1966, Lacan said, "The foundation of the surface is at the base of all we call the organization of form, constellation" (*L'objet de la psychanalyse*).The world, the visible world, is a world of images. That the surface be the principle of the image is what leads us to conceive of visible space as a superposition of parallel planes; the visible world is a layering of space, *feuilleté* (as in pastry). I would say scanned space, a thickness of planes. Henceforth, so that in such a *feuilletage,* or stacking of millithin leaflike planes on one another, an object can be delimited, we must pose a subject "that unifies the configuration" (*L'objet de la psychanalyse*). Question: Is it on a surface, the surface that is the retina of the eye on which the image is going to form itself—the image as form—that we can grasp the unifying principle? It is this question that makes an appeal to Descartes, to the distinction between extended matter and that of thought. One preliminary remark must be made: what Descartes produces his theory from in the *Treatise on the World,*[7] following the twelfth "Rule for the Direction of the Spirit," is an opposition in which the major upheaval introduced by the artistic conceptions of the Renaissance, two centuries earlier, will have consisted. This is to say that, in breaking with the Middle Ages, painters, such as Erwin Panofsky writing in *Idea,* would uproot the object from the interior world of the subjective representation to situate it in the exterior world.[8] We can date this from Cennino Cennini's *Trattato della pittura* (between 1350 and 1400), which, for the first time, counseled the painter to place himself—in painting a mountain—before a model.[9] Thus, the separation of the subject from the object was posed, bringing about the establishment between the two of a *distance* that the next perspective would materialize. We can therefore say that, in a sense, painting "anticipated" Descartes.

Let it remain that the opposition of thought and extended matter consists of a paradox because for Descartes, the area—that is to say, space as
homogeneous—is to be conceived of at the same time as *partes extra partes,*
which Lacan translates as follows: "Chaque point est identique à tous les
autres tout en étant différent" (Each point is identical to all the others, while
at the same time being different) (*L'objet de la psychanalyse*). This renders space
unthinkable. Lacan, it seems to me, raises the difficulty by reformulating the
Cartesian hypothesis on extended matter thusly: "Toutes ses parties se valent"
(All its parts are as good as each other). By the notion of value, he thus introduces the operation, which is no longer one of an aporetic imaginary identity
(a *semblable* or similar that would be not-similar) but that of an equality, which
supposes measure. By measure, what is different can be identical in having
the same value. (This constitutes the foundation of metrical geometry.) This is
of considerable consequence: Descartes's extended matter (or scope of space)
and thought are not separable but coherent. For, henceforth, he admits that
thought cannot unify space, for a good reason: Space as such cannot be
thought outside of thought; thought does not introduce measure into space,
supposedly conceived of as separated—it is constitutive of space. Also, says
Lacan, thought cannot explore space since it is that which builds it. There is
no space that is not measurable.

Notes

1.   The present text is a revision of a lecture given in Brussels, June 22, 1985, at the
invitation of *L'Ecole de la Cause freudienne* of Belgium.
2.   Cf. Jacques Lacan, "L'étourdit," *Scilicet* 4 (1973): 5–52.
3.   The status of Lacanian topology crosses paths here, as Jean-Claude Milner indicates
in "sur l'image" (Internet, <www.mle.asso.fr/banquet>), with two propositions from Ludwig
Wittgenstein's *Tractatus:* "7. That about which one cannot speak, one must remain silent" and
"6.522. There is surely an inexpressible. This shows itself . . ." (*Tractatus Logico-Philosophicus,*
trans. D. F. Pears and B. F. McGuinness [London: Routledge and Kegan Paul, 1961], p. 151).
4.   Ludwig Wittgenstein, *Tractatus,* p. 151.
5.   Jacques Lacan, *Le séminaire, livre XIII: L'objet de la psychanalyse, 1966–1967,* unpublished seminar, May 4, 1966; hereafter cited in text as *L'objet de la psychanalyse.*
6.   Jacques Lacan, *The Seminar of Jacques Lacan, Book XI: Four Fundamental Concepts of
Psycho-Analysis, 1964,* ed. Jacques-Alain Miller, trans. Alan Sheridan (New York: W. W. Norton, 1981); see especially chapters 6 and 7, pp. 77, 80–81.
7.   René Descartes, *Le Monde de M. Descartes ou le traité de la lumière, et des autres princi-
paux objets des sens* (Paris, 1664).
8.   Erwin Panofsky, *Idea: A Concept in Art Theory* (Columbia: University of South Car-
olina Press, 1968).
9.   Cennino Cennini, *A Treatise on Painting* [*Trattato della pittura*] (London, 1844).

The Hypothesis of Compacity
in Chapter 1 of *Encore:*
Seminar XX (1972–1973)

Geneviève Morel

With his illustration of the story of Achilles and the tortoise, Lacan discusses the male side of sexuation and shows the movement toward "embracing one another," clutching one another in bed, thereby defining what he calls "sexual *jouissance.*" In order to do this, Lacan appeals to the notions of succession, series, and real number, notions that are all the more necessary given that he argues that "embracing one another" is attained at a limit. To investigate this formulation, I shall comment here on chapter 1 of *Encore,* in which Lacan tackles what he calls the "hypothesis of compacity" on both the male and female sides of sexuation.[1] It is especially interesting that he states that this hypothesis, although designed for men, "verifies itself" for women. Lacan's formulation of the hypothesis represents, I believe, a reformulation of Zeno's paradox, although I will set aside this aspect for the present discussion.

WHAT IS A COMPACT?

A compact is defined in a space by the notion of closed and bounded aspects of these metric spaces. Here are some very simple examples: the numerical line, the real line, is a one-dimensional metric space; the plane, the back of the screen, is a two-dimensional metric space; space is a three-dimensional metric space; for a four-dimensional metric space, one could add the dimension of time, for example. A compact in a one-dimensional metric space is a closed interval: that is, its furthest points belong to it (a and b belong to the compact 1, as represented in diagram 1 by the arrow turned toward a and

From *Revue de l'Ecole de La Cause Freudienne,* no. 25 (Sept. 1993), pp. 99–123. The European School of Psychoanalysis. ECF–ACF; *Revista mondial de Psichoanalisis: Uno por Uno,* no. 38 (Summer 1994), p. 42 and following. Translated into English by the author; translation edited by Ellie Ragland.

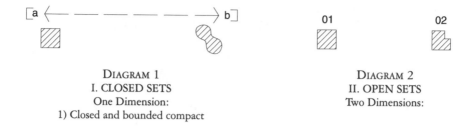

DIAGRAM 1
I. CLOSED SETS
One Dimension:
1) Closed and bounded compact

DIAGRAM 2
II. OPEN SETS
Two Dimensions:

toward b). A bounded interval means that one cannot extend all the way to infinity. One is blocked by the end points.

The property "open" is applied to those spaces that, on the contrary, do not contain their own limits. The open interval]a,b[does not contain its furthest points a and b, which are excluded. Lacan takes the property of compactness as a model for lovers "embracing one another" (*Encore,* 3). The meeting point, the space of sexual *jouissance,* is conditioned by the impasse caused by the presence of the big Other for both sexes; it can be represented as the segment [a,b]. There is a space that is common to sexual *jouissance:* both sexes, in "embracing one another," are in relation with the Other, although not in the same way, and they thus have different ways of assuming the *s'étreindre,* or "embracing one another." Here is the key problem of chapter 1 of *Encore:* How could one formalize the way in which each sex misses the target? It is always interesting to know how one fails, how one misses, even if knowing this does not give us the recipe for success. The impasse here is due to the presence of the Other, and Lacan asks the question: "What does the most recent development in topology allow us to say about this place of the Other, of a sex as Other, as absolute Other?" (*Encore,* 9). This expression of "absolute Other" is found in Lacan's earlier work in the 1958 articles in the *Ecrits.*[2] How should we understand the term *absolute*? I interpret it in its philosophical sense, as indicating an absolute alterity, something for which we have no standard of comparison, no access by identification, no access by the One.

Lacan's "hypothesis of compacity" consists of the supposition that the topological structure of embracing one another (to the extent that this relates to the Other) is a compact one. What are the consequences of this for women? Lacan proposes: "Let us follow here the complement of the hypothesis of compactness." The complement of the hypothesis of compacity is thus now the side of women. "Let us take the same limited, closed, supposedly instituted space—the equivalent of what I posited earlier as an intersection extending to infinity" (*Encore,* 9). He thus admits that there is a space in common for both sexes (the "embracing one another" with the presence of the Other) that gives the continuous structure of the compact. But what specifies the woman's side here? Lacan states that "the space of sexual *jouissance,* which thereby proves to be compact" (*Encore,* 10). On the woman's side, it is all the more surprising given that she belongs to the open sets]a,b[. Nonetheless, in the case of sexual *jouissance,* the space is limited and closed (*Encore,* 10). This way of speaking of a hypothesis of compacity for the man's side, following with the idea of woman as complement, and then considering that the latter functions as a proof—"It is verified."—is rather amusing. It means that, perhaps, Lacan started out from the woman's side in the first place! This is a well-known structure of reasoning: From one idea, one constructs something from its apparent opposite. But the idea of thinking that the point of truth is found on the woman's side, whereas the hypothesis had been posed on the man's side, might suggest to us that, as the Don Juan example at the end of the chapter shows so clearly, the whole elaboration had originally been founded on a consideration of the side of women. It seems all the more so in that Lacan talks so often about Don Juan, even as early as the *Object Relation* seminar.[3] In any case, analysts were discussing Don Juan well before Lacan, and others were analyzing him even before the existence of analysts. The phenomenon of Don Juan was a subject of debate from the sixteenth century on in operas, dramas, novels, and so on. What is sure is that, on the side of woman (even if it concerns a feminine man like Don Juan), sexual *jouissance* shows itself to be compact (i.e., limited and bounded).

To illustrate this, Lacan uses a different definition of compacity from the one he had used for the male side, this time in terms of open sets. There are many ways to define a mathematical set, and all these definitions are of course equivalent. There is thus another way to define compacity, another property, which is in fact its classical definition, using the notion of openness. Here is a second definition: a space F is compact if it is separated and if, for any open cover of F, one can produce a finite subcover. Instead of speaking in terms of intersection of open sets, we can speak in terms of unison. "Cover," covering a table for example, means that you put bits of paper on it until you can no longer see the color of the table but only the white of the paper. But the bits of paper may overlap or go beyond the edges of the table. This is called a cover.

If we take as our space F, the square in diagram 2 introduced earlier, and cover it with open sets on a line (diagram 1), or do the same with a plane, the following schema occurs (diagram 3):

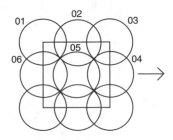

DIAGRAM 3
F(*emme*)/woman

The square in diagram 2 is covered in diagram 3 with discs 01, 02, 03, 04, 05, 06, and so on—F(*emme*)/ Woman—which do not contain their limits. This family of open sets, which may be infinite, covers the square (the sets are the bits of paper placed on the table). This is the sense of the term *cover*. I imagine the number of discs as infinite. I can do the same with intervals, as in diagram 1, by taking an open set 01, a second 02, and a third 03. Discs 01, 02, 03 cover the compact (a,b). This means that (a,b) is included (©) in the union of Oi: (a,b) C U Oi. U designates an infinite number of open sets. Thus, the formula (a,b) C, U Oi means that there is a cover of (a,b) by a family of open sets, the Ois.

What does the property of compacity tell us in this context? One thing the property of compacity tells us in this context is that the space must be separated; that is, one can include two different points with two open sets. (There are some spaces where two separate points may be infinitely close to one another.) We can thus say that a space F is compact if for any open cover on F, one may obtain a finite subcover; that is, only a finite number of discs is necessary to cover the plane, and there is therefore no need to refer to an infinite number of them. What is interesting about the property of compacity is that one can move from the infinite to the finite. The finite number of discs gives the same effect, then, as the infinite number.

With the male side, there is a requirement of the infinite; with the female, we move from the infinite to the finite. But this is the same compact space, and the definitions are in fact equivalent. Therefore, if the compact big Other is covered by an infinity of open sets, a certain, finite number of them will be enough to cover it; hence, the infinite collection is not necessary.

Lacan draws certain conclusions here as to feminine sexuality. The structure indicates the way a woman will approach the question of how she can be attained. How can we understand this? If the compact space allows one to transform the infinity of the big Other into the finite, an infinite number of open sets is no longer needed; we are able to cover our space of sexual *jouissance* (represented by the compact space) with a finite number of sets. These open sets, Lacan argues, represent women: "[T]he said spaces can be taken one by one (*un par un*) and since I am talking about the other pole, let us put this in the feminine *une par une*" (*Encore*, 10). If we take each woman/open set one by one, we will attain the compact space linked to the existence of the Other. That's the basic idea.

Lacan gives the mythic illustration of Don Juan. Don Juan, he says, is a woman's fantasy, or better, a feminine myth. After all, these are not identical: for Lacan, a myth aims at the real, at structure, and is always equivalent to a formalization, whereas a "fantasy" evokes something more imaginary.

Don Juan is thus a "character"—I believe that in the myth he does not really represent a man (a point discussed below)—who has the reputation of making a list of women (the famous *mille e tre*); he takes women one by one and makes his list. Lacan seems to be saying that women see things in this way (the feminine myth). This does not mean that they can only have relations with Don Juans, a reality confirmed by the clinic.

CONTINGENCIES

The question of contingencies can be examined with both the story of Don Juan and the idea of the compact property. Assume a woman as one of the open sets of the compact space. Within this infinite number, a certain finite number of open sets (or women) will allow one to attain the space A, the space of sexual *jouissance,* but one does not know which ones; the theorem fails to tell us. We do not know which open sets will end up as the cover. The theorem fails to tell us. We do not know where to start or finish, and, even worse, we could take an infinite number of open sets without any of them forming a cover. So we do not know how to proceed, and there is no method to tell us in what order to try. This introduces a dimension of contingency that is very strong for women. The finite number is aleatory: we don't know who the right ones are; we don't know what the right number is (1, 2, 3, 50, 000, 000, etc.). All one can do is to count the open sets that have already been used: we tried such-and-such an open set and it didn't work.

Lacan stresses the importance of the "one by one" in the compact: we try the open sets one by one, in a succession; we take one woman after another, but in an aleatory sense. And, he explains, this is what the masculine sex is for a woman. In other words, having placed oneself on the woman's side, the feminine myth starts to unravel itself. The feminine myth of Don Juan is the way in which a woman understands how the opposite sex proceeds to encounter her. What does this mean? Lacan specifies that the "one by one" has nothing to do with the One of universal fusion (i[a]), Freud's eros. The "one" in question is linked to the continuum of the Other (as illustrated by compacity, equivalent to this idea) and not to the One of love. It is a question of the One of succession, to the extent that this is required by the structure of the Other. Indeed, the structure of the compact space requires that one try out the open sets to produce the cover of the space one by one. The structure thus allows us to differentiate the "one by one" and the One of union and fusion. The One in question here is the One that is based on the continuum of the Other (the infinite aleph 1). As Lacan states at the end of the chapter, it is the Other that requires this "one by one" (*Encore,* 10).

So, what about the *mille e tre* of Don Juan? Rank, who wrote an essay on Don Juan, argues that he is a "fantastic figure."[4] What is fantastic is that Don Juan represents the aim of the infinite and the not-all, the aim toward the continuity of aleph 1. Don Juan's list is finite—*mille e tre*—at the moment when he is counting, but we don't know if he has covered the space. Perhaps, a woman may think, I will be the one needed by the list to attain the Other.

Perhaps I am the open set that is needed by the finite number to cover the compact space. This is possible. As we saw, with man, we are in the field of the impossible. For Achilles, it was impossible, with his necessarily repeated intersections, to attain or arrive at some point. Here, we are in the field of the possible, but on condition that we accept contingency. After all, it is certainly possible (even if rather difficult) that a woman, by some contingency, be the open set needed to cover the compact space. Hence the special importance of the contingency at play in the not-all. In other words, how does a woman situate herself in all this? In the list or outside the list? I think that the key to the story is that it is women who are outside the list and that they think they are outside it even if in fact they are within it. This is the case, moreover, for Dona Ana, the commander's daughter, the one whom Don Juan had at the start and who tries to find him again. Even if a woman has counted herself once on the list, she may still consider herself as not belonging to it. This situates a woman, one who has the myth in her head, as "minus one"; perhaps I am the "minus one" lacking from the list, the one needed to cover the compact, in order for him to make me Other. Lacan says, indeed, at the end of *Encore,* speaking of man: "[T]he Other cannot be added to the One. The Other can only be differentiated from it. If there is something by which it participates in the One, it is not by being added" (*Encore,* 129).

This is what Lacan has just been telling us, that the Other is not equal to $1 + 1 + 1 + 1 \ldots$, exactly what Achilles assumed: $1 + 1 + 1 + 1 +$ steps and perhaps I will get there? Lacan thinks that this is impossible. "For the Other—as I already said, but it is not clear that you heard me—is the One-missing (*l'un-en-moins*). That is why in any relationship of man with a woman—she who is in question (*en cause*) as object *a*—it is from the perspective of the One-missing (*l'Une-en-moins*) that she must be taken up" (*Encore,* 129). And now he refers to the start of the *Encore* seminar, where he had said, "But center him [Don Juan] on what I have just illustrated for you" (*Encore,* 10). That is, a woman situates herself as One-less on the list. What matters is not being in the list but trying, on the off chance (the same off chance that Lacan discusses in *Television*), to prepare herself to be perhaps the last open set needed to cover the compact space of the "to embrace one another."[5] This is one way of understanding why Lacan writes A/[(Other)] = (minus one, or the one less), that is, S(Ø). Ultimately, the compactification on the side of woman illustrates this very well.

In other words, if a man takes a woman from the perspective of the One-more (*l'Une-en-plus*), thus making her equivalent to phallic *jouissance* (what he always, in a sense, does because he follows the example of Achilles), he has ruined everything. The only way to take her correctly is to manage to always leave her in the place of the One-less (the one who is lacking from the list, needed to complete the cover of the compact), so that she will remain Other both for him and for herself.

We could also make a link here between the One-less, this "logical" feminine "requirement"—"the Other who is incarnated, so to speak, as sexed being [the woman]—requires this one by one (*une par une*)" (*Encore*, 10)—and the expression used in "L'étourdit" in which Lacan refers to the requirement "to be the only one."[6] Can we link these two requirements? I believe so; the One-less is unique, she is specified precisely as being the one who makes the finite equal to the infinite. The finite of the cover of open sets is equivalent, thanks to her, to the infinite of the initial cover represented by compacity— that is, the infinity of the not-all, the continuum. Now, the demand "to be the only one" in "L'étourdit" evokes an overstepping of the Other *jouissance* in relation to phallic *jouissance*. And the One-less is not the same as the One-more; there can be many One-mores, but there can only be one One-less.

The interest of this compacity property is thus clear, as it brings the infinite to the finite in an aleatory way and introduces contingency on the woman's side as something fundamental: the "on the off chance" of a woman who tries to lend herself to the man's fantasy. In other words, the not-all is not the infinity at the horizon; it is not the idea of the infinity of eros as union, universal fusion. It is next to you, between two doors as Lacan puts it so well in *Encore*: "You may have noticed—I am naturally speaking here to the few *semblances* of men I see here and there, fortunately I don't know them for the most part, and that way I don't presume anything about the others— that now and then, there is something that, for a brief moment, shakes (*secoue*) women up or rescues them (*secourt*)" (*Encore*, 74). Lacan is playing here on the words *secouer* (to give a jolt, to rouse) and *secourir* (to assist or save), and the "between two doors" (translated by Fink as "for a brief moment") clearly refers to something such as the brevity of an encounter: something sudden, improvised, contingent. This is not really the idea of infinite love on the horizon. It indicates that the infinity of the not-all implies; it is next to you, not in the distance, perhaps, but you don't know it—it is completely contingent. You might, for example, pick open sets at random an infinite number of times and you would never get the right ones. And there are certainly women who put themselves in this situation. If one sees Don Juan as a feminine myth, one may think of a woman strategy. One can imagine several variant cases here: those who avoid trying because they are too afraid of being One-less (or "One-missing," as Fink renders it); those for whom all that matters is being One-more, to be inscribed on a list and who will never be One-less, even if they collect lists. I want to stress the fact of contingency, which Lacan does not discuss in chapter 1 of *Encore,* but which is a consequence of the use he makes of the compactness property.

THE "FEMININE MYTH" OF DON JUAN

For Lacan, Don Juan is therefore a feminine myth, the logic required by the Other. Is he a man? I don't think so, even if Don Juan is provided with the phallic One and incarnates an inextinguishable desire. Lacan often puts man on the side of desire, even if he does grant desire to women—remember the famous sentence in the *Ecrits* in which he speaks about a *jouissance* that has to realize itself in the place of masculine desire[7] (*Ecrits,* 735)—but for Freud, desire is masculine libido. Don Juan incarnates a desire that is not satisfied because he is forever continuing the list: from this perspective, he is thus an incarnation of male desire.

But we have seen that the list only counts for the one who does not already include herself there. In other words, one must distinguish Don Juan from what Lacan calls the "At-least-one" of the hysteric, that is, the man with whom the hysteric identifies in order to approach femininity. This is, for example, Mr. K. for Dora, the one in whose eyes she is reflected, the one she always needs as a support. Thus, one encounters certain women in the clinic who fall apart when they don't have a man, as they need to have a medium for desire. For these women, desire is the desire of the Other, and thus they desire nothing if there is no man there desiring and allowing them to pose the question of femininity: What am I for you? Or what is she for you?

This shows us, furthermore, that it would be a mistake to interpret Don Juan in the light of the function of the Other Woman in hysteria. There is a delicate relation here between hysteria and femininity. It would be easy to say that the one for whom the fantasy is to have Don Juan as one's man would be a hysteric, as she could only desire when another woman is put in the place of the cause of desire for her (the hysterical trio). But Lacan does not say that Don Juan is a hysterical myth; he says that it is a feminine myth linked to "one by one" and not to the "At-least one." What counts in the logic of the story is the "one by one"—to be the One-less—and not that there exists an "At-least one." The woman is situated here on the side of a minus, whereas the hysteric situates herself rather on the side of the existence of the man, to pose the question of femininity through the figure of another woman.

Likewise, we cannot say that Don Juan is the big Other because he is on the side of the One. He is still the one who makes the list, one by one. Indeed, we could say that the matheme of Don Juan is that which Lacan gives for the not-all in *Encore* (diagram 4):

Lacan states that, if ~~The~~ Woman (from the sexuation graph and "A Love Letter") is not-all, it is due to her division between Φ and $S(\emptyset)$. This shows that the not-all is not equivalent to $S(\emptyset)$. The not-all is the "doubling" between Φ and $S(\emptyset)$ in terms of *jouissance*. Hence, we cannot situate Don Juan simply on the side of Φ or on that of the Other, even if this is the way

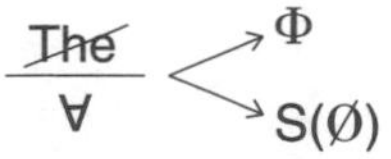

$$\frac{\text{T}\text{h}\text{e}}{\forall} < \begin{array}{l} \nearrow \Phi \\ \searrow S(\emptyset) \end{array}$$

DIAGRAM 4
Source: Encore, p. 78.

that the feminine myth accedes to the Other *jouissance* (this is how the Other *jouissance* of a woman could be logicized). Now we understand why Don Juan is a feminine myth. On the one hand, he is on the side of Φ. To the extent that we have the "one by one," there is a One involved (the One of repetition, of succession). On the other hand, however, this "one by one" only takes on its value due to the One-less $S(\emptyset)$ equivalent to the Other. We could thus write the following, which demonstrates that the minus $(S[\emptyset])$ is required to give the formula of the void as true in feminine sexuation, as coordinated in reference to the falsity of the nondialectical One (Φ):

(1) A/(Other) $= 1 + 1 + 1 + 1 + 1 + 1 + 1 +$ (false)
(2) A/(Other) $= 1 - 1$ (true)

On the first line is a false formula, according to which the Other would be equivalent to $1 + 1 + 1 + \ldots$, the schema of Achilles. On the second line is the formula deduced from the compacity on the woman's side; as an encounter, it is the infinity of compacity represented by $\_\_1$; (-1), being the point at which the woman situates herself, the One-less, and also the matheme of the proposition "The woman doesn't exist." Lacan says in *Seminar XVII* "privation of the signifier."[8] He refers to privation here not of The Woman but of the privation of the signifier of The Woman.

Lacan's evocation of the myth of Don Juan evolves in his teaching. In the 1957 *Object Relation* seminar, Lacan sees Don Juan as the one searching for the phallic woman; he is thus already looking for The Woman. And, Lacan says, he only finds her in the "silent guest," that is, the stone guest, the commander, Dona Ana's father, and hence, the dead father, which Lacan says is a beyond of The Woman (*La relation d'objet*, 418–19). This reminds us of the 1958 texts on feminine sexuality. Lacan is basically constructing an equivalence between The Woman and the point beyond the woman (the point beyond the veil) represented by the stone guest linked to the dead father. It is not exactly the 1958 link (in "Guiding Remarks for a Congress on Feminine Sexuality") between the "ideal incubus" and feminine *jouissance,* but almost.

THE STONE GUEST

In his seminar on *Anxiety,* Lacan stresses Rank's idea that there is a link between Don Juan and the priest who deflowers on the wedding night.[9] As Rank argues in this 1922 text: "It is inadmissible to consider the Don Juan legend only in the Freudian sense and explain it in terms of the father complex" (Rank, 123). In other words, Rank thinks that we are not in the Oedipal register. This is very Lacanian. Rank sees in Don Juan a superhuman figure who knows neither expiation nor repentance and who doubts God. Rank then notes the parallel between Don Juan and the specter who comes to visit the virgin. He refers to a play in which a grave digger, having disturbed a dead body that had protested, then, as a joke, invited the specter to his wedding night. On the day of the marriage, the specter arrives to enjoy the young woman before the grave digger does. This is the same structure as the ideal incubus who arrives before the partner. The link with the taboo of virginity is here: the idea that one cannot touch a virgin because she is dangerous and hence that someone has to do it first—a deflowering priest, an ideal incubus, or sometimes someone sent from God. Rank elaborates this train of thought. He refers to the "Book of Tobias," in which only someone sent from God can make a young woman accept a man when she always rejects them. Someone sent from God, someone divine, can come and visit a virgin to make her future sexual relations possible. We find once again the ambiguous figure of the ideal incubus, not a man but a figure of *jouissance* that authorizes desire; as we have seen already in 1958, this point involves an appeal toward God and the Other *jouissance* via the person of Christ. Indeed, this an ambiguous point situated between Φ and the $S(\emptyset)$. Rank also argues that "Don Juan's situation in relation to the husband is thus not strictly speaking that of a rival, but that of a God sure of his victory in relation to the mortal husband" (Rank, 123). According to Lacan, Rank had a good idea here. The divine person comes to give its soul to the virgin (Freud takes this up in the "Taboo of Virginity"),[10] so that she can transmit it to her child and so that the husband does not lose his own soul. This is amusing, as Rank concludes that the woman plays a very active role in the development of the character of Don Juan. Indeed, at the end of his discussion, he goes so far as to state that Don Juan is a liberator of women. He becomes almost the first feminist in history, because he deflowers women, doing them the service of making them women without wishing to keep them for himself; thus, he liberates women (Rank, 165–66).

Also interesting here is that the first Don Juan is called *el infamador* (he who renders infamous); Lacan often plays on the word *defame,* as *dit-femme,* and so on. We can thus say that Rank puts Don Juan on the side of God, of the soul, of spirituality and that, due to this, he opposes him to the sexual partner whom Rank puts on the side of pleasure in marriage. This is the very same dichotomy found in Lacan's 1958 formulation. To end his discussion, Rank quotes a poet, Lenau, in this very Lacanian passage: "My Don Juan is not a full-blooded man eternally chasing after women. In him there lives the desire to find the unique woman who incarnates the femininity in which he could *jouir* with all the women on earth, because he cannot possess them all individually one after the other" (Rank, 176). There is thus the idea that Don Juan is searching for The Woman because he cannot possess them all individually one after the other; he hadn't had the idea of compacity that turns the infinite to the finite.

Given these developments, Lacan remains, even as early as the *Anxiety* seminar, quite close to what he says in *Encore,* insofar as there is the idea of

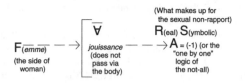

DIAGRAM 5

someone who incarnates The Woman: Don Juan is a feminine fantasy. He is like a woman because, like her, you can't take anything away from him (woman because she doesn't have anything of the phallic One to castrate, him because he can always *jouir* with another woman); he is thus an uncastratable figure.

In the conclusion of the first chapter of *Encore*, Lacan links the sexual *jouissance* of women to the not-all; and what characterizes this, in contrast to men (for whom *jouissance* passes via the object *a* as *jouissance* of the body as asexual), is that *jouissance* does not pass via the body. Already in the 1958 text, Lacan constructed a circuit that was not anatomical. How does the woman make up for the absence of the sexual relation? By means of a logical demand—A (other) = (−1), the demand for "one by one" or for the One-less— which results from the logic required by the compacity of sexual *jouissance* due to the presence of the Other. He says elsewhere in *Seminar XX* and other texts as well that a woman has a relation with the unconscious and with the object *a*: One shouldn't exclude her relations to them, as diagram 5 suggests.

It is my personal opinion that psychoanalysis is not very effective for making up for woman's relation to her unconscious or to the object *a* insofar as sexual *jouissance* is concerned. Of course, it allows Lacan to formulate the structure of feminine sexual *jouissance* in its relation to the presence of the Other. But it remains true that, to the extent that psychoanalysis effects the unconscious, it works on the fantasy and does not really go far in effecting this essential compensation. This does not mean that we cannot know anything about it when a woman is in analysis, but it remains rather on the side of something that we can glimpse, perhaps between two doors, but which cannot be constructed in the analysis itself.

Notes

1. Jacques Lacan, *The Seminar, Book XX: Encore, On Feminine Sexuality, The Limits of Love and Knowledge, 1972–1973*, ed. Jacques-Alain Miller, trans. Bruce Fink (New York: W. W. Norton, 1998); hereafter cited in text as *Encore*. Cf. chapter 1, "On *Jouissance*," 1–13, especially 8–9.

2. Jacques Lacan, *Ecrits* (Paris: Seuil, 1966); hereafter cited in text as *Ecrits*. Cf. "La signification du phallus" (1958), 685–95 (the Other/*l'Autre*) (also translated by Alan Sheridan

in *Ecrits: A Selection* [New York: W. W. Norton, 1980]); "Jeunesse de Gide ou la lettre et le désir" (1958), 739–64, 751 (the Other/*l'Autre*).

3.   Jacques Lacan, *Le séminaire, livre IV: La relation d'objet, 1956–1957,* ed. Jacques-Alain Miller (Paris: Seuil, 1994); hereafter cited in text as *La relation d'objet.*

4.   Otto Rank, *Don Juan et le Double, Etudes Psychanalytiques* (Paris: [Petit Bibliothèque] Payot, 1983), 135; cf. chapter 9; hereafter cited in text. All translations, from French into English, are by G. Morel.

5.   Jacques Lacan, *Television,* ed. Joan Copjec, trans. Denis Hollier, Rosalind Krauss, and Annette Michelson, with *A Challenge to the Psychoanalytic Establishment,* trans. Jeffrey Mehlman (New York: W. W. Norton, 1990), 40.

6.   Jacques Lacan, "L'étourdit," *Scilicet* 4 (1973): 5–52; cf. p. 23.

7.   Jacques Lacan, "Guiding Remarks for a Congress on Feminine Sexuality" (1958), in *Feminine Sexuality: Jacques Lacan and the École Freudienne,* ed. Juliet Mitchell and Jacqueline Rose, trans. J. Rose (New York: W. W. Norton, 1985), 97. See also Lacan's *Ecrits* (Paris: Seuil), 735.

8.   Jacques Lacan, *Le séminaire, livre XVII: L'envers de la psychanalyse, 1969–1970,* ed. Jacques-Alain Miller (Paris: Seuil, 1991), 180.

9.   Jacques Lacan, *Le séminaire, livre X: L'angoisse, 1962–1963,* unedited seminar.

10.   Sigmund Freud, "The Taboo of Virginity (Contributions to the Psychology of Love III)," *SE* 11 (1919 [1917]): 192–208.

Selected Bibliography

◆

Primary Works

Translated into English

"Desire and the Interpretation of Desire in *Hamlet*." *Yale French Studies* 55–56 (1977): 11–52. Trans. James Hulbert. Ed. Shoshana Felman. The seminar of April 29, 1959. This seminar is taken from *Seminar VI: Le désir et son interprétation, 1958–1959,* an unedited seminar.

Ecrits: A Selection. 1977. Trans., with notes, Alan Sheridan. New York: W. W. Norton, 1980.

"Kant with Sade." *October* 51 (Winter 1989): 55–104. Trans. James Swenson.

"Introduction to Jacques Lacan's Lecture: 'The Neurotic's Individual Myth.'" Trans. Martha Evans. Psychoanalytic Quarterly 48, No. 3 (1979): 386–425.

The Seminar of Jacques Lacan, Book XI: The Four Fundamental Concepts of Psycho-Analysis, 1964. Ed. Jacques-Alain Miller. Trans. Alan Sheridan. New York: W. W. Norton, 1981.

Télévision. Trans. Denis Holier, Rosalind Kraus, and Annette Michelson, with *A Challenge to the Psychoanalytic Establishment,* Trans. Jeffrey Mehlman. Ed. by Joan Copjec. New York: W. W. Norton, 1990.

The Seminar of Jacques Lacan, Book I: Freud's Papers on Technique, 1953–1954. Ed. Jacques-Alain Miller. Trans., with notes, John Forrester. New York: W. W. Norton, 1991.

The Seminar of Jacques Lacan, Book II: The Ego in Freud's Theory and in the Technique of Psychoanalysis, 1954–1955. Ed. Jacques-Alain Miller. Trans. Sylvana Tomaselli, with notes by John Forrester. New York: W. W. Norton, 1991.

The Seminar of Jacques Lacan, Book VII: The Ethics of Psychoanalysis, 1959–1969. Ed. Jacques-Alain Miller. Trans., with notes, Dennis Porter. New York: W. W. Norton, 1992.

The Seminar of Jacques Lacan. Book III: The Psychoses, 1955–1956. Ed. Jacques-Alain Miller. Trans. Russell Grigg. New York: W. W. Norton, 1993.

The Seminar of Jacques Lacan, Book XX: Encore, On Feminine Sexuality, The Limits of Love and Knowledge, 1972–1973. Ed. Jacques-Alain Miller. Trans., with notes, Bruce Fink. New York: W. W. Norton, 1998.

In French (not translated into English)

Ecrits. Paris: Seuil, 1966.

"De la psychose paranoïaque dans ses rapports avec la personnalité." Doctoral thesis, Faculté de Médecine de Paris, 1932. Paris: Seuil, 1975.

Les complexes familiaux dans la formation de l'individu. Paris: Navarin éditeur, 1984.

Le séminaire de Jacques Lacan, livre VIII: Le transfert, 1960–1961. Ed. Jacques-Alain Miller. Paris: Seuil, 1991.

Le séminaire de Jacques Lacan, livre XVII: L'envers de la psychanalyse, 1969–1970. Ed. Jacques-Alain Miller. Paris: Seuil, 1991.

Le séminaire de Jacques Lacan, livre IV: La relation d'objet, 1956–1957. Ed. Jacques-Alain Miller. Paris: Seuil, 1994.

In French (not officially edited)
Le seminaire de Jacques Lacan:
livre V: Les formations de l'inconscient, 1957–1958.
livre VI: Le désir et son interprétation, 1958–1959.
livre IX: L'identification, 1961–1962.
livre X: L'angoisse, 1962–1963.
livre XII: Problèmes cruciaux pour la psychanalyse, 1964–1965.
livre XIII: L'objet de la psychanalyse, 1965–1966.
livre XIV: La logique du fantasme, 1966–1967.
livre XV: L'acte psychanalytique, 1967–1968.
livre XVI: D'un Autre à l'autre, 1968–1969.
livre XVIII: D'un discours qui ne serait pas du semblant, 1970–1971.
livre XIX: . . .ou pire, 1971–1972.
livre XXI: Les non-dupes errent, 1973–1974.
livre XXII: R.S.I., 1974–1975.
livre XXIII: Le sinthome, 1975–1976.
livre XXIV: L'insu que sait de l'une-bévue s'aile à' mourre, 1976–1977.
livre XXV: Le moment de conclure, 1977–1978.
livre XXVI: La topologie et le temps, 1978–1979.

These officially unedited seminars may be found in the psychoanalytic book-stores in Paris. Most, if not all, have also been translated into other languages (such as Spanish and Italian) in other countries. They can be obtained in psychoanalytic bookstores in those countries. Many portions of these seminars are available in the *Bulletin de Psychologie* or in *Ornicar?,* as well as in various books and journals in several languages, when permission has been given to print. Although such books or journals are too numerous to list, the following have included translations of unedited texts in English: the *Newsletter of the Freudian Field* (editor, Ellie Ragland), *A-nalysis* (editor, Leonardo Rodriguez), and *lacanian ink* (editor, Josefina Ayerza). Unofficial English translations of all the seminars also exist.

Secondary Works

Books
Apollon, Willy, and Richard Feldstein, eds. *Lacan, Politics and Aesthetics.* Albany: State University of New York Press, 1996.

Aubert, Jacques, ed. *Joyce avec Lacan.* Paris: Navarin, 1987.

Bracher, Mark, and Ellie Ragland-Sullivan. *Lacan and the Subject of Language.* New York: Routledge, 1991.

Clément, Cathérine. *Lives and Legends of Jacques Lacan.* Trans. Arthur Goldhammer. New York: Columbia University Press, 1983.

Copjec, Joan. *Read My Desire: Lacan against the Historicists.* Cambridge, Mass.: MIT Press, 1994.

Feldstein, Richard, Bruce Fink, and Maire Jaanus, eds. *Reading Seminar XI: Lacan's Four Fundamental Concepts of Psychoanalysis* (The Paris Seminars in English). Albany: State University of New York Press, 1995.

————. *Reading Seminars I and II: Lacan's Return to Freud* (The Paris Seminars in English). Albany: State University of New York Press, 1996.

Fink, Bruce. *The Lacanian Subject: Between Language and Jouissance.* Princeton: Princeton University Press, 1995.

————. *A Clinical Introduction to Lacanian Psychoanalysis: Theory and Technique.* Cambridge, Mass.: Harvard University Press, 1997.

Granon-Lafont, Jeanne. *La topologie ordinaire de Jacques Lacan.* Cahors: Point Hors Ligne, 1988.

————. *Topologie Lacanienne et clinique analytique.* Cahors: Point Hors Ligne, 1990.

Leader, Darian, and Judy Groves. *Introducing Lacan.* New York: Totem Books, 1995.

Lefort, Rosine, in collaboration with Robert Lefort. *Birth of the Other.* Trans. Marc du Ry, Lindsay Watson, and Leonardo Rodriguez. Urbana and Chicago: University of Illinois Press, 1994.

Leupin, Alexandre, ed. *Lacan and the Human Sciences.* Lincoln: University of Nebraska Press, 1991.

MaCabe, Colin, ed. *The Talking Cure.* New York: St. Martin's Press, 1981.

Metzger, David. *The Lost Cause of Rhetoric: The Relation of Rhetoric and Geometry in Aristotle and Lacan.* Carbondale: Southern Illinois University Press, 1995.

Muller, John, and William Richardson, eds. *The Purloined Poe.* Baltimore, Md.: Johns Hopkins University Press, 1988.

Ragland, Ellie. *Essays on the Pleasures of Death: From Freud to Lacan.* New York: Routledge, 1995.

Ragland-Sullivan, Ellie. *Jacques Lacan and the Philosophy of Psychoanalysis.* Urbana and Chicago: University of Illinois Press, 1986.

Samuels, Robert. *Between Philosophy and Psychoanalysis: Lacan's Reconstruction of Freud.* New York: Routledge, 1993.

Schneiderman, Stuart. *Jacques Lacan: The Death of an Intellectual Hero.* Cambridge, Mass.: Harvard University Press, 1983.

————, ed. *Returning to Freud: Clinical Psychoanalysis in the School of Lacan.* New Haven, Conn.: Yale University Press, 1990.

Turkle, Sherry. *Psychoanalytic Politics: Freud's French Revolution.* New York: Basic Books, 1978.

Zizek, Slavoj. *The Sublime Object of Ideology.* London: Verso, 1989.

————. *Looking Awry: An Introduction to Jacques Lacan through Popular Culture.* Cambridge, Mass.: MIT Press, 1991.

Articles

Felman, Shoshana. "The Originality of Jacques Lacan." *Poetics Today* 2 (Winter 1980–1981): 45–57.

Miller, Jacques-Alain. "The *a* and *A* in Clinical Structures." In *Acts of Paris-New York Workshop (1986),* ed. Stuart Schneiderman, 1–5. New York: Schneiderman Publication, 1987.

————. "Another Lacan." Ed. Helena Schulz-Keil. *Lacan Study Notes* 1, no. 3 (1984): 1, 4.

————. "To Interpret the Cause: From Freud to Lacan." *Newsletter of the Freudian Field* 3 (Spring/Fall 1989): 30–50.

Suggested Readings

Freud, Sigmund. *The Standard Edition of the Complete Works of Sigmund Freud,* ed. James Strachey. 24 vols. London: Hogarth Press and the Institute of Psychoanalysis, 1953–74.

Lacan, Jacques. The volumes and essays by Lacan listed under primary works.

Miller, Jacques-Alain. The unpublished courses of Miller (when they can be obtained) and chapters and articles published in various psychoanalytic journals, either taken from the courses or separate. Miller has given approximately 18 courses, each one or two volumes in length. They are available to those who attend his courses and engage in the work surrounding them. Contact Dan Collins in the English department at SUNY–Buffalo for Miller's bibliography.

Notes on Contributors

◆

Jacques-Alain Miller is professor and director of the Department of Psychoanalysis at the University of Paris VIII, Saint Denis, and the editor of Lacan's seminars. He has given a course every year since 1981 to an international audience. He is the director of the European School of Psychoanalysis and the World Association of Psychoanalysis, as well as an analyst in private practice. He has written numerous publications in various languages.

Richard Glejzer, professor of English at Albertson College, has written a book on *Lacan, the Middle Ages, and the Epistemology of WOMAN* (currently under consideration by a press). He has also coauthored two collections of essays—on rhetoric and Holocaust studies—and published several essays on Lacan and epistemology and Lacan and gender studies.

Charles Shepherdson, professor at Emory University in the Psychoanalytic Studies Program is currently Fellow at the School of Social Science, Institute for Advanced Study, Princeton, New Jersey. He is author of the book *Vital Signs and the Place of Memory in Psychoanalysis* (1998), has just completed a book on Lacan's *Ecrits,* and has written numerous essays on literature, psychoanalysis, and gender studies.

Colette Soler is professor of Psychoanalysis at the University of Paris VIII, Saint Denis, and analyst in private practice. She has conducted weekly courses since Lacan's death and is known for the numerous essays she has published on Lacan in many languages, as well as the collections she has directed. Many of her courses may be bought in bookstores in French or Spanish.

David Metzger, professor of English at Old Dominican University, is author of *The Lost Cause of RHETORIC: The Relation of Rhetoric and Geometry in Aristotle and Lacan* (1995) and *Lacan, Psychoanalysis, and Trauma* (under consideration by a press). He is also editor of *bien dire,* a journal of Lacanian *orientation* and author of numerous essays on medieval studies, Lacan and analytic philosophy, Lacan and gender, and Lacan and the study of the Bible. He has also edited and coedited two medieval volumes and one psychoanalytic volume, *Proving Lacan,* with Ellie Ragland.

Stuart Schneiderman, psychoanalyst in private practice in New York City, wrote a doctoral thesis on Shakespeare at Indiana University (1975). He has published *Returning to Freud: Clinical Psychoanalysis in the School of Lacan* (1980), *Death of an Intellectual Hero* (1983), and *An Angel Passes* (1989), as well as numerous essays.

John Holland, doctoral candidate in psychoanalysis at the University of Paris VIII, Saint Denis, has also completed his doctorate in English at Princeton University. He has written *Henry James and the Question of Subjectivity* (under consideration by a press). He works as a translator and reader at the Sorbonne and has published numerous essays on Lacan, the *sinthome,* and Henry James's fiction.

Gérard Wajcman, professor of Psychoanalysis at the University of Paris VIII, Saint Denis, is known for his work on Lacan, topology, and art. His articles are numerous, his book on Lacan's object *a* forthcoming, and his work builds a bridge between Lacanian topology and his rethinking of form itself.

Geneviève Morel, is professor in Psychoanalysis at the University of Paris VIII, Saint Denis, and lecturer in the clinical section at the Universities of Lille and Bordeaux. She is known for clarifying Lacan's work on sexuation and on topology (having trained as a topologist before becoming a Lacanian analyst). Her published articles are numerous and in many languages. Many of her courses may be obtained if one is working in her area and she gives her permission.

Index

◆

The Volume Editor

◆

Ellie Ragland is professor and former department chair of English at the University of Missouri (Columbia). She received her Ph.D. in French and Comparative Literature from the University of Michigan and has taught in the Department of Psychoanalysis at the University of Paris VIII, Saint Denis (1994–1995). She is the author of *Rabelais and Panurge: A Psychological Approach to Literary Character* (1976), *Jacques Lacan and the Philosophy of Psychoanalysis* (1986), and *Essays on the Pleasures of Death: From Freud to Lacan* (1995). She coedited *Lacan and the Subject of Language* with Mark Bracher (1991). She is editor of the *Newsletter of the Freudian Field* and author of numerous essays on Lacan, psychoanalysis, literature, and gender theory. Her forthcoming books are *Proving Lacan: Psychoanalysis and the Force of Evidentiary Knowledge*, coedited with David Metzger, and *The Logic of Sexuation—Aristotle to Lacan*.

The General Editor

◆

Robert Lecker is professor of English at McGill University in Montreal. He received his Ph.D. from York University. Professor Lecker is the author of numerous critical studies, including *On the Line* (1982), *Robert Kroetch* (1986), *An Other I* (1988), and *Making It Real: The Canonization of English-Canadian Literature* (1995). He is the editor of the critical journal *Essays on Canadian Writing* and of many collections of critical essays, the most recent of which is *Canadian Canons: Essays in Literary Value* (1991). He is the founding and current general editor of Twayne's Masterwork Studies and the editor of the Twayne World Authors Series on Canadian writers. He is also the general editor of G. K. Hall's Critical Essays on World Literature series.